Common Sense Training

Common Sense Training

A Working Philosophy for Leaders

by

Lt. Gen. Arthur S. Collins, Jr., U.S. Army

PRESIDIO

Library of Congress Cataloging-in-Publication Data

Collins, Arthur S., 1915–1984
    Common sense training.
    1. Military education—United States. 2. United States. Army. I. Tile.
    U408.3.C64   355.5'0973   77-19077
ISBN 0-89141-676-5

Printed in the United States of America

To the soldier,

from whom I learned so much,

and to whom we owe so much.

Contents

List of Figures

Introduction to the Second Edition

When the United States Army dominated and crushed the vaunted Iraqi armed forces in a hundred-hour blitzkrieg, many civilian observers wondered how it happened. How did an army that crawled home from Vietnam with its fighting prowess in tatters become the world standard for ground combat forces? Many attributed the resurgence to wonder weapons, or enthusiastic popular support, or good generalship. Indeed, all of these contributed to victory in the Gulf War. But in the opinion of professional soldiers, the major cause for the great American ground triumph can be summarized in three words: common sense training. If you wonder how America's Army won so convincingly in the Gulf, this book offers the reason why.

Written by Lt. Gen. Arthur S. "Ace" Collins and first published in 1978, *Common Sense Training* is simply the best book ever written on how to train American soldiers. In lucid, clever prose punctuated by terrific anecdotes and provocative examples, the general describes the tough, realistic training techniques that our Army used to prepare for war in the Gulf and still uses today. Written for an army struggling with dwindling strength and reduced funding, Collins's book speaks eloquently to today's force, which faces so many of those same challenges.

For my own part, I have seen this camouflage-covered little gem on so many bookshelves and in so many rucksacks that I thought for a long time that the Army issued Lieutenant General Collins's masterful work. In the most important sense, the Army granted the book an even greater tribute by adopting outright so much of Collins's thinking. As old readers will rediscover, many of General Collins's key ideas are now U.S. Army policy. New readers, already schooled in present-day Army training techniques, can see the logic and insights that underlie these now-accepted ideas. Unlike long-winded field manuals, however, you can actually read this book. It's funny. It's interesting. And if you try this stuff, it works.

This second edition introduces Gen. Ace Collins to a new generation of soldiers, students of military affairs, business leaders, and concerned citizens in general. The author's thoughts are as timely today as when written. You can read hundreds of books about war and how to fight. But this book, the only one of its kind, tells you something more important—how to win.

Daniel P. Bolger
Colonel, Infantry
United States Army

Publisher's Note

This edition of General Collins's seminal work on training military units is being reissued without change to the main text, because in the twenty years since it was first published in 1978 it has become a genuine classic, more widely read than any other book like it. It is as indispensable today as when it was first published (as Dan Bolger's new introduction attests). Naturally, with the passage of time, some things have changed, even in the Army.

This note lists these changes in page-by-page order. There are also a few paragraphs that contain information that is now obsolete. Rather than deleting them, we have employed a gray screen to highlight them for the reader. On these and other detailed notes, we are indebted to Colonel Daniel P. Bolger, USA, who reviewed *Common Sense Training* for changed procedures, modified nomenclature, and other anachronisms.

DETAILED NOTES

Page 13. The Annual General Inspection is no longer conducted in the U.S. Army. Today, a similar inspection is done by the chain of command as a *"Command Inspection Program"* (CIP).

Page 16. Many of the complaints about Army schools remain valid, but changes in the officer basic and advanced courses now stress small group instruction by experienced former commanders.

Page 17. U.S. Army units are no longer nuclear capable.

Page 21. General Collins's comments on this page remain valid today, despite some minor changes to the readiness reporting system. The discrepancies between AR 220-1 and the technical manuals no longer exist, but there is still confusion between Fully Mission Capable (FMC) and 10/20 (in accord with the −10 and −20 technical manuals) standards. These issues still hobble sound maintenance, and the matter of integrity still arises.

Page 28. General Collins refers to first echelon maintenance. There were actually five echelons when this book was written: 1st = company or drivers. 2nd = battalion or unit mechanics. 3rd = direct support unit or technicians. 4th = general support or post civilians. 5th = depot or arsenal. Although officially out of date, the idea persists in the Army today. Mechanics regularly refer to direct support as "third shop."

Page 33. The ARTEP is now commonly called an EXEVAL (external evaluation), if done by another unit or a CTC (combat training center) rotation if done at Fort Polk (JRTC), Fort Irwin (NTC), or Hohenfels (CMTC). The term ARTEP still survives as ARTEP-MTP (Army Training and Evaluation Program-Mission Training Plan), the evaluation standards for tasks like "assault" and "defend."

Page 35. Please see the footnote. Current training doctrine is contained in the following Army publications: FM 25-100 *Training the Force* (1988), FM 25-101 *Battle Focused Training* (1990), FM 25-1 *Training* (1984), FM 25-2 *How to Manage Training in Units* (1984), FM 25-3 *How to Conduct Training in Units* (1984), FM 25-4 *How to Conduct Training Exercises* (1984), FM 25-5 *Training & Mobilization for War* (1985). These continue to be used, although issued prior to the 25-100/25-101 series.

Page 43. Current examples of inspection/courtesy/assistance teams are pre-Ranger cadre, unit school cadre, standing teams to check maintenance of machine guns and radios, range inspectors, and barracks inspectors. Umpire teams are now called "observer/controllers (O/Cs).

Page 45. FM 25-100/101 requires training schedules to be "locked in" six weeks early. In reality, changes are made in too many units, *unless* the commander really puts his/her foot down.

Page 47. Equally important is locking in resources (land, ammunition, and training aids) when the schedule is made. FM 25-100/101 is emphatic about this.

Page 48. Relative to timing, the current buzzwords are "Train to Standard, Not to Time," but experience tells unit commanders what the usual times are.

Page 52. The "two-up" rule is now doctrine (25-100/101 series).

Page 79. The current doctrine (25-101 and MTP manuals) refers to STX (situational training exercise) lanes based on this chapter. General Collins's technique has thus been institutionalized.

Page 91. Catchwords and slogans continue today. Current favorites are "multiechelon training," "high-resolution training," and "lane training." Under Checklists, ATT equals EXEVAL. See Page 33.

Page 93. Critiques are now called "after-action reviews" (AARs).

Page 94. The questioning technique illustrated here is now mandatory for AARs.

Page 99. General Collins refers to live-fire problems, developed by the 75th Ranger Regiment and conducted by the British Army. This is now the approved Army method.

Page 104-105. Since Army units are no longer nuclear capable, this section is now obsolete.

Page 110. On training requirements imposed by higher headquarters, this continues to be a common problem, although FM 25-100/101 suggests that it is not.

Page 111. BDUs (battle dress uniforms) originally were not permitted to be starched by Army Regulations. Today, they are routinely starched. This ruins some of the radar reflective and light-scattering properties of the material, but the practice is still prevalent in the Army anyway. BDU shirts are designed not to be tucked in.

Page 113. The "training NCO" is still very much present in the Army today for all the reasons cited by General Collins.

Page 115. Security is a common weakness noted at NRC, JRTC, and CMTC. The example shown here is constantly repeated, with great friendly losses.

Page 120. SQT has been discontinued. Now the Army relies on the NCO Education System (NCOES) schools and duty performance. Under individual awards, the current correct names are EFMB (Expert Field Medical Badge) and EIB (Expert Infantryman Badge).

Page 127-128. The devices and accessories listed on these pages no longer typify the Army's night-fighting technology.

Page 130. The Unit Conduct of Fire Trainer (UCOFT) combines turret training concepts with an "aircraft simulator" environment to train current tank and infantry fighting vehicle gunners.

Page 131. MILES (Multiple Integrated Laser Engagement System) and the Army's great combat training centers have replaced SCOPES/RETRAIN with a massive force-on-force "laser tag" game.

Page 136. The programs here are now known as the ARTEP-MTP. See Page 33.

Page 138. The short-range air-defense missile is no longer organic to a battalion. The missile described here has been replaced with the "Stinger."

Page 141. Tailoring the soldier's load is battalion commanders' business.

Page 143. Terms shown are now obsolete—replaced by MILES and the CTC system. See Page 131.

Page 148. EXEVAL or CTC rotation. See Page 33.

Page 152. Brigade commanders' branch of service indicated here is true for today's armored and mechanized forces, but not for light infantry brigades.

Page 158. The obsession for tank gunnery excellence now also characterizes training of Bradley Infantry Fighting Vehicle battalions.

Page 168. The Redeye has been replaced by the Stinger.

Page 171. This section on inspections is now obsolete.

Page 173. This part on readiness tests is still valid; the tests are done from time to time.

Page 187. The Army now has an approved PT uniform, including sweats.

Page 189. Army Readiness Regions and Readiness Groups are now called "Readiness Training Detachments."

Page 193. During the mobilization for the Gulf War, three Army National Guard mechanized brigades were federalized. None of the three was deployed, however.

Page 200. Insofar as training of women in the Army is concerned, it is a "given" today.

Page 205. There are, or course, no longer any "Soviet" soldiers.

Page 214. Although references in this chapter to the Soviet Union, Communism, or the Soviet soldier are out of date, the positive attributes of the American soldier still inspire confidence in the United States Army and the nation.

A book is necessarily locked in time. By the time you read *Common Sense Training*, it is likely that other changes, large and small, will have occurred. We at Presidio Press believe, however, that the soundness of General Collins's advice will continue to be recognized by soldiers and their leaders far into the future.

Foreword

The key word with respect to proper military training is, and always will be, *interest*. But the problem is not simple. It has two parts.

The first is interest on the part of the soldier being trained. Much training is so poorly conceived and presented that the troops are bored stiff and therefore fail to derive any profit from it. The Army has unfortunately earned its reputation for hurry-up-and-wait, and for dull presentations, usually to a too-small fraction of the unit in a "classroom"—a word a combat unit could well do without—instead of quick and concise instruction in the field. Training interest, which can be augmented by unusual and imaginative exercises interspersed with short periods of critique and instruction, is of the first importance, but I shall leave further discussion of this vital matter to the author of this book.

The second half of the problem is interest on the part of those who run the Army—the generals. Interest must start with the Chief of Staff and be maintained throughout the higher echelons of command. Whatever the requirements for administration, maintenance, and education, if training for combat is not vigorously pursued the Army will lose its meaning and its reason for being.

An individual's real personal interest in any skill is directly dependent on his competence in it. A child won't tolerate lessons on the violin for long if he can't get some reasonable approximation of music out of the thing; a boy who can't learn to throw or bat will shuck baseball—maybe in favor of the violin. But at least a measure of skill can be inculcated in a person who genuinely wants to learn it. Good military teaching, therefore, will usually develop competence in the subordinate commander being taught. Once he begins to understand the principles and techniques of combat, the young officer worth his salt will generate great interest in improving, on his own initiative, his ability in the military art of command.

But let it be stressed that I am talking mostly of the *senior* commander's interest. From my experience, I would cite as one of the Army's worst characteristics (among many good ones) an all too pervasive indifference among senior officers to the requirements for combat proficiency. There was (and I suspect still is) a pronounced tendency among army and corps commanders, with some obvious exceptions, to become so enmeshed in administrative and social problems that all the emphasis of their written and oral directives was (and is) placed on those problems. Even today it is not unusual for a young lieutenant colonel to feel that his efficiency rating is dependent not on whether his battalion is ready for war, but on how he supports his education and racial-relations programs.

Presumably most of our current division commanders harbor a genuine desire to have a battle-ready outfit. But I venture to say that no commander of a corps or division has any real *personal* understanding of the state of training of his command unless he *personally* spends at least two or three twenty-four periods a year—without benefit of sleep during such periods—with a combat company in the field on a tactical exercise. He should take his next two subordinate commanders with him, but not his bedding roll. It will be a pretty exhausting period for everybody, but if the company is kept solidly at work for the twenty-four hours, in a succession of varying combat problems, the several commanders present will learn more of the company's state of training, physical conditioning, esprit, and discipline than a mountain of written reports can provide. If each corps, division, and brigade commander devotes such a twenty-four hour period to *one* company of each of his immediately subordinate commands (with a minimum warning as to what company is to be observed), and if battalion commanders are required to do the same thing with each of their remaining companies, *then* we may be reasonably confident that our troops will rediscover what their real mission is, and that all the echelons of command will know how well they can perform it. The lesson to be remembered is that the competence of any combat force can be judged mostly by *looking at it* in the field. No one can evaluate a force by using a mathematical formula, by simply putting it through various firing tables on the range, or by ritualized testing administered by hordes of umpires with check sheets. Tactical *inspection* by highly interested and competent senior commanders is absolutely essential to any military force. Without it, the emphasis of command will inevitably dwell on other matters.

But for commanders—at all levels—to train their forces properly and in the course of training to inspect them properly, they must themselves be properly inspired and motivated. This can come only through personal interest in the tricks of the trade—an understanding of, and even a fascination with, the military art. Such an understanding, brought about through an intense lifelong interest, is what qualifies General Art Collins to write this book.

Understanding—and often fascination—can be developed partly by reading. That familiar little book, *The Principles of War*, by von Clausewitz should be slowly and carefully read by every combat branch officer about once a year—it takes only an hour. *The Rommel Papers* will show one how a master of the art works; it is the finest book to come out of World War II.

Let me quote one of the best paragraphs ever written on the military art. It was taken from a lecture by a German Captain von Bechtolsheim at Fort Sill in 1931. Bechtolsheim later became a corps commander in the great war. If we had studied carefully the text of his four lectures before our Artillery School we could have anticipated the overwhelmingly effective tactics which allowed the German Army to overrun Europe so quickly in 1939 and 1940. In part, this is what he had to say about mobility:

> *Our supreme tactical principle therefore is* Mobility. . . . *Mobility is aided by* surprise, *by the* independence of the subordinate commander *within the mission of the higher unit, and what we call* tactics by mission. . . . *Mobility means quick decisions, quick movements, surprise attacks with concentrated force; to do always what the enemy does not expect, and to constantly change both the means and methods and to do the most improbable thing whenever the situation permits; it means to be free of all set rules and preconceived ideas. We believe that no leader who thinks or acts by stereotyped rules can ever do anything great because he is bound by such rules. . . . War is not normal . . . We do not want therefore any stereotyped solutions for battle, but an understanding of the nature of war.*

Perhaps I should not indulge myself this way, but I cannot help saying that if those words do not excite and inspire the reader he should not be in the combat echelons of the Army. This was the philosophy which guided Patton and Manteuffel and Rommel and Harmon and the finest of our division and brigade and battalion and company commanders in heavy combat. It is a philosophy which will escape the lover of the routine and the norm, and the plodder. For to really understand and apply it requires intense interest in *training*, and that is the subject of this book.

Hamilton H. Howze
General, United States Army, Ret.

Preface

This is more than just a book on training. The ideal treatise on training would be shorter by a third—better still by a half—and would contain only suggestions to stimulate thought and action by commanders in the field of training. But the training environment that now exists is not conducive to good training. This environment must be analyzed critically, and this book attempts to do so.

Two major themes predominate in this work: first, that training is the number one business of a peacetime army but that it has suffered neglect; and, second, that the senior commander sets the tone on training in an army organization. The training atmosphere the commander creates prevails over all the efforts of his subordinates. This book is aimed at him and those who respond to his orders and attitudes. There is a message here for all levels of the chain of command, from the civilian secretaries who influence the quality of the soldier to the noncommissioned officer who is involved in most of his training.

The focus is on training at battalion level and below with major emphasis on company/battery/troop level.[1] Although many suggestions on practical down-to-earth training techniques are to be found here, few detailed charts or specific programs are included. In every unit, conditions vary with respect to training areas, experience, and a host of other variables, not the least of which is the

---

[1] In the interests of brevity, the following terms are used: *company level* for company, battery, or troop; *battalion level* for battalion or squadron; and *brigade level* for brigade, group, or regiment.

commander's attitude. Therefore, training guidance from a distance is not much help to the trainer at the unit level. The details of particular training programs are spelled out in appropriate field and technical manuals. But no matter what is in the manuals, junior leaders cannot be effective trainers if a healthy atmosphere is not created where the training takes place. Training flourishes only in an atmosphere that invites it to do so, and only the generals and the colonels can extend that invitation.

If the senior commanders improve the training environment, training will improve rapidly. Ideas and attitudes conducive to good training are pervasive since they come from a true recognition of the importance of training to an army. All ranks, from the general officer to the NCO, can use these ideas and attitudes within the scope of their respective responsibilities. These ideas on training are internally consistent, and the basic themes apply to the National Guard and Reserves as well as to the active Army.

The most notable training achievement in Army history was the creation of a great Army and Air Force between 1940 and 1945. Churchill said, "The rate at which the small American Army of only a few hundred thousand men, not long before the war, created the mighty force of millions of soldiers is a wonder of military history . . . This is an achievement which the soldiers of every other nation will always study with admiration and envy." The pre-World War II Army that accomplished that feat did not have nearly the capability or expertise that today's Army has. The leaders of that Army, however, had a training knack that has been lost. The task at hand is to recapture the art.

In addressing a new generation of leaders, I cannot emphasize too strongly that the fundamentals of training do not change. Weapons change, technology advances, and tactics adjust to what is new. The fundamentals of training, however—to prepare an army to fight in some national crisis with whatever means are at hand—change but little. The major changes in training come from the social changes that affect the human condition. The enlightened trainer takes advantage of these changes to forge a better fighting force.

This book is a dialogue with my fellow soldiers on a subject vital to the Army's future. The soldier knows that death, sacrifice, and hardship are daily companions in combat; only good training or an end to the fighting alleviates them. My prejudices on training are strong, as my colleagues in the service are well aware. Although I do not presume that my training prescriptions are the best, they have been tried at every level of command—and they work. A host of solid professional soldiers taught me what I know. Few of these men were famous, but all of them were dedicated to the military profession and the Army. This book will repay a small part of my debt to them and to the Army, whose virtues far outweigh its faults.

If this volume illuminates the training environment, helps its readers to overcome the neglect of training, and kindles an imaginative interest in training in the new generation of officers and noncommissioned officers, who have to train an Army far more complex than the one I joined in 1938, it will have served a useful purpose.

Acknowledgments

In the writing of this book I received help and comments from many officers and noncommissioned officers of all ranks from sergeant to general. If there were voids, they had ideas on how to fill them. If there were errors or lack of balance, they suggested sources or examples to put things in perspective. I am deeply indebted to them for their help and my gratitude is great.

Mr. Joseph R. Friedman, formerly of the United States Army Center of Military History, edited the manuscript and gave me valuable advice as this work went from manuscript through publication.

ASC

COMMON SENSE TRAINING

A Working Philosophy for Leaders

1

Training is all-encompassing and should be related to every-thing a unit does or can have happen to it.

A Philosophy of Training

The essential characteristics of a good army are that it be well trained and well disciplined. These two characteristics are apparent in every unit achievement, whether in peace or in war. Discipline derives and flows from training and serves to emphasize a fundamental point essential to a philosophy of training: that training is all-encompassing. Training permeates everything a military organization does.

If training is so important, why is it so often neglected? There must be some inherent contradiction when commanders fail to devote adequate attention to the activity which can do so much for every aspect of a unit's operations, maintenance, administration, and esprit. In trying to analyze this contradiction, I have come to the conclusion that perhaps a misconception exists as to what is meant by training. Through the years, I have noticed that when commanders and staff officers discuss training, they most often talk in terms of tactical exercises, firing of weapons, and those aspects of military operations that focus on "move, shoot, and communicate." Seldom do they talk or write about training in the context of personnel and administrative procedures, maintenance, and safety. They fail to relate the serious-incident reports, which tell of accidents and injuries resulting from a broken towbar or poor rigging, to the training that might have prevented the accidents. Too many commanders are not aware that training is all-encompassing and should be related to everything a unit does—or can have happen to it.

A professional soldier, be he officer or noncommissioned officer, must learn early in his career not to think of training as the insatiable enemy that endlessly consumes his time. True, he and his troops will be training most of every day. But training is not just a priority to be emphasized this week because a senior commander is now pushing it, as he was "maintenance" last week and "safety" or "equal opportunity" the week before. Training affords a commander the opportunity to explore the variety of problems and missions that will always confront him. When a commander of a military unit takes this attitude, most of his problems—and those of his unit—will be met and solved in the course of daily training, and thus will cease to be problems. The same attitude will prevail again over new problems.

A good example of a comprehensive view of training comes from *The Patton Papers*.[1] General Patton's flamboyance in the context of training is irrelevant, a matter of personal style. Sometimes it works; most often it doesn't. What really bears on the issue of training is that General Patton was a keen student of the military art and gave much thought to weapons, tactics, training of the individual and the small teams, as well as to physical conditioning. He stressed the fundamentals and made maximum use of limited resources:

> *The arrival of the new tanks, giving the center 25 in all, made it possible to have company maneuvers. Patton consequently modified the drill schedule in order to have the companies, in rotation, train as a unit every afternoon, and the platoons, each in turn, work on night maneuvers every day after dark.*
>
> *From seven until noon, some men from each company took driving instruction while the rest trained on the guns and practiced such activities as message writing, grenade throwing, and gas-mask wearing; from one in the afternoon to six, one company held a maneuver as a unit while the other troops worked physically. From seven-thirty to midnight, each platoon had an exercise that featured night driving.*[2]

This passage might suggest ideas to National Guard and Reserve units on what can be done by concentrated training in back-to-back drill periods. But using time efficiently takes a lot of thinking, good organization, and an effective chain of command.

Another principle basic to my philosophy of training is that the key to all successful training lies in raising the quality of individual and small-unit skills. Success in battle is dependent on the coordinated effort of a number of small units of several arms and services working together to accomplish a mission. Other things being equal, the army with the best trained small units will prevail.

---

[1] Martin Blumenson, *The Patton Papers 1885-1940*, vol. I (Boston: Houghton Mifflin, 1972).
[2] Blumenson, pp. 545-46.

Even when other things are not equal, the army with skilled soldiers and determined small units will sometimes defeat bigger and better equipped armies and will often confound and outlast their adversaries. The modern Israeli Army is a good example of the former; the Viet Cong and the North Vietnamese Army are good examples of the latter. The importance of small-unit training to mission accomplishment cannot be overemphasized.

Still another principle of this philosophy is, don't put on a show. The best way an army can gain the confidence of the people, not to mention the confidence of those who are in the army, is to do the best job it can every day. It does not necessarily follow that everything will be right. Human nature being what it is, there will be errors enough to go around. But commanders who accept the odds and decide that they are going to have confidence in their subordinates can look forward to the visit of senior commanders to their units without a flurry of activity that makes needless work for everyone. It has been my personal experience that maintaining such an attitude of calm in the face of a VIP's appearance is no easy feat. The competitive spirit in our society naturally carries over into the service. This is not all bad, but the pressures on commanders are great and too many are preoccupied with simply looking good. It is a rare commander who has enough confidence to look with pleasure on the opportunity to show an unexpected visitor how his unit goes about its daily routine. We love to put on a show, and most commanders with any advance warning will do just that. But in so doing, they don't fool the troops, and they don't fool any senior commander who knows his business. The troops and the company-level commanders are the ones who pay the bill for the shows put on for visitors. The extra effort plays havoc with the training already scheduled. The Army as a whole must look critically at the things that create this worried state of mind.

Finally, this philosophy is based on four requirements for training. The first requirement is soldiers, and you have them in every unit. The second is equipment, and you have that in abundance—too much of it, in fact. The third requirement is a place to train, and generally you can find that once you learn to look at your surroundings and make the most of whatever is available. The last necessity is all in the head: a combination of brains, imagination, interest, and initiative that enables you to put everything together and do the training that has to be done. The first three requirements—the men, equipment, and place—are there for the using. The last requirement, mental and of the spirit, is intangible and is the hardest one to provide. But an able leader can provide it if he has in his military soul a genuine concern for the soldier and the Army's many missions.

From experience I know that few trainers relish the term philosophy when it is associated with the action-filled world of training. However, I have used the term purposely with respect to training because one definition of philosophy is "the general principles or laws of a field of activity ordinarily with implication of their practical application." Thinking of training in those terms might stimulate the interest in training that is needed. Training is hard work, but it does not have to be dull. Much military training is presented in boring fashion. The troops lose interest and do not absorb the instruction, the training program fails, and the morale of the troops drops. Good training requires a lot of mental effort; the commander must devise ways to make training intellectually and physically challenging to the troops. The unfortunate thing is that so many commanders don't recognize dull training. But their troops do.

2

I have never seen a company, platoon, or squad take a hill at 100 percent strength.

Common Excuses
for Inadequate Training

The most common excuse for poor training I have heard over the years is a shortage of troops: "I don't have enough men," "Half of my men are on detail," or "I need a full strength unit to train properly." You may have used these excuses yourself. I suggest you forget them if you are a company-level commander. If you are a field-grade-level commander and you hear these comments, start doing something about them, but don't accept them as excuses for poor training.

Obviously, full strength is most desirable. Full crews and squads make training easier, and if you are going into combat, higher headquarters should see to it that your unit is at full strength so you can get everyone well trained before the bullets start flying. Generally, this will happen in time of war. In time of peace, which is the condition any intelligent soldier hopes for, the Army will never have enough men to keep all units at full strength. With leave, education programs, and sick call, to mention only a few everyday realities that account for absent men, rarely will a unit be at full strength for training. With good training management, however, enough men will be there to make training worthwhile. Regardless of the number, a leader dedicated to training will find that much good training can be accomplished for the many, or the few, who are available. A little imagination at the company-command level and good organizational management at the field-grade level will make it possible.

When you begin to think you cannot train because some of your men are not available, just remember this: I have never yet seen a company, platoon, or a squad take a hill at 100 percent strength. Many of the objectives I have seen taken were seized by units that combat had reduced over a period of time to 55 to 65 percent of their TOE strength in the forward-fighting elements, and those reduced-strength units went on to take their objectives with a minimum of casualties. I don't know of any artillery units that stopped giving fire support because a couple of guns were knocked out or because some gunners were casualties. The drivers and ammunition bearers took positions at the remaining guns and kept them firing in the tradition of the artillery. When a tank is destroyed in a tank platoon, the other tank crews go on fighting. If that is what happens in combat, what is to stop you from conducting meaningful training in peacetime despite the fact that some of your men are not there? The problem here is that commonly the commander believes that the return on the training time spent will be inadequate if a number of the troops are missing. If you can accept the principle that the key to successful training is to raise the quality of every individual's and every small team's skills, then the excuse that training is poor or cannot be conducted because some members of the unit are absent will just not bear hard scrutiny.

When you hear a subordinate complaining about absent men your question should be, "What are you doing for the troops you do have?" Remember, individuals from your unit will step forward when there are combat casualties, and they will carry out the mission if their noncommissioned officers (NCOs) and officers have taken advantage of the time available to teach them all there is to know about their military specialty. A soldier needs to know much more than most people realize. That need is what makes a command assignment so demanding, and a trainer of soldiers must train them all well because he never knows which one of his soldiers will save the day.

An example with which I was personally familiar will help make this point. Private First Class Dexter Kerstetter from Centralia, Washington, was a most unlikely hero. He was a cook's helper in C Company of the 130th Infantry during World War II. The strength of the rifle platoons was down to eighteen to twenty men and the company commander scoured the company to get riflemen in the front line. Kerstetter, small, gaunt, thirty-seven years old—an old man to most of his nineteen- and twenty-year-old company mates—picked up his rifle and stepped forward. The citation he received tells the rest of the story:

CITATION: Medal of Honor. He was with his unit in a dawn attack against hill positions approachable only along a narrow ridge paralleled on each side by steep cliffs which were heavily defended by enemy mortars, machineguns, and rifles in well-camouflaged spider holes and tunnels leading to caves. When the leading element was halted by intense fire that inflicted five casualties, Private Kerstetter passed through the American

6

line with his squad. Placing himself well in advance of his men, he grimly worked his way up to the narrow steep hogback, meeting the brunt of enemy action. With well-aimed shots and rifle-grenade fire, he forced the Japs to take cover. He left the trail and moving down a cliff that offered only precarious footholds, dropped among four Japs at the entrance to a cave, fired his rifle from his hip and killed them all. Climbing back to the trail, he advanced against heavy enemy machinegun, rifle and mortar fire to silence a heavy machinegun by killing its crew of four with rifle fire and grenades. He expended his remaining ammunition and grenades on a group of approximately 20 Japs, scattering them, and returned to his squad for more ammunition and first aid for his left hand, which had been blistered by the heat from his rifle. Resupplied, he guided a fresh platoon into a position from which a concerted attack could be launched, killing three hostile soldiers on the way. In all, he dispatched 16 Japs that day. The hill was taken and held against the enemy's counterattacks, which continued for 3 days. Private Kerstetter's dauntless and gallant heroism was largely responsible for the capture of this key enemy position, and his fearless attack in the face of great odds was an inspiration to his comrades in their dangerous task.[1]

PFC Kerstetter was of course a brave man. Also he was a well-trained soldier. He was perhaps the last man anyone would have picked in C Company to accomplish what he did. But war is like that. So train well the men you do have, and fight to get back those who are missing.

Having said all this, I can hear some harried, overburdened, young commander mutter, "Well, that's easy for you to say." Having analyzed and examined thousands of understrength situations on the ground I feel strongly that lack of men is a poor excuse for inadequate training. But quite often the fault is not that of the company-level commander. Battalion, brigade, and higher level commanders and staffs often create a host of competing activities that make it most difficult for the company commander to concentrate on the training of his unit. Examples?

Commander's call during prime training time.
Inspection teams formed from subordinate units.
Unannounced surveys that could have been scheduled well ahead.
Sergeant Major calls to send police detail "right now," because "someone is coming."

Any company/battery/troop commander can cite fifty more such examples.

---

[1]*Medal of Honor Recipients, 1863-1973*, 93rd Congress, 1st Session (Washington: U.S. Government Printing Office, 1968) pp. 598-99.

Quite often the staff imposes these demands without the commander knowing about it or without realizing the full impact. But the senior commander should be aware of the conflicts if he is properly checking training and conditions in his units. Higher level commanders, especially general officers, can do much to create a frame of mind in which everyone is thinking about having as many soldiers at training as possible. That is what training management is all about. It will be discussed at length in Chapter 6.

Another common excuse is, "The training area is inadequate." The training areas are either too small, too far away, too wooded, too open, or too something. What has happened is that we have lost our eye for terrain. In a school on training conducted for battalion and brigade commanders in Europe, we made it a point to look for a small piece of ground within a stone's throw of the headquarters or the barracks that we could walk to. After a brief look at the surrounding terrain we would discuss types of training that could be conducted from that point. The commanders were always surprised by the number of things they concluded could be done. Open your eyes; the terrain is there if you know how to use it. Keep in mind that it is individual and small-unit training that needs special attention; that type of training can be done most anywhere by the imaginative leader.

Other common excuses are complaints about the size and frequency of large training exercises and insufficient training ammunition: "It's not big enough," "We don't have enough of the large exercises so essential to training the Army," or "We need more ammunition and blanks." Officers of all ranks pronounce these sentiments so often that they have come to have the authority of almost total acceptance. But they are myths. Generally the bigger the exercise the poorer the training at the small-unit level. In my thirty-six years of service I saw no exception to that observation. As for liberal ammunition allowances, they do not necessarily lead to better training. Some people think that noise makes up for thorough preparation. Too much ammunition frequently leads to the expectation that the course can be fired one more time in the event of a poor score. Stringent ammunition allowances encourage better preparatory training and better range firing. Some individuals or crews may not qualify, but that hazard is an incentive to better training and more dry runs before the next chance comes around.

It would be enlightening for anyone who believes that developing a good army requires large training areas, big maneuvers, and large quantities of ammunition to study the training of the German Army before World War II. Note how much of the training of that very effective fighting force was conducted in local training areas close to the *kasernes*. Note how much of the preparation for larger operations was accomplished by war games and command-post exercises or map exercises.

The type of training I consider essential to developing a professional fighting force does not depend on a full complement of troops, or large training areas, or lots of ammunition. Developing individual skills, which we tend to neglect and which always need attention, does not require much in the way of space or resources. There are hundreds of situations that provide the opportunity to train the crew—of a tank, a gun, or a mortar—in most of the fundamentals of the weapon's operation. All that is needed is the number of men available to be taught. This may be only two squads or two tank crews out of a platoon, but these men can be trained if you do not look for an excuse not to train them. Then, if proper training-management procedures are established, the platoons and company-level units will have adequate opportunity to train. Once the procedures are established, the battalion, which is the basic fighting unit in an army, is all but ready to go.

Good small-unit training demands thinking, and a lot of it, to plan, organize, conduct, and evaluate. It does not require a lot of paper or great logistical and personnel support. All that really counts is what is available: the men actually present, their equipment, a piece of ground, knowledge of weapons and tactics, and, most important, a little imagination and initiative. Now, having dispensed with the myths, it might be well to pause and reflect on what has contributed to a poor training climate in the U.S. Army.

3

A command assignment was a race to be run only when absolutely necessary—and then as swiftly as possible.

What Happened? Where Did We Go Astray?

There was considerable unanimity among the junior officers about Army problems in the late 1960s and early 1970s. This extract from an Army War College study sums up a prevailing criticism:

> *A scenario that was repeatedly described in seminar sessions and narrative responses includes an ambitious, transitory commander—marginally skilled in the complexities of his duties—engulfed in producing statistical results, fearful of personal failure, too busy to talk with or listen to his subordinates, and determined to submit acceptable optimistic reports which reflect faultless completion of a variety of tasks at the expense of the sweat and frustration of his subordinates.[1]*

---

[1]USAWC, *Study on Military Professionalism*, (Carlisle, PA, 30 June 1970) p. iv.

This study was one of several directed by the Chief of Staff of the Army in what was a most difficult period for the Army. The study was critical of the Army officer corps. Some of the conclusions were relevant and valuable, others were questionable. The study test was "exploratory" and stated it was used on a small, skewed sample of respondents. The study was done quickly by direction, and an in-house privacy characterized the study. It was in the family and amounted to a segment of the officer corps letting off steam by bawling itself out. The study noted that some comments were "naive" and "idealistic" which is normal when juniors are talking about how much better their seniors can be. There was one glaring weakness in the study: its absurd rejection of trends in the whole society as causative factors in the Army's difficulties in the late Vietnam period (from discussions with Dr. A. L. Wermuth, a retired infantry colonel—see his comments in the journal *Armed Forces and Society*, Spring, 1977).

I dwell on this study because it has been singled out for selective extracts by those who want to attack the military. Seldom do they note who directed the study or cite reservations of the study group.

Young officers expressed similar views at symposia at the Command and General Staff College and at West Point. If the criticism was valid, and my assessment is that there was some merit in it, these conditions did not emerge overnight. They had their beginnings much earlier.

Fifteen years before the War College study appeared I was commanding the 10th Infantry Regiment in Germany. As a result of my experiences I wrote an article "intended to highlight some of the problems that make a command assignment a dubious honor."[2] Statistics, administrative requirements, mandatory training, and reluctance of commanders to explain shortcomings to superiors came in for comment. A review of that article shows that some current problems were headaches in the mid-fifties.[3]

About ten years after commanding the 10th Infantry, I took command of the 4th Infantry Division. Several of the statistical and administrative problems had improved greatly, but the training situation was not any better. In one respect it was worse. Soon after taking command, in the summer of 1965, I observed that many dedicated field-grade officers did not even notice the fundamental deficiencies in their own units. Field-grade officers should have seen and corrected these deficiencies as if by second nature, but they either did not recognize the deficiencies or lacked the confidence and knowledge required to dive in and set things right. In a note prepared for the Chief of Staff at the time, I pointed out that there was an apparent weakness in the background of some lieutenant colonels and colonels on basic weapons, tactics, and supervision of training, and that infantry training was particularly weak. I wrote that after mulling it over with the Assistant Division Commanders and a few other senior officers, we could come to no clear conclusion as to why this was so, though someone had suggested that these grades were suffering from the period of the Army's pentomic structure. To fill what seemed to be a void in their professional development, we set up a school program of tactical walks, sand-table sessions, and "how to train" exercises. The officers learned quickly, conducted similar schools for their junior officers and NCOs, and took well-trained units to Vietnam where they were good combat commanders.

In June of 1971, after visiting units on an almost daily basis for more than two years—one year as a field-force commander under combat conditions in Vietnam and the other as Deputy Commander-in-Chief, United States Army

---

It is a sign of strength in an organization when it can look at itself critically and then do something about it. This study was an example of the Army doing just that. A number of officers of great talent left the service in this period. Had they remained in the Army they could have done much to make it better. In spite of all that is said to the contrary the chance is there if one has the guts to speak his piece, and many do.

[2]Arthur S. Collins Jr., "What Are We Doing To Our Commanders?" *Army* (January 1957), p. 22.

[3]For another view see portions of letter from General Anthony McAuliffe to General Henry Hodes at start of Chapter 5, this book.

Europe, an assignment which provided an unparalleled opportunity to observe a large number of units from every branch of the service—I sent a memorandum to my boss that summed up my observations as follows:

As I looked over units during the past year and tried to account for the shortcomings in operations overall, and training in particular, I was persuaded that our problems stemmed from a lack of perception of proper standards and a lack of knowledge on the demands of their jobs on the part of many of our lieutenant colonels and colonels. I am more certain than ever that this is a major factor we must recognize.

These daily visits to units continued for another two years until my retirement in July 1974. By that time I had no doubt that the weakness lay with a large number of field-grade officers, and some general officers too, who lacked an understanding of the fundamentals of training as well as with the complex personnel, logistic, and maintenance systems that had been introduced into the United States Army. In the United States Army Europe (USAREUR) we established a school for field-grade commanders, as we had earlier established a company-commanders course. The schools helped, but they only scratched the surface of the Army's need to develop an understanding of what had happened down at the unit level and what had gone wrong in our efforts to develop competent commanders.

When visiting units, I always talked to officers and enlisted men about what they were doing, what their problems were, and what could be done to make things better. I frequently asked officers of all grades what had happened in the Army that had dulled the desire to command except as a "ticket punching" assignment that one should get away from as soon as possible, hopefully with a good rating. One response, from virtually all battalion and brigade commanders, was striking. They repeatedly spoke of the "crisis management" that stemmed from emphasizing too many programs simultaneously. Maintenance, equal opportunity, training, accidents, roadside spotchecks, and a host of other on-going programs all competed for attention. They said if they had only one or two priorities at a time, instead of the great number that confronted them, they would not have much of a problem commanding their units. The individual activities the commanders were most concerned about at that point were recited like a litany, and "training" was always one of them. This repeated reference to "training" as one of the competing priorities suddenly made me realize what low esteem training had fallen into in the Army. I had been taught that when a problem arose more emphasis was given to the training that pertained to that subject area. Now, "training" was one of a list of activities or events competing for attention.

I spent a lot of time trying to put over the idea that training is comprehensive, that it encompasses everything an Army does. You train mechanics in maintenance and operators in their duties, and this is reflected in the vehicles that pass the roadside spotchecks and in the rating in the Annual General Inspection (AGI). You train drivers in defensive driving as part of the safety program. You train officers and NCOs to look out for the well being of their men as part of the equal-opportunity program.

These examples may at first appear oversimplified, but they are not. Basic to a philosophy of training is the recognition that training is comprehensive and relates to all that is done in a military unit. This idea was hard to communicate and equally difficult for harassed commanders to accept in the early 1970s. During this period the Department of Defense prescribed a mandatory program for equal opportunity, and commanders were directed to appoint a series of councils that tended to undermine the chain of command. A host of programs reflecting a Madison Avenue approach to a volunteer army, some poorly conceived and others too hastily imposed, eroded the confidence of the noncommissioned officers. A commander's lot is never an easy one, but in this period the pressures and problems were greater than any I had ever encountered in my years of service.

Since the officers I am talking about were hardworking, intelligent, and eager to do an outstanding job, I spent a lot of time thinking about what circumstances had changed that would leave so many dedicated and ambitious officers, at this critical juncture in their careers as field-grade commanders, insufficiently exposed to the fundamentals of the military art to train their units properly. What follows is a condensed version of some of the thoughts that came to mind.

The first thing to emphasize is that one change by itself might not make much difference, but the effect of a number of them can be overwhelming. They creep up on you, and they emanate from deep-rooted changes in our society: in technology as well as social, economic, and other conditions. For instance, it became obvious that leaders, both officers and NCOs, were losing an appreciation for terrain. This factor had its roots in technological developments with respect to transportation. In the late 1930s, before World War II was expected by many people in the United States, the officers and enlisted men who came into the service walked with their men or rode horseback, depending on their rank and their branch. In this age of advanced technology, that form of transportation sounds almost antique. But in 1938, when I was assigned to a machine-gun company, I had a horse, which was a great luxury for an infantryman. The jeep might have been on a drawing board somewhere, but I didn't see one until after 1941. Those who came to command in World War II knew terrain naturally. They had a keen appreciation for the difficulties in passing over it and they could use its many variations for attack or defense. They were better tacticians and better trainers because of this knowledge.

After World War II, the internal combustion engine took over, and the automobile became more American than apple pie. When this happened, we began to lose touch with the ground. The Sunday afternoon drive took the place of a walk in the countryside. Youngsters then, the commanders and trainers of today rarely got more than a glimpse of the woods and fields along their route of travel as the family car sped over ribbons of concrete at high speeds. With the advent of television, they began to spend less time playing outdoors in the local fields and woods. The boys from the farms and the country—the Sergeant Yorks of World War I and Audie Murphys of World War II, who were credited with being close to the ground—were moving to the cities. Therefore, leaders of this era do not come by terrain appreciation as naturally as their forebears did. Couple this fact with the trend in service schools to move training from the outdoors into the classroom, and it should surprise no one that a new generation of leaders lacks the affinity for the ground that is essential for an officer or NCO of the combat arms in the conduct of training. I wonder how many foresaw this problem as the emphasis and teaching techniques in the service schools slowly changed along with the society at large.

The changes in the service schools did little to enhance training. Beginning in about the mid-1950s, the Army War College tended to look at distant horizons as it adjusted to the United States's shift from pre-World War II isolationism to its role as leader of the free world. The roles that a few senior service commanders filled during and just after World War II—Marshall, Eisenhower, MacArthur, Clay—provided the rationale for much greater emphasis on international affairs and national strategy in the service schools curricula. The new Department of Defense organization created the need for emphasis on management, and on combined, joint, and general staff procedures. These are all important subjects, and the leaders of the Army should have some acquaintance with them, but the emphasis on political science, Department of Defense, and joint-staff concerns pushed study and analysis of Army problems into the wings. The Army War College curriculum, perhaps in an effort to match the prestige of the National War College, seemed to be designed to develop military statesmen for the National Security Council, future Supreme Allied Commanders, or chairmen of the Joint Chiefs of Staff (JCS).

But those positions are few in number, and the leaders selected to fill them could be counted on to learn what was needed by using their ability to absorb the big picture. Meanwhile, the large number of students who were to become battalion, brigade, and division commanders were learning little about the leadership, logistics, and similar problems confronting all the units of the Army. A close personal friend of mine, who was on the faculty of the Army War College at the time, still calls me his "favorite military mechanic" because of my insistence that we were not paying enough attention to the Army's business. He naturally felt that the curriculum was going in the right direction.

14

Within a few years the Command and General Staff College (C&GSC) felt the pressure to catch up with the new look. The curriculum was revised to incorporate an inordinate emphasis on nuclear warfare and to address itself more fully to the social- and political-science aspects of military matters. Advanced degree programs were stressed, as they had been at the War College. At the same time, although the Army had more sophisticated equipment, complex systems, and world-wide commitments, the C&GSC devoted less time to the problems these changes created in the fields of training, personnel management, maintenance, and leadership.

A major selling point for newly commissioned officers was how soon they could get an advanced degree. At West Point, this factor was more important to some about to be commissioned cadets than what branch or station they were going to. Some of the officers selected for degree programs had little or no troop duty. Advanced degrees are essential if the Army is to keep pace in this day and age, but when young officers obtain them at the expense of troop duty, the wisdom of the program is open to challenge. In times past officers had worked hard to get degrees, often on their own time and after they had matured in the service. Now the degree was becoming more important than the duties that come with service to men, unit, and country. Selection for Command and General Staff College and the War College is a recognition of competence, ability, and work well done. The opportunity to get an advanced degree is recognition of intellectual qualifications and future potential. Acquiring these credentials placed the officers with them in the top brackets of the Army at least as far as these indicators of competence were concerned. They were indicators that stood out in career summaries.

While all these developments were going on, the Department of Defense, Joint Chiefs of Staff, a host of military advisory groups, missions, and headquarters were expanding and placing demands on the services for their best officers. These agencies had top priority for assignment of graduates from the top service schools and graduate courses. As a result, over a period of years some of the most talented officers had a succession of assignments to schools, high-level staffs, executive posts, and as aides to top civilian secretaries, and then went back to school—all at the expense of duty with troops, which is what the Army is all about. The units suffered, since they did not get the best officers —except for an occasional brief assignment for which front-runners were probably requested by name. The officers suffered because they had not learned about the complex ramifications of their own profession. They were not learning about training, the mud, and the dark night. They were not conscious of the leadership, training, and personnel problems that were simmering in the units, under the pressures of the Vietnam conflict and a revolution in our society. The Army was successful in developing the military statesmen, staff planners, and management experts, but it had neglected the "military mechanics." The results were beginning to show in the units.

While the senior Army schools were devoting more and more attention to matters other than Army business, advanced courses of the service schools were unobtrusively undergoing changes. Emphasis shifted to staff procedures and training on sophisticated devices that were not available in troop units. Training was taking place more in the classroom and on TV, and less out on the actual ground. Though no one gave it much thought, this was a further curtailment of the opportunity for young commanders to learn about terrain and tactics, subjects a commander must be familiar with before he is qualified to train or fight. The subject of training in a unit got scant attention in the form that might be valuable to a company-level commander. An article by an armor company commander stated that " the advanced course is not designed to train officers for company level command duties."[4] Neither did any other course.

The Huntley-Brinkley form of presentation, and the sight of an immaculately dressed officer pulling a collapsible pointer from his pocket and ceremoniously extending it at precisely the right moment were the hallmarks of success in the service-school circles. But you don't teach soldiers by talking at them. Unfortunately, this penchant for the lecture was carried over to training in the units where it had no place.

By way of comparison, a three-month battalion commanders course at the Infantry School from January through April of 1942, left me a memory not of lectures and classrooms, but of days spent in the open—most were raw, cold, and wet and a few were pleasant and warm. We looked at and organized defensive positions on hills, in draws, and in the woods, and then figured out how best to attack them. We spent days on the range learning about weapons, what caused stoppages, and how to keep the weapons firing. We learned about supporting fires and how to adjust them when we could hear the shells whirring overhead. If the subject was transportation we were in the motor parks or checking vehicles in the field. This was the most practical and valuable course I ever took. Though only a captain with four years of service, it prepared me so that I was able to command a battalion by May of 1942 and a regiment in August 1944.

The readiness reporting system made its debut in the mid-1960s. It promptly contributed to the deterioration of training. Each passing year it has created other problems as well. This system, originally devised for management purposes, had some value in that limited role. But in time it became the monster that threatened commanders' careers and eroded standards of integrity—at least if the junior officers' view is valid. This reporting system had some ridiculous aspects, and the field-grade and higher commanders who could bring a judgment to bear on the combat readiness of their units were suspected

---

[4]Alphonso Pearson, "The Neglected CO," *Armor* (September-October, 1973), p. 44.

by some subordinates of painting optimistic and inaccurate reports. This problem was made more intense because of a vendetta between the Stennis Preparedness Subcommittee of the Congress and Secretary McNamara and his systems analysts. The charge was the same at this level as it was in the service. The Secretary of Defense was charged with trying to paint a rosy picture on service readiness, and Congress was using the statistics from the readiness reporting system to prove this picture false. This placed a terrible burden on battalion and brigade commanders and it was a monkey they could not get off their backs, because general officers felt the pressure of the statistics and their concern rattled right down the chain of command.

A different type of readiness check, pertaining to nuclear weapons—the Technical-Proficiency Inspection (TPI)—produced even more severe tremors in units with a nuclear capability than those created by the readiness report in other units. Great pressure was put on commanders not to fail a TPI, and battalion- and company-level commanders believed that if they failed even one such inspection their careers were in jeopardy. In some cases this belief was confirmed. General officers put the pressure on and many commanders were relieved.

The inevitable result of these readiness checks at battalion and company level, since this was where commanders felt the pressure most, was an emphasis on the maintenance of materiel and the reports rendered on them as opposed to a concern for the men and for the way systems operated and could be used most effectively—that is, for operations and training. Training deteriorated because the commanders emphasized what they considered a threat to their careers: training was not much of a threat and is not easily quantified. Commanders had too many other things to worry about that could be quantified.

The centralization of command, management, and information systems to meet the demands for data on operations, logistics, personnel, and readiness by burgeoning DOD secretariats added to the pressures. Seldom noticed was the gradual loss of professional military expertise as Army officers in large numbers spent years developing and practicing new technical, analytical, and managerial skills. Military preoccupation was with planning and studies at the expense of training, tactics, and traditional military expertise. The longer talented officers stayed away from troops, the less confidence they had in their ability to command in these troubled times. A command assignment was a race to be run only when absolutely necessary—and then as swiftly as possible.

Finally, the demands of the Vietnam conflict and the concurrent revolution in manners, morals, and beliefs took their toll on the training environment. Units had more than a 100 percent turnover every year, and some units had two or three commanders in the same time frame. The counterculture of the 1960s culminated in protest marches and anti-Vietnam demonstrations in the late 1960s and early 1970s. Racial animosities, the spread of the drug culture, and an emphasis on individual freedoms combined to create serious morale and leadership problems in all the armed forces as well as in other sectors of society. Add these social pressures to the instability in units due to the demands of Vietnam, and the wonder is that the Army functioned as well as it did.

If training was the main casualty of the period, we have much to be thankful for, because that deficiency can be corrected in a few years with the right leadership. The matters of integrity, the systems that put undue pressures on commanders, and the disoriented school programs are already under review by the Department of the Army. Now is the time for action. Enough study has been done, and the most glaring example of a prolonged deficiency is the readiness reporting system. Senior officers have long been criticized for failing to understand the system, and the latest studies say the situation still exists.

To summarize, I saw hundreds of middle-level commanders in the early 1970s who reflected the deficiencies noted in the War College study. These men had pride and wanted to do well, but the pressures on them often blurred their sense of responsibility for their subordinates. Some of the most able had acquired several degrees and had fine reputations. They were the ones general officers received letters on, saying that they were being released from some staff position only if they could get a command. When they did get command of a unit, they did not stay long enough for senior commanders to evaluate the unit over a prolonged period. The talent of some of these men was such that they put on a great front and a good show as a commander, but they did so at the expense of their troops. As they had advanced in rank and returned to units in higher grades, they simply had not learned the fundamentals of their profession. They knew their weakness and lacked the confidence to fight back up the chain of command when the pressures mounted.

Since the objective of this book is to improve training, I have touched only lightly on my beliefs and reflections without trying to produce detailed proof. I am convinced, however, that the evidence is there for the historian who wants to pursue it. I hope that historian is in the War College or Command and General Staff College now, studying these Army concerns. It is important that the Army attempt to identify and comprehend clearly those undercurrents and conditions of our society that had so adverse an influence on operations and morale in the late 1960s and early 1970s. The Army War College and the Command and General Staff College should continue their recent investigation of these matters, while the Army Staff makes appropriate policy changes. Several such changes have already been announced—for example, assignment of more C&GSC graduates to troop units, selection and designation of commanders by Department of the Army, emphasis on training at Command and General Staff College, orienting advance school courses to the "how" of training, and placing more emphasis on command responsibility.

4

Without exception, the units which had the most maintenance hours on the training schedule had the poorest maintenance.

Maintenance and Training— the Chicken or the Egg?

Social and organizational changes as well as heavy demands on the Army contributed to the deterioration of training. To appreciate the depths of this problem, take a close look at a functional area important to operations and see how staff and command actions can compromise the system and the objectives the Army hopes to achieve. The maintenance function provides a good vehicle for examination, so take a ride.

An extract from a service-school course says, "Good training includes good maintenance." Should the maxim have more realistically read, "Good maintenance includes good training"? Maintenance problems originated with man's first weapons, and good maintenance has always been essential to an effective military organization. By the early 1970s, conditions which had been building since the early 1960s combined to create what some called the "motor pool" or "maintenance syndrome." It had an adverse effect not only on training, but also on maintenance itself. Distortions of what maintenance is and how it is performed were pervasive in the early 1970s. It is clear that a number of factors contributed to the problems: the amount of equipment and its complexity; the unit readiness reporting system with its emphasis on statistics and the tendency it engendered to compare one unit with another; the commander's concern about numbers and his natural desire to make his unit look good; and a failure to differentiate between primary-function maintenance, performed by skilled mechanics, and secondary-function preventive maintenance, performed by the driver or crew member.

With respect to the first factor, equipment, it suffices to say that too much complex equipment is being placed down at the company/battery/troop level. An army must prepare for all types of crises, but it has to take a calculated risk in some areas. I doubt that anyone has accurately assessed the effect on a unit of the maintenance burden for all this equipment, or the pressures such a burden places on a commander. Many unit problems and many millions of dollars could be saved by a persistent paring down of the Tables of Organization and Equipment by a few hard-headed realists. Some will say that this process goes on all the time, but if it does the knife has grown dull.

The unit readiness reporting system has probably contributed more to the distortion of the maintenance function, and in turn to training, than any other single factor. It has also led to many assertions of questionable data and contributed to an undermining of confidence in the Army's integrity. Originally devised as a management tool to keep the Army informed on the availability, condition, and distribution of equipment, the readiness reporting system had merit and filled a real need. However, as the Office of the Secretary of Defense and the Department of the Army began comparing the status of units based on the reports, and then later as the system was incorporated into the Joint Chiefs of Staff forces-status reporting system, the management objectives were subordinated. Then systems analysts, service secretaries, representatives from the Office of the Secretary of Defense, congressional committees, and Department of Army staff elements began to use the unit readiness reports to show how good, or how bad, things really were. Harassed unit commanders bore the brunt of this struggle. In the Air Force and the Navy, the elements reported on are planes and ships and their crews, rather precise elements. But in the Army a division commander might be reporting on almost as many items as the entire Navy or Air Force.

It is not practical to keep the mass of statistics on Army equipment up to date. The condition of equipment in a unit changes continually and its readiness status is subject to change if replacement parts and mechanics are available and the equipment can be repaired in forty-eight hours. The validity of the statistics and the reports is therefore a matter of perspective and is frequently under challenge. Largely, interpretation of the figures depends on who wants to prove what. Just wade through Army Regulation (AR) 220-1 and finish up with Appendix D, Logistical Data, and you will quickly see why. The unit readiness report consists of four parts: personnel status, training, equipment on hand, and equipment status. Though the first two caused some minor flurries, they were nothing compared to the debates that developed on the equipment.

The debates and misunderstandings resulted because the Army developed two systems for evaluating and reporting equipment readiness. The first system is described in Appendix D, AR 220-1; it ultimately yields a unit rating, called the equipment status readiness condition (REDCON), which is part of the unit readiness report. The basis for this equipment status rating is the Equipment Serviceability Criteria (ESC), which rates equipment items into green, amber, and red categories. The percentage of total items rated red, or not ready, determines the monthly unit rating as of the date of the report.

The second system is the Materiel Readiness Reporting System, or 2406 Report, which rates items of equipment, not units. A different set of rules was developed for this system to categorize equipment items as either OR (operationally ready), NORS (not operationally ready for supply), and NORM (not operationally ready for maintenance). The 2406 Report yields the percentage of days an item of equipment was available for a three-month period; that is, the OR rate or average availability rate. The rates for each type of equipment are then compared with DA standards established in AR 750-52. Units and commands are also compared.

If this situation confuses you, you are beginning to get the blurred pieces of the picture. The criteria for the two systems are different. On a given day, an item might be ready, green, or amber for AR 220-1 purposes, but NOR for materiel readiness. A jeep without turn signals or a horn might be unsafe and technically unavailable for peacetime use—that is, NOR for materiel readiness—but fully capable of performing in combat—green for AR 220-1 purposes. In addition, the operators use the 2406 criteria, which come from the appropriate technical manual (TM) every day, but they use the ESC criteria only once a quarter. This mishmash prevents ESC/2406 correlation and underscores the incompatibility of the parallel systems. Nevertheless, senior officers, civilian secretaries, and members of Congress still compare the two types of data.

The conflicting pictures of equipment readiness depicted by the two systems cause confusion among those unfamiliar with all the ground rules, which is just about everyone. Worse yet, the differences provide an opportunity for those who want to fish in troubled waters. In the past, the varying purposes for which the civilian secretaries, DOD systems analysts, the military staffs, and the Congress used the data from the reports put the commanders in an impossible position. Requests to explain the discrepancies were continuous and so hard to answer that commanders found the effort a losing proposition. The burden and confusion at troop unit level can be imagined.

The readiness reporting system can easily lead one astray, but it relates directly to what happened to the maintenance function and, in turn, to training. Although one may marvel at some of the Alice in Wonderland absurdities the system engendered, it should be clear that the burden on the commander was created by outside pressures. To condemn him for wanting to look good is to ignore the fact that the system had him so much on the defensive that he had no other choice unless he was blessed with a very knowing, confident, and understanding boss—a rare combination of qualities.

Thus, a slow erosion of confidence and integrity occurred as commanders tried to compensate for statistics which said their units were not ready while their professional judgment told them their outfit could do the job in a pinch. Both the statistics and judgments were close to being right, but the difference between the standards for materiel, the time factors, and a few other quirks of the readiness reporting system created a jungle that the commander constantly had to fight his way through. The nuances and niceties of the system were such that any commander attempting to defend his judgment ratings appeared to be playing the old shell game to hide deficiencies. In time, careers were jeopardized and credibility was compromised as congressional committees and representatives from the Office of the Secretary of Defense argued over what the statistics meant. Each group was trying to prove a point for political purposes, and commanders as well as the Department of Army staff got caught in the meat grinder. That the rules of the system were constantly being changed, and that they were much more complex initially than they are now, made the task no easier. This is an area in which the DA staff has not served the units well. For almost ten years the basic faults of the system have plagued the units in the field, and the staff has not yet cleared the air.

As the concern for the statistics and the need to explain them grew, commanders felt pressured to put more time on the training schedule for maintenance than was warranted. The first place to look for this imbalance is in the training schedules themselves. I have visited numerous battalions in which the training schedules for two or three weeks running showed "Maintenance." Figures 4.1 and 4.2 are examples of training schedules that reflect the maintenance syndrome. I have seen hundreds like them—or worse. The hope of the commander in designing such schedules was that maintenance readiness reports would look better because of this all-out effort.

This hope was seldom realized because the commanders who made the effort rarely set up a comprehensive training program to solve their maintenance problems. The soldiers in these units always complained about the time wasted in the motor pool. The result was boredom, resentment, and the accepted practice of the soldiers drifting away, or in their own term, "ghosting off." The term was most descriptive, since they meant to disappear. The ultimate effect on attitude toward training and maintenance should be obvious. Without exception, the units which had the most maintenance hours on the training schedules had the poorest maintenance.

A major defect in this sort of attempt to improve maintenance was a failure to differentiate between maintenance to be performed by skilled mechanics as their primary duty for most of every day, and the preventive maintenance and before and after operations checks that drivers and crew members are qualified to do under supervision of the chain of command. The latter is an important feature of an effective maintenance program in a unit, and requires training for

FIGURE 4.1
TRAINING SCHEDULE, CAVALRY TROOP

MON	0820-0920		Morning Parade
	0920-1200		Maint of Track and Wheel Vehicles (Automotive)
	1335-1500		Maint of Track and Wheel Vehicles (Automotive)
	1500-1700		Intraunit Athletics
TUE	0820-0920		Morning Parade
	0920-1200		Maint of Track and Wheel Vehicles (Cleanliness)
	1335-1700	Sel Per	Day SCQC
	1335-1700		Maint of Track and Wheel Vehicles (Suspension)
	1730-1830	Officers	Conduct of Ranges
	2000-2400	Sel Per	Night SCQC (Night Driving and Crew Duties)
WED	0001-0730	Sel Per	Occupation of NDP (Security)
	0820-0920		Morning Parade
	0920-1200		Maint of Track and Wheel Vehicles (Batteries)
	1335-1700		Maint of Track and Wheel Vehicles (Oil Levels)
	2000-2400	Sel Per	Night SCQC (Night Driving and Crew Duties)
THU	0001-0730	Sel Per	Occupation of NDP (Security)
	0820-0920		Morning Parade
	0800-0900	Sel Per	Movement to Home Station
	0920-1200		Maint of Track and Wheel Vehicles (Cleanliness)
	1000-1130	Sel Per	AM Radio Training
	1335-1500		Maint of Track and Wheel Vehicles (After Operation Checks)
	1500-1700		Intraunit Athletics
	1730-1830	Officers	TBA
FRI	0820-0920		Morning Parade
	0920-1200		Maint of Track and Wheel Vehicles (Oil Levels)
	1335-1500		Prep of Track and Wheel Vehicles for Inspection
	1500-1700		Squadron Commander CI

FIGURE 4.2

TRAINING SCHEDULE, AIR DEFENSE ARTILLERY BATTERY
(CHAPPAREL/VULCAN)

MON	HOLIDAY (LABOR DAY)		
	0700-0800		Commander's Formation
TUE	0800-1130	Sel Per	TI & PM of Vehicles
	1230-1630	Sel Per	TI & PM of Vehicles
	0800-1600	Co (-)	TI of Weapons & Gas Masks
	0700-0800		Commander's Formation
	0800-1130	Sel Per	TI & PM of Vehicles
WED	1230-1430	Sel Per	TI & PM of Vehicles
	0800-1430	Sel Per	TI & PM of Nonmounted Comm
	1430-1630		Intraunit Athletics
	0700-0800		Commander's Formation
	0800-1130	Sel Per	TI & PM of Vehicles
THU	1230-1530	Sel Per	TI & PM of Vehicles
	0800-1530	Sel Per	TI & PM of Generators
	1530-1630		Command Information
	0700-0800		Commander's Formation
FRI	0800-1430	Sel Per	TI & PM of Vehicles
	0800-1430	Co (-)	TI of Tentage & Other QM Equip
	1430-1630		Intraunit Athletics

the drivers and crew members. It also requires a vigorous application of a well-trained chain of command in checking to see that drivers, operators, and crew members perform their duties. Where this training is not done and where the chain of command does not check, the troops are just putting in time and the maintenance effort starts to deteriorate at the most critical point, the operator and crew level.

There is another drawback to letting so many members of the unit get involved in maintenance. Any commander who has seen his youngster take apart the old alarm clock or get ready for the local soap-box derby should need no warning about the American soldier's penchant for tinkering with anything mechanical. A soldier who is scheduled to be in the motor pool for long hours with little to do will do what comes naturally: He'll tinker. As drivers and crew members who are amateur mechanics take parts off or put them on, the bill for spare parts soars and creates just another headache for commanders and comptrollers.

Sometimes commanders unwittingly lend a helping hand that only makes things worse—for example, by requiring roadside spotchecks, supposedly to aid maintenance efforts. As senior commanders received more and more critical reports from DA on maintenance deficiencies, a favorite solution was to set up roadside spotcheck teams. This meant taking experienced mechanics, maintenance NCOs, and warrant officers from the units to form the inspection teams. With the loss of the supervisors and skilled mechanics who should have been helping the units work out their own maintenance difficulties, maintenance in the units got worse and roadside spotchecks showed the blemish. When commanders began to get letters about unsatisfactory vehicles, new pressures were felt by the commanders and new directives were put out, even at general officer level, prescribing that before a vehicle could be dispatched there had to be a technical inspection (TI).

A TI in this case was ridiculous. The mechanics in a unit are the ones who do technical inspections. They are not in a unit to insure that a dispatched vehicle will pass some inspection on the road. The mechanic's job is to do the scheduled or emergency maintenance so that a certain percentage of vehicles in a unit are available to carry out the unit mission. In reality, almost everything being done was the reverse of what was intended. The situation would have been comic opera if it had not been so sad to see how few commanders recognized what their own policies were doing to them and how self-defeating they were. In a note to commanders I made this observation:

We should not fool ourselves on how well units are doing on roadside spotchecks. It has become a practice throughout most of the command to have a vehicle TI'd before it is dispatched. This TI is done by a mechanic who should be working on the vehicles that need repair. Since the TI takes 40 minutes to an hour for each vehicle, the vehicles that are in the shop for maintenance get short shrift.

I am a great believer in letting the commander decide how he uses his own resources and if this is the way he chooses to improve the record on roadside spotchecks, so be it. However, we must not delude ourselves into thinking it is an efficient operation nor does it make us as good as the statistics make us out to be. The day we can depend on the drivers and the dispatchers to do their part in dispatching a vehicle and the maintenance personnel to do their jobs on the vehicles that require maintenance, we will be closer to being a professional force. When mechanics spend a major portion of their time on the supposedly green vehicles that have been designated for dispatch, we are using band-aids.

I would hope the time will soon come when we can begin to take the risks involved in dispatching a vehicle without a complete TI by one of the mechanics.

It is easy for someone standing off at a distance to disparage the judgment of commanders who let these things happen. But such a critic is a bystander who is not subjected to the daily pressures of a commander. Commanders' decisions, no matter how peculiar, often reflect the need for change in the system. I put many of them in the "games and gimmick" department, and the TI before dispatch was one of them. Two more examples on the maintenance function follow.

Some battalion and brigade commanders, concerned about their efficiency reports, started to develop a game for avoiding a poor score on a roadside spotcheck. Knowing how to use intelligence, being tactically minded, and well aware of the value of a reserve, they had a plan. As soon as a report came in that a roadside spotcheck team was in the area, the battalion commander would give the word to dispatch "Six," the command vehicle, in the right direction in the hope that it would be caught in the net. Naturally "Six" was always in great shape and if stopped the vehicle and driver would get a top score. Then "old number 10," another vehicle saved for such emergencies, would be sent out. After enough vehicles from one unit were stopped, the roadside inspection team, which was out to get a representative sample, would start looking for vehicles from other units. If the game plan worked, that unit looked good in the report. Some might say that the ploy worked well. But how many vehicles were dispatched unnecessarily or on a roundabout route, just so the unit could look good? How many commanders wasted valuable assets such as helicopters to keep tabs on the roadside spotcheck teams?

Gimmicks are common and are used by all commanders for many things, but throughout my service the gimmicks that made the least sense, at least to me, were those that commanders used to impress visitors with their devotion to maintenance, particularly motor maintenance. One popular such gimmick was the "hoods-up routine." One commander had a standing operating procedure (SOP) for every time a vehicle stopped. The hood went up to show that the driver had done his after-operations check. It stayed up until the vehicle moved. The first time I observed this routine it was in a dusty area, and when I asked the drivers about it they explained the unit SOP. I thought it was absurd, since clouds of dust were settling over the engines as other vehicles went past, but how to get the message over to the battalion commander with a little education thrown in! I soon met up with him. As we approached the first vehicle, the driver hurried into view and started brushing at something under the hood. "What is he doing, Colonel?" "Sir, in this outfit whenever we stop the hood goes up and the driver does his after-operations checks. We have a great maintenance program, Sir." I suggested that we stop and just watch. The driver looked at us and then brushed furiously at something. When he looked up again, to his dismay we were still standing there. He then brushed some more, looked up, and there we were. By this time the battalion commander was most anxious to show me something else, but I was in no hurry. After watching this little show for about five minutes, which probably seemed like hours to the battalion commander, I suggested we go talk to the soldier to find out what he was doing. Again, the answer was that he was doing his after-operations check. When I observed that I hadn't seen him check the oil, the soldier replied, "I did that when I first stopped, Sir." "Then why were you puttering around with the cloth for the past five minutes?" He got that grin on his face, so typical of the soldier involved in one of those command-directed charades, and said it was to be sure visitors would know how serious his outfit was about maintenance.

If the soldier were asked if this SOP made any sense he would be the first one to answer "no." Stopping to observe this performance and talking to the drivers of two or three vehicles was generally enough to get the message across to the battalion commander. A brief suggestion that he check one or two specific items on occasion—oil, batteries, tires—so that he would know what the driver had done, and would also let the drivers know that those items would be checked, was always good for the commander's education.

One last point on the maintenance function, the mental attitude of commanders, and distortions that develop in the system. I recall it from visiting an armor battalion, but this example also applies to infantry, artillery, engineer, signal battalions and cavalry squadrons. When I asked the battalion commander why the training schedule for the week was "maintenance," he explained that he had just returned from a major training area. A check of the training schedules showed "maintenance" all day every day for three solid weeks. When I asked the commander "Why?" he explained that the unit had to "recover" from the visit to the major training area. This is an old story, and the same answer has been given by unit commanders after returning from major training exercises for many a year. The commander who "recovers" this way doesn't know much about the Army.

In combat you maintain as you go. Mechanics work at their maintenance tasks every day. The crews do their preventive maintenance every time they stop. If a unit has to have a lot of maintenance recovery time after going to a major training area or on a maneuver, its troops, in bald terms, are not caring for their equipment each day as they should, and its maintenance and support elements are failing to participate in the best training they can get, supporting the tactical elements in the field.

The law of the land says that the Army's role is that of sustained combat. It is time for unit commanders to recognize that the Army functions through the full range of its capabilities both as it fights and as it trains. In Chapter 3, I commented on the tendency of the Army War College and the Command and General Staff College to cover many subjects that are not particularly pertinent to the Army's business. If these schools devoted more time and emphasis on teaching future Army leaders about complex systems—logistics, maintenance, personnel—and how they affect Army operations, their graduates would bring more know-how to their tasks. Further, some of the pressure that derives from these systems would be eased, or at least they would be better understood. This part of the overall Army training program is beyond the control of local commanders. It is in this area that effort at the two top schools would be beneficial.

Maintenance will always pose problems for commanders because it requires good organization, sound training programs, and plenty of supervision. It will not respond to patchwork programs which peak at stated intervals to make the unit readiness report look good. The result of the patchwork has been deterioration in maintenance and training as commanders sought solutions in a lot of special programs, games and gimmicks that were self defeating.

Maintenance in earlier days placed great emphasis on teaching the operator how to conduct his first-echelon or preventive-maintenance checks. The chain of command pulled hard at motor stables or just plain spotchecks along the road or in the field in all echelons. Unit schools contributed by developing an awareness of how to check the state of maintenance. There was also a lot of on-the-job training (OJT) in the actual maintenance function in the shops. It didn't seem as if maintenance were something separate from the normal functions of the unit. Maintenance was a chain-of-command responsibility that was reinforced by training.

I believe the strong support of the chain of command was a holdover from the days of the horse. In World War II and through the 1950s there were still many officers and NCOs who had been in units which had horses and mules. They knew that the animals had to be cared for at the end of the day before their own creature comforts were accommodated. To them a vehicle was a gas burner instead of a hayburner. While the care may not have been as sentimental—or profane—as it was for the horse and the mule, the idea of bedding the vehicle down was strong. We had better get back to that frame of mind.

5

Training is not good when command assignments are not popular.

Who Is Responsible for What?

Misunderstandings, as they pertain to terminology and responsibility, have been major sources of training problems in recent years. Some discussion of the misunderstandings might help clear the air.

On 26 June 1954, General Anthony McAuliffe wrote to General Henry Hodes expressing his thoughts "upon an urgent and vexing problem which faces both the US Army as a whole and the Seventh Army in particular." The problem was the strictly professional aspects of life within the combat units of the junior officer and the senior noncommissioned officer.

> *It is my understanding that assignment to command of a company or a battery is not a popular one, a pronounced contrast to the attitude existing prior to World War II. . . . We must give emphasis to the decentralization of command. . . . We must not preach decentralization and at the same time punish the commander for practicing it. . . . In the matter of training, all higher headquarters must seek to cut to a proper minimum the required hours for specified subjects, in an endeavor to leave the company or battery commander a reasonable latitude in the training of his unit in subjects which he selects as requiring greater emphasis. . . . In training it is also necessary to avoid over-supervision. By this I do not mean that battalion, regimental, or higher commanders should spend any less time in the field and in inspection of training, but the company commander must have the feeling that he is being trusted with the training of his company and that each move he makes is not being supervised by a hovering*

senior. . . . We have made the routine tactical problem a pretty dull affair. Troops spend long periods doing nothing, thinking nothing, learning nothing. . . . At all costs we must avoid the false front.

How familiar do these concerns sound to the commanders of the late sixties and early seventies? Or to today's commanders? Some two decades later the same problems are still with us, only they are more pronounced. The command of a battalion or brigade is now included in the unpopular command assignments except as it might improve one's chances for promotion.

The unpopularity of command assignments reflects poor training. Conditions that degrade training frustrate commanders. But a major contributing cause to the unpopularity of command was the centralization of command, management, and information systems at higher and higher levels. Some senior commanders believed that decentralization of training would correct some of the training problems and counter some of the undesirable features of overcentralization. It might also make a command assignment more desirable. Acting on this belief the Chief of Staff directed in May 1971 that training be decentralized.

Note that when General McAuliffe wrote about training in 1954 the emphasis was on "decentralization of command." Naturally, when a true decentralization of command took place training was also decentralized. In 1971, after years of emphasis on centralized management and a decade in which centralization of all aspects of operations had accelerated, the Army had to explain what was meant by "decentralized training." As different echelons of command tried to explain what was once routine but was now just an idea or concept, misunderstanding was inevitable. The weakness in our institutional memory was once again apparent.

Misunderstanding cropped up at both levels of responsibility. At company-command level, some lieutenants and captains interpreted decentralized training to mean, "I should be left alone," "I shouldn't be inspected," and "I should be allowed to do the training I want without any supervision." At the other extreme, some battalion or brigade commanders felt that decentralized training meant they no longer had responsibility for training. Thus, if the training was bad, it would be because the company officers were doing a poor job; since the training was decentralized, the company-level officers were responsible. Both of these attitudes give hard evidence that both senior and junior leaders can lose sight of the fundamentals.

There is no activity at any level that does not require supervision and inspection. If the supervisors and inspectors carry out their assignments ably they will benefit the junior officers and NCOs who themselves have so much to supervise, and the field-grade officers who have so much to teach. At the battalion and brigade level, the commanders define training objectives, allocate range facilities, apportion training space, provide staff support, and, above all, they teach. The company commanders should then have leeway to determine in what manner, in what amount of time, and with what emphasis the training objectives will be achieved. Battalion and brigade commanders have a continuing responsibility to check on the training of their subordinate units to see that objectives are being achieved and standards maintained. More important, the colonels and lieutenant colonels should make the most of opportunities to suggest new ideas or alternative approaches to the young officers. Constructive criticism is the means, and improved training is the objective. Leeway allows for innovation and emphasis by the company commander in the execution of training. Assistance, teaching, and maintenance of standards are the province of the field-grade commanders. This division of labor is what decentralized training has always meant to me.

By 1974, the extreme views were no longer a problem, but it took a lot of effort at the highest command levels to bring about a better understanding. Whenever a misunderstanding develops on so basic a point, discussion between the field-grade commanders and company-level commanders is needed to spotlight, define, and solve the difficulty. Simply put, there is a lot of learning to be done at the level of the junior officer, and that requires a bit of humility; there is a lot of teaching to be done by the field-grade officers, and that requires a solid background in the military fundamentals as well as patience and understanding.

The report of the USAWC study group on military professionalism stated that a favorite theme in seminar sessions conducted at the service schools was the senior officer who didn't listen to his subordinates. It is unfortunate that in a period when so much was being written about communication and generation gaps no forum, such as a unit school, was available to generate discussion on so important a subject as decentralized training. For field-grade officers ready to listen, a question certain to bring about a lively interchange on training is, "Who is the key man in a decentralized training program?"

Everyone in the chain of command has a training responsibility, but training is especially important for NCOs, platoon leaders, and commanders at company, battalion, brigade, and division levels. For training to be effective, however, a more precise identification of training responsibility is necessary.

Traditionally, field-grade officers have been expected to maintain the quality of training. Lieutenant colonels and colonels are the training managers and teachers at battalion, brigade, or group levels. They set the standards and manage the resources and facilities. They supervise and guide the efforts of the company, troop, and battery commanders. Above all, they teach lieutenants and captains how to train. Field-grade officers must lead the way in establishing the high training standards required in peacetime so that the Army is ready for any national crisis. The senior officer's job is teaching at every level of command. The general officers, too, can make a tremendous contribution if they develop a method of operation that will contribute to a quiet businesslike approach to training rather than creating conditions that will result in Hollywood-like performances.

But I still haven't identified the key man in a decentralized training system. Participants in a battalion and brigade commanders' course conducted in USAREUR spent a lot of time discussing this subject, and the favorite answers ranged from the NCO to the brigade-level commander, a full colonel. In discussions with about fifty different groups, no one ever voted for the general officer as the key man—an assessment with which I agree.

In most groups, one or two people considered the NCO to be the key man. After some discussion it was generally agreed that, while the NCO was vitally important to training, he could not be the key man. The best rationale for saying no on the NCO was that field service regulations and field manuals prescribe how things are to be done. The NCO's job is to see that the soldier does things strictly according to the book. This is essential for the proper care and functioning of weapons and equipment and especially important to safety. The NCO does not have the flexibility that the key man in training must have. For similar reasons, the lieutenant was considered vital but not the key man.

The brigade commander was the senior individual put forward as a candidate, but he fell by the wayside in the discussions because of the variety of units that might fall under his command: a cavalry squadron, a mechanized infantry battalion, an artillery battalion, and an armor battalion. He would be a rare individual if he knew enough about the fundamentals of the different branches of the service to be the key man in the training chain of command. He might be a great help, or a headache, to the commander of the battalion that corresponded to the brigade commander's basic branch, but not much help to the others in training their units. The brigade commander has an important role to play as the buffer, organizer, and manager. As a full colonel he ranks high enough to argue with the higher level staff when they impose unrealistic requirements and short suspenses on the subordinate units. He should be the one to fight for range and other facilities, and to use his staff to manage the resources and conflicting demands of the battalions. When there is a need to approach the general-officer level to defend battalion programs or point out that directives from above are inappropriate, that is the time a full colonel can earn his pay.

A number of votes invariably went to the company/battery/troop level commander. He should know the strengths and weaknesses of his unit, and he is the one to determine where the emphasis should be in the training of his unit. At this point it was generally clear that the key man had to be the company or battalion commander. The discussions brought out that at the company level the commander would have little to say about assignment of training areas and allocation of resources. That was the province of the battalion- and brigade-level commanders, both of whom had staffs. Though knowledgeable, and certain to be a good trainer in the best armies, the company-level commander would not have the background and knowledge of a battalion commander, who had already been a company-level commander. By the time a lieutenant colonel becomes a battalion commander he generally has had additional schooling and should have developed a degree of maturity and understanding that would help him teach and develop his young commanders.

Other factors tipped the scales strongly toward the battalion commander. He is basically concerned with one arm of the service, and does not have several types of units under his command, as does the brigade commander. He visits different units of the same type on a daily basis and what he sees in one company, battery, or troop that is innovative he can pass quickly to the other units with the same equipment and same mission as he makes his rounds. When he sees something consistently wrong in units with similar missions he knows there is a need for special effort and inquiry as to the root cause.

The discussions tended to support my own belief that the battalion commander is the key man in the training of an army. I would carry that a step further by saying that he is the key commander in combat too. It was always my experience that division commanders fought battalions. A larger unit is difficult to disengage, and most often when the going is tough it is the shifting of a battalion to the left, right, or around a flank that pushes an attack to a successful conclusion or shores up a shaky defense. With this outlook, I always give my vote to the battalion commander by a wide margin. The new series of Army Training and Evaluation Programs (ARTEP) reinforces the importance of the battalion commander with this statement:

> The battalion commander is not responsible for following a standardized training program. He is responsible for determining and pursuing a training program uniquely designed to prepare his own battalion to meet successfully or to surpass the training and evaluation standards set forth in this ARTEP.[1]

In discussions with the German Infantry and Armor Schools on this subject, it was suggested that the question of who is the key man be rephrased. Students agreed with all the points on the battalion commander and said he was of primary importance, but they added the company-level commander has such stature in the eyes of his men and is so close to them that he has to be considered a key individual in training. All company-level commanders would agree with that view, and I do not know any senior officers who do not look back on their days as a company, battery, or troop commander without a sense of nostalgia and accomplishment. Therefore, perhaps the question would be

---

[1] U.S. Department of Army, ARTEP 7-45, September 1975.

better phrased, "Who are the key individuals in training?" The answer would then be the battalion commander and the company-level commander. This version makes even more sense when you consider the number of separate companies that do not have a battalion commander, or the support battalions which are often so spread out that the troops seldom see their battalion commander. Having provided this fertile stamping ground for debate by future generations of commanders from corporal to general, let us consider how commanders can make training better than it has been of late.

Senior Army officials make too many speeches about being ready to fight tomorrow. Actions and directives flow that make the training job more difficult.

Training Management

Training management involves time, people, equipment, facilities, money, and the wisdom to determine what training needs to be done. Since most of these factors are in a constant state of change and since the results are not easy to quantify, training is a difficult program to manage. But it is manageable if enough thought is given to it, and if it is not neglected. Inadequate training most often results from poor training management.[1]

LENGTH OF TRAINING PROGRAM

A recurring question is the proper length of the training program. Should it be four months long? Six months? A year? Budget planning almost demands an annual training program. Besides the budget cycle, which drives almost everything an organization does, a host of agencies are going to influence the training program: for example, the Unified Commanders' Joint Exercise Schedule and specialized training areas that have to be assigned to units in rotation. Such requirements lead higher staffs to think in terms of an annual training

---

[1]TC 21-5-7, *Training Management in Battalions*, is in draft form. When it is validated and published it will be a great help to trainers.

program for staff reasons. My experience as a commander convinces me that annual training programs are in the best interest of the commander too.

In recent years some units appeared to program training in three-, four-, or six-month cycles. Many commanders set their sights on an Annual General Inspection (AGI) in one period, a Command Management Maintenance Inspection (CMMI) in another, then on a field training exercise (FTX), and finally on a range season. Activity peaked when the major event was scheduled and the commander concentrated all his efforts on that event and even canceled scheduled training in the process. Overall readiness was not the objective; rather it was readiness for the current crisis. The objective for the year was to be sure to get by each hurdle, and little thought went to an overall training program tailored to the missions, training deficiencies, and resources of each unit. Some commanders put their priorities first on the inspections and tests which would subject them to close scrutiny, and next on staff procedures and planning for the higher unit tests and field exercises. They gave comparatively little attention to individual and small-unit training. At times some field-grade commanders appeared more at home with community projects and the planning and staff effort for the big exercise than they were with the execution of unit training. This apportionment of their attention to the needs of their units could well be a product of the staff emphasis and the classroom orientation in the service schools.

The reason given by many senior officers for the abbreviated cycles was that high turnover required frequent training of the elements from battalion through division. The turnover *was* high. Commanders could never catch up because they were always training a new team for whatever period that team was under their command. While greater instability would seem to dictate a greater need for teaching the fundamentals to individuals and small units, the pressures of the time, or possibly the lack of a coherent philosophy of training, forced commanders to focus on the upcoming event or the big exercise, which got more visibility.

From about 1968 to 1971 the demand for replacements in Vietnam was so great that all Army units other than those in Vietnam were little more than replacement depots. Soldiers stayed only a short time in any unit, and experienced officers and NCOs were in short supply. Instead of limiting training to the perfection of individual skills and the improvement of collective and tactical training up through platoon level, which would have helped in the development of noncommissioned officers and junior leaders, units carried on with battalion-training tests and brigade and division field-training exercises. At the same time dissent, drugs, and racial animosities were creating almost insurmountable problems for the NCOs and company-level commanders.

Good training at the lower unit levels would not have solved all the problems, but having the men work together to improve individual skills and collective effort at the crew level—reasonably attainable objectives—would have brought the troops closer together in a team effort. A better understanding of some of the sociological problems confronting the Army at ground level might have resulted, and some of the serious morale problems might have been alleviated. Surely the life of the young commanders would have been better.

Planning training at least on an annual basis helps to establish long-range objectives and can help to alleviate a crisis mentality. But planning training annually does not mean something is done only once a year; rather, it means that time and funds are scheduled for a year. What goes into an annual training program is for the immediate commander to decide, and his decision must be based on the unit's mission, state of training, and general needs. A commander must be sensitive to weaknesses in his unit as they develop and, within his annual training plan, adapt his program to overcome the weaknesses as he reinforces the strengths. Senior commanders must recognize that adjustments in the program will be needed when conditions change. If adjustments are not made, serious problems will result, both for the units and the company-level commanders. Therefore commanders must put the emphasis in the right place.

The importance of individual and small-unit training has already been stressed. Figure 6.1 shows an annual training program that was used in educating battalion commanders before they went to their units. Note the reinforcement of individual training in every quarter, the repetition of small-unit and weapons training, the company athletics—in brief, the basics. The "company commander time" provides for adjustment due to changing conditions or to differences in units. Field-grade commanders should encourage this flexibility. This type of annual program helps to avoid the peaks and valleys that are so prominent in shorter cycles; it also sustains individual and small-unit capabilities and provides a plateau from which training can move forward into another annual program. It provides time for supervision and quality control. During the Vietnam conflict a program of this type, with most of the emphasis on the individual and small unit, would have been a boon to the commanders providing the replacements.

INSTANT READINESS AND
A REALISTIC TRAINING POLICY

Many things contribute to the training problems faced by battalion and company commanders that they can do nothing about. Commitments made by the Department of Defense and pronouncements by Department of the Army on instant readiness create most of the management headaches, as well as a lot of

FIGURE 6.1
TANK BATTALION ANNUAL TRAINING PROGRAM

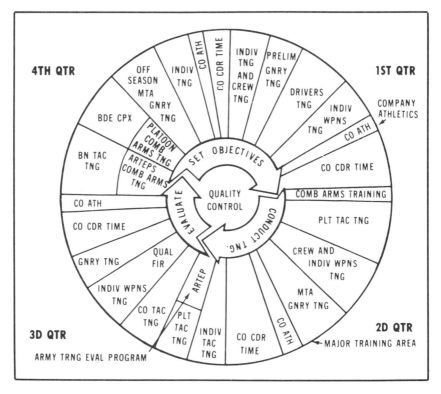

THERE ARE SEVERAL ADVANTAGES TO AN ANNUAL TRAINING PROGRAM DEPICTED IN CIRCULAR FASHION. THE SENSE OF REINFORCEMENT AND SUSTAINMENT OF INDIVIDUAL AND COLLECTIVE SKILLS THROUGHOUT THE YEAR IS APPARENT; IF PROGRESSION FROM LEVEL TO LEVEL IS REQUIRED, IT IS CLEAR. EACH SLICE ALLOTS A CERTAIN NUMBER OF HOURS TO A PHASE OF TRAINING, BUT THE SPECIFICS ARE LEFT TO THE UNIT COMMANDER. COMPANY COMMANDER TIME ALLOWS THE UNIT COMMANDER AN OPPORTUNITY TO ADJUST AND EMPHASIZE THE TRAINING HE THINKS HIS UNIT NEEDS. AS TIME PASSES THE TRAINING FOR THE NEXT QUARTER IS REFINED. EMPHASIS THROUGHOUT THE YEAR IS ON REINFORCEMENT OF SKILLS, SUSTAINMENT OF CAPABILITY, PROGRESSION, EVALUATION, AND QUALITY CONTROL.

individual heartaches that are too often ignored. Senior Army officials make too many speeches about being ready to fight tomorrow. Actions and directives flow from the speeches, making the training job more difficult. Too many commanders, reacting to the oratory, try to accomplish everything usually required of a unit before overseas deployment in a wartime situation. This is impossible in peacetime because the personnel, equipment, and money are not available to most units.

Any unit, ship, or plane will fight when it is necessary. These essential elements of our defense establishment may not have every weapon or individual that they would like on hand when the moment of truth arrives. But they will surprise a lot of people by how well they will fight if they have been thoroughly trained in the fundamentals of their weapons systems and combat environments.

Therefore, just as realism is needed in the conduct of training, realistic policy is needed in the management of training. Throughout my service the demands on the Army and organizations in it have often been out of proportion to the people and resources available. The Army seldom adjusted goals that had been established prior to reductions in force and budget cuts. The missions, exercises, and tests were left on the books. Too many "can do" commanders at brigade level and above tried to do them all. Only great sacrifice and hard work by commanders, especially those from battalion on down, kept units operating. A few units with a high priority could function effectively, but most units just barely survived. The troops and the Army as an organization paid the price. The periods 1946-50, 1953-60, and 1970-74 come to mind.

When budgets are lean or unexpected commitments for national security arise, realistic training policies are more necessary than ever. One policy well within the Army's capability at such times would be to maintain the highest standards of training and discipline from the individual through the company level. As time and resources permit battalion standards could be raised. When the Army has to fight or go on a peace-keeping mission, the soldiers down in the companies are the ones with the toughest jobs—and they had better know how to do them well. Both the Army and the country would be well served by such a policy, because the effectiveness of the units would be at its highest under the circumstances. In these crisis periods, developing the leadership qualities of noncommissioned officers and junior officers so that they can take on greater responsibility when emergencies arise is of paramount importance.

Often crises are short-lived—sometimes a month or two in length—and changes cannot be made in regulations and directives in these short periods. This fact is important in the management of training resources, and must be clearly understood at the highest levels of the Department of the Army and through all levels of the chain of command. Senior officers—especially two-, three-, and four-star generals—should recognize when adjustments should be made in established goals. It will be better when brigade commanders see the need for change and become the bulwarks they should be, to shield battalion- and company-level commanders from unrealistic demands. This may require some changed perceptions on what is required to succeed as a career officer. Education on this point at the Command and General Staff College and the Army War College would help spread the faith.

MAXIMUM STRENGTH FOR TRAINING

As noted in the preceding chapter, soldiers absent from a unit is a common but poor excuse for not training. Still, the persistent absence of a large number of troops who need training is discouraging to company-level commanders and NCOs. It is also an indication that battalion, brigade, and division commanders are not managing their resources properly. Senior commanders must vigorously support the principle of maximum strength for training. Here are a few suggestions that may help.

Designating a "prime time" for training

In day-to-day life at home station, units will find that they are unable to train all out eight hours a day. Some service support units—maintenance, finance, Adjutant General, and other similar organizations—can come close, but even they need time for physical fitness, weapons familiarization, and other exercises that do not pertain to their basic support function. Combat and combat support units must accomplish their mission-essential training on days when educational, administrative, medical, and other matters make demands for personnel who should be available for training. Also, the officers and NCOs who must devote time to preparation for instruction cannot fulfill these duties and still be with their unit if it is striving to devote a full eight hours a day to training. The answer to these conflicting demands is to designate a "prime time" for training during which everyone present for duty will be out for training with the unit.

A few cautions on establishing a prime time: Remember that prime time does not have to be the same for all elements of a division or even a brigade. With all units out at once, training areas would be congested, so there has to be flexibility. The installation itself is the key. Some adjustments can be made with civilian working hours in the Post Exchange, barber shops, medical and educational facilities, and the host of other activities important to a soldier on the installation, but there is a limit. A division on one installation can rotate brigades or a certain number of battalions through prime time cycles at different hours of the day. In the United States, where the Army has large division posts, rotating units might provide the best solution. Overseas, where there are brigade- and battalion-size installations, the problem is harder to solve.

X and Y concept

Try General Hamilton Howze's X and Y concept. General Howze used the "full strength training" concept in units he commanded; he said he was never able to think up a better name for it. Admittedly, "full strength" is a dream, since if nothing else a certain number of personnel are going to be on leave all the time. But the term describes the objective, and that is the important thing to keep in mind. This concept also became known in some units as the X and Y concept; the reason is clear from General Howze's description:

> *The scheme is simply one in which units are paired off to allow one of the pair to do as much as possible of the other's chores while it trains in the field at full (or as full as possible) strength, after which the two units swap. The week is divided into halves: for the first half, unit X goes out into the woods with nearly everybody present while unit Y does all the guard and fatigue for both; unit Y goes out the second half. The scheme lightens the load on officers and noncommissioned officers because they are not repeatedly instructing a small percentage of the unit, which demands of them more preparatory and training hours. Moreover, while a unit is in the field, be it only a couple of days, it can do much more with the time than it can while under the distractions of garrison life; and of course, night training, a neglected art, becomes easy to schedule and do. While there are also fewer hours of formal training in the week, much more training gets done. The only real problem in all this is that visiting inspectors have got to get used to seeing a troop baseball game in progress on a training morning.*[2]

This subject merits considerable attention from those who wear stars, bars, or stripes, and who do not understand fully the prime time concept, the X and Y concept, or its first cousin the XYZ concept. The basic objective is to get the maximum number of troops out to training. Sometimes people get technical as to what should be done in prime time, and debates develop on mission-related training. In fact, the latter includes just about everything. Two good examples are motor stables and unit schools, which are clearly mission-related but which in my opinion should not be conducted in prime training time. When

---

[2]*Howze on Training* (Fort Benning, Ga., 1971), p. 1.

these questions came up in my units, I told commanders not to get wrapped up in a lot of definitions, but to use this rule of thumb:

> When all the officers, NCOs, and soldiers had to be present to do the training or perform a task—armor maintenance is a good example—that was the training to be done in prime time. When the activity was a unit school for officers or NCOs, or motor stables, which called only for drivers and certain supervisory personnel, it was not the type of training effort that merited prime training time.

This sentence from a Forces Command training guideline seems to hit the mark: "Prime time is defined as that time devoted to mission related training during which, insofar as practicable, 100% of present for duty personnel attend and unit integrity is maintained."[3]

The best solution when policy guidance is not clear is to have division, brigade, and battalion commanders discuss the objectives thoroughly enough so that they are operating on the same wave length. Next, the battalion commanders should follow suit with company-level officers and senior NCOs. Then, when general officers and brigade commanders are inspecting training, hopefully they will ask the company-level officers how the concept is working and what the problems are. Get that dialogue going. Getting the maximum number of troops out for training, for whatever period is practical, has never been easy, but it will improve the quality of training and is well worth the effort.

Recognizing the need and the objective, the installation commander in conjunction with the unit commanders can set a prime time for training and gear other activities—sick call, education, finance visits, and the rest—to achieve minimum interference with training. It is surprising how sick call drops off when it is timed so that the soldier does not miss half the training day by going to the dispensary.

Prime time can be any time during the day or night. When a unit has night training, for example, the designated hours in the night constitute the prime time for that training. On a day-to-day basis, prime time should be a period of 4 to 6 hours. For the XY or XYZ proponents it should consist of blocks of hours or days in which a unit is freed from outside commitments and details. It is essential that senior commanders—colonels and generals—think through the prime time concept, decide on the program best suited to their units and missions, make sure that the objectives are clearly understood from top to bottom, and coordinate all the support activities so as to detract as little as possible from the training effort.

Coordinating support activities is not easy because it involves civilians and other groups whose working hours may have to be changed, a process that

---

[3]Training Guidelines, FY 75, 5 July 1974, Headquarters, FORSCOM.

runs into union problems and lifestyles that have not varied in thirty years. Installation commanders can manage the job with persistence, patience, and with the cooperation of the unit commanders. The commanders benefit from the prime time that gets a maximum number of men out for training as a group. Unit commanders in turn must assist installation commanders by seeing to it that the troops keep their appointments in other than prime time when the appointments might conflict with motor stables, fatigue details, and other similar commitments that must be met the rest of the day.

INSPECTION TEAMS AND ASSISTANCE, OR "COURTESY," TEAMS

The number of inspection teams has an influence on the number of people who are absent from training. In recent years inspection teams have proliferated and the senior commanders—general officers—are responsible. These teams add to the pressure on commanders and contribute to the peaking for special events. The offspring of inspection teams, courtesy and assistance teams, provide commanders a crutch which reduces the daily effort they should expend on the activities of their units. A few weeks before a big inspection commanders stop most of their training and other activities to get ready. Offers of "preinspection Technical Assistance Visits" and a "Courtesy TPI to those installations unable to conduct their own"[4] are welcomed by a commander who believes he might be relieved if his unit fails an inspection.

The undesirable features of inspection teams are considerable, but most of them can be held in check by a strong commander. The worst feature is the number of skilled personnel absent from unit training. The most stubborn problem is that few inspection teams are provided for in the tables of organization; so personnel for the teams are taken from the units, which need those same people to get their own tasks done. Another drain on unit resources are the special programs generated by the Department of the Army and the Department of Defense.

I am not referring here to umpire teams or groups organized to monitor or conduct small training exercises at battalion or even brigade level. Such teams generally exist for but a short time, and everyone profits from the effort. My reference is to the teams organized by higher headquarters which often become permanent even though no provision has been made for them. Maintenance, administration, and other functional areas are adversely affected when well-qualified NCOs and specialists are used by higher headquarters in creating

---

[4]These phrases can be found in many Division, Corps, and Army Training Directives.

such teams. If most of these teams were eliminated, how many E–6s, E–7s, E–8s, warrant officers, and officers would be released back to their units where the work has to be done?

This area needs critical scrutiny by all commanders. If the Department of the Army cannot provide the spaces for these activities, then perhaps it is time to puncture the inspection bubble. A lot of officers have taken courses in systems analysis and operations research. Perhaps they could analyze the inspection effort to get a judgment on the value of all the inspections and what might happen if the inspectors are returned to the units. I realize there is no easy solution to this problem, since some inspections are essential, but in the interest of resource management—which includes making more personnel available for training—a reappraisal is necessary.

USING THE STAFF

Field-grade commanders could be a great help to company commanders if they used their staffs, especially the S–1, to take a hard look at the details that have been requested by installation commanders. There is no question about the need for support of installation activities. It is unfortunate, but until the Department of the Army can convince Congress that funds and spaces for installation support are grossly inadequate, units will continue to pay the bill. The requirements for details, however, change frequently. What is needed this month may be dispensable next month. Personnel once needed all day may now be needed only in the afternoon.

A good way to eliminate this uncertainty is to have the battalion or brigade S–1 take the lists of individuals on special duty and drop by the hospital, warehouse, or wherever they are supposed to be working to see if they are there. How busy are they? What time do they come to work? What time are they released? Quite often this kind of on-site inquiry will show that these people are no longer required and can be returned to duty with their units. Additional requirements, like some government agencies, take on a life of their own, and go on long after need for them has ceased. Battalion and brigade commanders should use their staffs to make these checks, which would be a great help to the heavily burdened company commanders.

MAINTAINING THE TRAINING SCHEDULE

One of the most serious and common violations of sound training management is changing the published training schedule. Changes are seldom warranted;

most often they are examples of poor planning or poor judgment on the part of the one who makes the change, and poor leadership on the part of the next highest commander who permits or directs the change. Frequent schedule changes result in poor training and bored soldiers, who lose confidence in the Army's ability to carry out its own plans. Training schedules should be followed as published, changed only on rare occasions, and then only with good cause.

In recent years the training schedule has been looked on as a general guideline that might be followed if all went well that week. Changes frequently result from actions taken at corps or higher level down through the company-command level. Some junior officers seem to equate decentralized training with the right to change training schedules at will, on short notice, and frequently. Battalion and brigade commanders sometimes change the schedule in order to concentrate on some "priority." They direct immediate action to correct some reported deficiency by calling a unit in the evening and saying, "Complete all equipment serviceability criteria tomorrow morning." They are concerned about the crisis of the moment instead of developing a training program to correct shortcomings through routine daily actions. Corps or army most often causes changes by sending a survey team or a research group into a unit without advance notice, but experience indicates that most changes are generated between brigade and company level.

When battalion and company commanders are asked about these changes in schedule they tend to blame the "they" at higher levels of command. If "they" are responsible, lieutenant colonels and colonels in particular must earn their pay. They should call up the chief of staff or G–3 of their unit and ask "How come?" or "Why can't we do that two weeks from now?" If that doesn't work, they should ask to speak to the division commander and explain that short-notice announcements play havoc with the training already scheduled. But they must first be certain to check the people on their own staff to be sure responsibility for the fault does not lie there; quite often it does. Firmness both up and down the chain of command will bring unwarranted changes to a halt.

When commanders find it easy to change training schedules, the scrambling begins. Let's say the change develops the night before or about 0500 because the instructor's wife is just about to have a baby, or there is a conflict in use of the training area. A change is approved and someone asks what will be substituted.

"A training film," is the answer.

"On what?"

"Let's see what they have."

Next someone has to find out if the projector is working and where the film will be shown. While this instant training is being firmed up someone forgets to tell the first sergeant who has just seen the troops off to the south forty, and an NCO is dispatched to guide them back to where the film will be shown. This comic-opera approach to training is what happens when changes to training schedules become commonplace. It does not impress the troops, since they are the victims of the haphazard training that ensues and do not like to have their time wasted.

Some changes are unavoidable, however. They will occur because there can be an unannounced alert, random urinalysis, or some future type of check that no one yet knows the need for. In these cases the training schedule should be picked up where and when the commander thinks best. However, these unanticipated requirements should be kept to a minimum, and it is the responsibility of the general officers to do that. When are changes justified? Here are a few examples that meet my criteria:

(1) An unannounced alert by the highest headquarters, by which I mean above corps. OK, that's the training for the day. But, please, no rehearsals. I stress the "highest headquarters" because of the tendency to have a series of practices or rehearsals at lower levels of command that result in an enormous loss of training time.

(2) A natural phenomenon makes a scheduled activity impossible. I once made a visit to a tank company which had ranging exercises on the schedule. The company was not at the designated site, but a guide was there. He said that the company was in the woods and led me to the company commander. The company commander reported and said, "Sir, we're not doing the ranging exercises. We can't see the silhouettes because of the fog hanging in the valley, but that happens every so often so we have a package of crew exercises for these days while we wait for the fog to lift." He took me around to see men replacing the machine-gun barrel against time, setting the headspace on the 50 calibers, and going through a few other drills. It made my day to meet a young commander who knew his training environment and planned for problems that might arise. It was time to pat that company commander on the back and say, "Great, captain," and go on about my business, which I did.

(3) Unforeseen events. I recall visiting a cavalry squadron I had observed two weeks before, when no one had been following the training schedule and no training worthy of the name had been going on. On my return there were still no signs of training. I asked a charge of quarters, "Where are the troops?"

"Sir, they are down at the chapel."

"Why?"

"The sergeant in charge of the dining hall died Saturday and the whole squadron is at his funeral service."

You can't beat that for a reason to change the training schedule. People are what the Army is all about, and I am certain it meant a lot to the family of that NCO to see the whole squadron at the funeral service. Also the soldiers new to the service were no doubt impressed to learn that an individual meant that much to the commander and the unit. This was proof that soldiers are not faceless numbers in the Army. I went on to check training in another unit and later saw the squadron marching back from chapel. They were dressed in greens, guidons flapping in the breeze, officers and NCOs in their proper positions in the formation. They looked good, and I respected the commander who made that decision in a climate that definitely stressed "No changes to the training schedule," especially since he knew me well enough to know I'd be back.

Changes should be few indeed. If you do make one and you can look any higher commander in the eye and tell him why you did it, he will recognize the merit if there is merit in it. If the change is due to poor planning, lack of preparation, or other self-inflicted wounds, he will no doubt recognize the absence of merit too, and the commander who changed the schedule will probably learn the error of his ways. Unfortunately, the answer too often is something like, "The lieutenant was not prepared," "The training film was not available," "Someone else was on the range," or "They wouldn't give us the ammunition," all of which are examples of poor planning and poor training management.

If training schedules are not to be changed, the point in time at which they are prepared is important. Generally training schedules for company-level units should be approved from two weeks to ten days before the date the schedule is to be effective. Schedules submitted three or more weeks in advance result in too many changes that cannot be anticipated. Submission fewer than ten days before the effective date limits the time commanders and instructors have for obtaining training aids, looking over the training area, studying the manuals, and preparing worthwhile, interesting training.

Company-level commanders should be able to adhere to a training schedule prepared ten to fourteen days in advance. If a commander thought the training was necessary when the schedule was made out, it will still be necessary on the effective date. If not, the training plan was poor to start with. When company-level commanders cannot adhere to their training schedules, they should look critically at their own training plans. The field-grade commanders should be looking into the reasons too, in order to eliminate the causes for change and create a better training climate for their subordinates.

The results of a better training climate are significant. There is a tremendous improvement in the quality of training if it is preplanned. When the soldier knows what to expect he is more receptive and mentally prepared for the training. The chain of command can devise checks at the end of each week or at the end of each day to determine if the soldier has learned what he was supposed to learn during that period. Planned training helps the chain of command focus on the training objectives and permits feedback to improve ongoing training. For these reasons, whenever a senior officer visits training he should make it a matter of habit to determine if the training he is watching is going on as scheduled. Changes should be challenged and the changemaker required to defend the change in the face of searching questions.

FLEXIBILITY IN TRAINING SCHEDULES

At this state of the discussion someone is certain to ask, "How about a little flexibility?" Suppose the subject is not adequately covered in the time available? The answer is, incorporate reinforcing training in other related subjects; reschedule the training. But if the subject needs more time perhaps the original presentation was inept or poorly planned. In that case training requires a little more thought. Changing the next day's schedule to repeat the subject seldom helps; it is generally much better to reschedule the training about two weeks later in the next schedule the commander prepares.

What do you do when training went so well that it was completed an hour ahead of schedule? On those rare occasions, I believe the company-level commander should report to his battalion commander and request permission to terminate the training. He may even want to reward the troops for a job well done. If a commander consistently wants to move on to something else because the training has been finished early, it is time for the battalion commander to start looking at the schedule closely.

EVALUATING A TRAINING SCHEDULE

The training schedule is where the training program begins to take on reality and training moves from plan to execution. Learn to look at a training schedule quickly and comprehend the good and bad features at a glance. By the time you are a field-grade commander you should have acquired this talent or you do not know your business. This capability grows along with the development of a healthy philosophy of training and bits of training doctrine that derive from it. Over the years I have force-fed my commanders the following bits of advice:

Get troops out of barracks and classrooms and onto the ground.
Don't talk about it—DO IT.
Watch the tempo; keep tactical problems short.
Be specific.

When I would visit a unit and glance at the training schedule, these guidelines would determine my itinerary. If the training was in the attic, dayroom, or a classroom I would go there first. On the way up or downstairs there is always the opportunity to look in a few living or work areas—a day room, a supply room —and begin to get a picture of the unit's discipline and standards. A judgment can also be made on the number of men in the barracks area who are not at training. A lecture or training film in the post theater always drew my attention because there a brief look would suffice to tell me whether the training was interesting. If it wasn't, the appearance and demeanor of the troops would reflect that fact.

Next in order of priority was determining the kind of training going on. I always looked in on the subjects that experience had taught me were neglected —first aid, interior guard, and organized company athletics. Emphasis on these subjects varies in each unit and reveals the strengths and weaknesses of subordinate commanders. A battalion or brigade commander should quickly learn to judge the content of the training if he is checking it every day as he should.

"Maintenance" as an item on the training schedule always attracted my attention. The location and the length of the period devoted to it were both pertinent. If maintenance was not taking place where the equipment was likely to be, I would be curious as to how the subject was being taught. If it was scheduled for a prolonged period of two to three hours, I'd be certain to look in on it. Long, dragged-out training sessions get tiresome; people drift away and it is surprising how often, particularly in maintenance, no one is at the scheduled location after a certain point. Also, it is easy to tell how much was done before they left by a quick look at some of the equipment. Commanders of armor and other units that have heavy equipment make a case for two- to four-hour blocs for maintenance because of the time it takes to get at the equipment. There is no magic to the number of hours, the test is what is happening during that period. Are the troops there? Are they supervised? Is their training meaningful? Those are the criteria.

These are all ideas on how to make a quick judgment on the quality of a training schedule by looking at the product. Once you know what to look for, the habits that lead to poor training jump out at you from the schedule. One indicator that stands out in my mind is described by the word *specificity.*

Roll that word around on your tongue a few times. At first you'll probably have trouble with it because it is not easy to pronounce, but that will help you remember it. Being specific as to what training is to be conducted will do as much to improve training as anything I know. When entries like "Tank Gunnery," "Infantry in the Attack," "Communications," "Maintenance," or "Gunnery," a favorite with the artillery, clutter up a training schedule start asking questions. If the entry is tank gunnery, ask what aspect of gunnery? If it is an infantry attack, attack of what? By what size unit? Day or night? Once you learn what specificity is all about the questions will automatically come to mind. I had always discussed this aspect of training with subordinate commanders, but never as well and as clearly as it was portrayed to me on a visit to the German Infantry School.

One of the questions I had asked the Germans was what they taught their officers about training in the school. They taught them a lot. One thing that caught my attention was the following chart:

SPECIFICITY

- MAJOR SUBJECT AREA:
  Mechanized Infantry Tactical Training
- LEVEL OF TRAINING:
  Squad Training
- SEGMENT OF TRAINING:
  Reconnaissance Security
- LESSON:
  Reconnaissance Patrol
- SPECIFIC EXERCISE:
  Employment of the Dismounted Reconnaissance
  Patrol in Wooded Areas

They taught their officers to go through a checklist like this every time they made out their training schedules, emphasizing that once an officer learned to think through each subject proposed for training in this fashion training time would not be wasted. The trainers—officers and NCOs—would know just what the soldier was expected to learn and just what manuals were needed. This knowledge almost guaranteed that the specific exercise would be well presented. The checklist was also an aid to selecting terrain and breaking the training into progressive blocks of instruction.

Once you have developed a coherent philosophy of training and are familiar with the training requirements of your branch of service and your level of command, you should be able to identify at a glance the strengths and weaknesses of the schedule you are looking at as well as the commander who approved it.

One final note on the relationship between the training schedule and management has to do with the time of the company commanders. On several occasions I asked battalion commanders how much help they were giving their company commanders in preparing training schedules. From their replies I sensed that they were trying to do entirely too much. I recall one battalion commander who told me how much help he was giving a battery commander to improve his training schedule. "Sir, we started on the schedule at 1600 Friday afternoon and we worked on it until 2000. I still wasn't satisfied so we got together again Saturday morning." That poor battery commander was not to be envied. He was getting the kind of help that battery and company commanders can do without. If they need it, something is wrong. The company-level commander, it should be kept in mind, has all the responsibility for executing the weekly training schedule. His time is valuable, and he cannot afford to spend several hours in conference with the staff or field-grade commander discussing the details of a training schedule. If you are spending long hours "helping" company commanders make up a training schedule, take a look at your own leadership techniques. Teach subordinates a little each day while observing training, and the format and content should soon fall in place.

CENTRALIZED CONTROL

In recent years there has been a tendency to centralize supervision of training tests at higher and higher levels in the chain of command. In the early 1970s it was routine for one brigade commander to be responsible for supervising the tank-crew qualification course for all tank crews in a division; another brigade commander would be responsible for setting up a mechanized infantry squad problem for all infantry squads in the division. In effect this is committee training in its worst form, although no one ever calls it by that name. Committee training is effective in basic training and in training centers, but it has no place in unit training except with respect to an occasional short-term training deficiency.

There were several reasons for this centralized control. One concerned competition: Someone wanted to designate the best squad or tank crew in a division, and centralization provided a "fair" way to do it. Other factors were the lack of stability and experience due to the demands of Vietnam, the brigade commander's branch of service, and a need to consolidate support because of personnel shortages. Well-organized, stereotyped training supervised by one brigade for all like elements in a division has some value, but the gain does not begin to compensate for the degree to which the chain of command is undermined.

Officers and noncommissioned officers, as well as those in support roles, learn a great deal from the problems they improvise, supervise, and umpire. It is often hard to see your own mistakes while conducting training, but when you are in the role of umpire it is easy to learn from the mistakes of others. Support of other units in training can be a burden, but throughout my service I always believed that my officers and noncommissioned officers learned as much from setting up, controlling, and umpiring problems as they did from going through them. They also learned when they went through the problems that they could make mistakes too. When one brigade supervises a phase of training for all like elements in a division, the valuable learning and training that comes from the supervisory responsibility is confined to a small segment of the division, and the rest of the chain of command suffers. But if each company or battalion sets up its own test problems and supervises qualification of appropriate levels of the unit, many more leaders are involved in preparing and supervising, a most important phase of training. This is the best possible school for developing the leadership, tactical knowledge, and training techniques of young leaders, since a greater variety of tactical situations and a healthier training climate will emerge as more commanders contribute ideas. More emphasis, it is to be hoped, will be given to teaching and training, and less to competition.

The objective in training should be to let battalion commanders train and test their own commands to the extent of their ability. During range seasons, or when unit tests are being conducted, brigade commanders should give all possible support to the battalions. This effort provides training opportunities for the brigade staff and supporting elements of the brigade and division. Within a battalion, a unit that needs help can get it from similar units in the battalion. Coordinating this support is good training for battalion staffs. When senior commanders centralize control and evaluation of subordinate elements of company level units—squad, tank crew, gun section, or platoon—at a level above battalion, their action reflects a lack of faith in the battalion commanders.

Experience indicates that there is merit in placing control or supervision of tests two command echelons above the element being tested. For squad, tank-crew, or gun-section tests, control should be at company level; for platoon tests, control should be at battalion level. For company or battery tests, control should be at brigade or group; for battalion tests, at division. Support of training tests at one echelon is generally beyond the capability of the next echelon up the chain of command; however, it is almost always within the capability of the second higher echelon. There will be exceptions, but for elements below the company level the more that can be done within the battalion, the stronger the links for building the chain of command.

TRAINING RECORDS

Current Department of Army policy is that training records are not subject to audit. This policy is designed to encourage commanders to maintain useful and factual records to assist in the development of sound training programs without fear that the reports might be used against them. However, a note on training records is pertinent, because policies change and the request for training records is persistent.

One hardy perennial is the maintenance of individual training records. My viewpoint has not changed on that since I was a company commander. It has been my experience that individual training records at company level are mere eyewash and are seldom, if ever, up to date. If kept up to date, the system requires the full time effort of at least one member of the unit, who is therefore not available for training. I believe that individual training records should be kept only at the level of the first commander or supervisor in the chain of command responsible for the individual—for example, squad leader for the infantry squad, tank commander for the tank crew, section chief for gun section, communication chief for communication section, and so on. The best way to keep such records is in a small pocket notebook. This method distributes the work load and allows each noncommissioned officer to spend only a few minutes a day on the training status of his or her troops. An important bonus is that when the immediate leader keeps the record it reinforces the leader's position in the chain of command.

While I do not advocate any comprehensive system of training records, some commanders feel a need for something recorded. If the need exists use the same procedure as on the individual training records: Maintain records at the level of the responsible commander in the chain of command. Platoon commanders maintain records on the state of training of their noncommissioned officers and the results of tests of elements of their platoons, company-level commanders maintain the results of platoon or section tests, battalion commanders the result of company or battery tests, and so on up the chain of command. By this means useful and simple training records can be maintained and kept in the proper channel. No effort is wasted, since each level of command maintains its own record of training. But don't let the G–3s ask for reports; they will if given the chance.

Senior officers can ask immediate commanders for a training status report as they visit a unit. Again, such a policy adds to the prestige of subordinate commanders, many of whom believe their responsibility has been eroded in recent years. It also reminds those same commanders of their very real responsibility for their troops. This is one small but important way to build up the pride and prestige of commanders who carry a heavy, and too often unrecognized, load.

TRAINING HIGHLIGHTS

It is all right to have training highlights, but do not publicize them. The typing wastes the company clerk's time and the advertising does not help a unit's overall training program. Many high-ranking people in the chain of command tend to gravitate to the highlights; if they don't, they get pushed, pulled, or invited in that direction, and the highlight turns into a demonstration. Meanwhile, what is going on in the maintenance bays, or the interior guard and first aid classes? When I knew all commanders were headed for a training highlight, I frequently dropped in on some other training in that brigade or division. Try it sometime; it is quite enlightening and often disappointing.

Training highlights ought to be the best training for miles around. The training that leads up to the highlight will get lots of attention from the immediate commander and no doubt from one to two levels above, so a flock of visitors will not help that training very much. When training highlights are not published, subordinate commanders begin to realize that everything they have on their training schedule is important, and they start giving the entire schedule the attention it needs. It is not difficult for members of the chain of command to pick out training of special interest just by looking at the training schedule. Remember, we want to encourage commanders to do just that.

Until senior generals get control of their aides, chiefs of staff, and secretaries of the general staff, training highlights will continue to survive. Invariably when a general officer is planning a visit to the troops, the aides and staffs automatically start asking for the training highlights so that the boss can see the best. All you need is one or two of these requests whenever a senior general is about to visit a unit, and you can be sure that army, corps, and division commanders will be asking subordinate units for training highlights. If the Army Chief of Staff instructed his aide not to call in advance of a visit for training highlights but rather to pick up a bundle of unit training schedules so that on arrival the Chief could say, "I want to see that," such action would soon put a stop to training highlights. All company clerks would appreciate this approach, and the training in the Army would suddenly improve.

MAKING AN ARMY AT THE HOME STATION— EVERY DAY

Closely associated with the deemphasis of the training highlight is the balance in the commander's mind between the daily training in garrison and local training areas, and training at field firing ranges and major training areas.[5] Senior commanders—full colonels and generals—tend to be much more in evidence when units are on the range or in major training areas than during routine daily training. Since battalions and brigades are rotated through the field firing and major training areas, if the senior commanders believe that is where they should be, then the training of the units back at the home posts tends to be neglected.

The major training area is the graduation exercise for a well-trained unit in a properly managed training program, because in that type of program the label "well-trained unit" is earned at home station. Day-to-day training on subcaliber ranges, ranging exercises, weapons training, first aid, and other individual and collective training on the fundamentals is what creates a unit's operational capability and enables that unit to integrate all aspects of training at the field firing areas. Certainly the senior commanders should visit the field firing areas, and visiting each battalion-size unit in a major training area would also be worthwhile. But if senior commanders slight the units in their home station training, things get out of balance. From long experience, I am convinced the most important training is the work a unit does every day on the fundamentals at the home station and the local training areas. If a unit trains well at home it will do well when it goes to the ranges and major training areas. If the training at home station has been neglected, the trip to the major training area will not be worth the money the taxpayers provide for transportation and ammunition.

---

[5]Major training areas and field firing areas are used in the same context. In these areas major weapons systems—tanks, artillery, mortars, and other supporting weapons—can be fired; the terrain lends itself to tactical exercise and maneuver. Overseas these training facilities are some distance from where the units are stationed and most often are called "major training areas." Units of the host country train in these areas and scheduling is very tight. In the United States the field firing ranges are most often adjacent to the installation where the major units are stationed.

Garrison and local training areas refer to the areas close to barracks which can often be reached by a short march from barracks. In many installations in the United States the known distance ranges for small caliber weapons are often close to the barracks areas.

7

It is astounding what well-trained and dedicated soldiers can accomplish in the face of death, fear, physical privation, and an enemy determined to kill them.

Training Yourself and the Chain of Command

Two vital parts of training are seldom taught: training yourself and training the chain of command. There is a lot of talk about these subjects, but most of it amounts to lip service. We seem to expect that happenstance and experience will do the job. Often experience is the only teacher, but learning from experience is often slow, painful, and expensive. In training yourself, improving your grasp of what is right and wrong and being able to relate what you see to other activities are paramount. Teaching about the interaction of one type of endeavor with another is easy when relationships can be demonstrated and when opportunity exists for discussion and an exchange of ideas. I do not know of any profession that provides a better opportunity for this type of teaching than the military.

The commander's ability to command a unit, the quality of his leadership, and his methods of training are interdependent. The good commander is always teaching and training, and one activity complements the other. The examples that follow may appear at first glance to be of little consequence, or even a form of harassment to younger officers who do not yet recognize that little weaknesses should alert a commander to major problems in the making or already existing.

Too often those who should be solving problems do not even know they exist. The pintle in the towing eye of the quarter-ton vehicle is an example.[1] If it

---

[1]See below, p. 58.

is not properly placed, the message conveyed to the commander should be that the driver did not do his job thoroughly and his noncommissioned officer and his company officers either did not notice the failure or did not check. The commander must realize there is a faulty link in the chain of command and he had better do something about it. Minor deficiencies that he sloughs off as unimportant are sure to become major.

Attention to detail is of primary importance in military operations. These operations take place in a hostile environment where adversaries are determined to thwart your every move. Terrain may be neutral, but a well-trained enemy will defend ground that is not easily traversed. Weather too becomes hostile to operations that go on in the cold, snow, rain, or jungle and desert heat. Given all the adverse factors that are present in a military action, precision in performance and execution must be the goal of every member of a unit. Total precision is hard to attain, but it is what training is all about. It is astounding what well-trained and dedicated soldiers can accomplish in the face of death, fear, physical privation, and an enemy determined to kill them. Only by habitually doing the little things right can soldiers maintain and retain a semblance of order in the combat environment.

If you have ever seen a mortar or artillery round fall short in the midst of your own men, you realize the importance of insuring that each soldier does his duty properly, and that a chain of command exists that is trained to check on his performance. Only by learning the obvious indicators of poor performance and by learning to train a chain of command so that each member of it strives to do his best can a commander be assured of success in his daily undertakings. Once he learns these lessons, his command assignments will be a pleasure, but he has a lot of homework and fieldwork to do in order to reach such a state of grace.

LEARNING TO SEE

Certain qualities contribute to an individual's competence as a trainer, and the young officer should start developing them early. One that stands out is the ability to see—that is, the power of observation. It is surprising how unobservant most people are. Because a military commander is ultimately responsible for the lives of his soldiers, he can ill afford to be unobservant. Here are some ideas on developing the power of observation.

For a start, get out from behind that desk. So many reports have to be prepared or reviewed that it is easy for a commander to justify devoting an inordinate amount of time to paperwork. And there is something comforting about paperwork; it does not have anything to say and does not question correction. Not so with troops. A new commander who has not been with troops for a long time—a common situation in the United States Army—naturally suffers from a lack of confidence. His concern about troop attitudes and his limited knowledge of new equipment make the office a comfortable place to be. Don't fall into that trap. Get out where the troops are, and learn by watching what is going on. Limit the paperwork to a time of day that is not prime training time. During prime time, visit the units and training areas and take the time to talk with the troops. I do not mean give a speech. Just talk to a private here, a sergeant or junior officer there, a mechanic in the maintenance bay. You will get ideas on what the troops are thinking and what to be on the lookout for.

Once out there, how do you learn "to see" in a meaningful manner? There is no book big enough to contain all one needs to know. The modern army has too much equipment for anyone to be knowledgeable about all of it. The same goes for the variety of operations. And the equipment, operations, and situations are always changing. But the pamphlets, field manuals, and technical manuals that do exist can be of great help. There is one problem, however; the field manuals that used to fit conveniently into the pocket of a field jacket now fit better into a brief case. But they seem to be getting smaller again, so when the one you need is pocket-portable start carrying it with you. Technical manuals are a little bigger, but there is supposed to be one with each vehicle and weapons system. If you have to check something, ask to see the manual. Just finding a technical manual where it is supposed to be tells something about a unit.

Let's take a specific example. All units have quarter-ton vehicles. Reach for *The Commander's Guide to Preventive Maintenance Indicators*[2] and look at the pictures pertaining to the quarter-ton on the way to the motor park or the training area. Select a few items that are easy to see. Take two—say, the pintle in the towing eye and the intervehicular connecting cable on the trailer—and by looking at the picture in the manual note their correct position. When you inspect the vehicles, are there pintles out of place? They are quite noticeable when they are hanging down. The intervehicular connecting cables on the parked trailers—where are they? Hanging on the ground? Draped over the front of the trailers with the plug lying in the bed? If so, are they suspended in water that was not drained after the last rain?

Enough for one day. As you visit a unit and look for specific items for which the manual has given you the correct picture, the things that are wrong will catch your eye and what is right will soon be obvious. And as you point out

---

[2]DA Manual 750-1, January 1971. This small manual is a great help when an officer reaches battalion-level command and above.

deficiencies to the senior member of the unit present, a picture of the unit's chain of command will begin to emerge. Why didn't a noncommissioned officer or lieutenant see the error and get it corrected? If the cables are not properly suspended, how many are broken or rusty? Improper stowage affects the maintenance effort and the cost of spare parts; it might suggest a look at the supervision of motor stables in that unit the next day. If the quarter-tons you checked are correctly maintained as prescribed in the manual, mentally chalk up a plus for that commander and his chain of command.

More important, you have learned to know the correct configuration on a common but important type of equipment. From what you have seen, you will know whether the driver is doing his job and if his supervisors are checking on him. Soon what is right or wrong will be obvious not only on that type of vehicle, but on a whole series of vehicles with similar parts. Deficiencies will jump out at you as you pass vehicles on the road, or wherever you see them. When you go into a motor park or a maintenance area where there are several vehicles of the same type, you will automatically notice different configurations when someone has erred. When you see these variations, you can be 99 percent sure that something is wrong. And you ought to know the reason for variations that are not errors. If you have no manual with you—and often you will not, since you would need a pack horse to carry them all, particularly as you get to higher rank and see all types of units—just ask the noncommissioned officer for the appropriate manual. While he is getting it, point out the two configurations to another officer or noncommissioned officer from that unit and ask him which is right. Then you can all look at the manual together to get the right answer. The same goes for weapons systems, generators, or any other type of equipment. This is a good way to get noncommissioned officers and young officers into the habit of using the manuals. It also develops in the senior officer the confidence that comes from knowledge and a facility for easy interchange with the troops.

I have said the office is a haven for some officers because paperwork does not talk back. It's a rare officer who does not have a queasy feeling in the pit of his stomach when he takes command of a unit. I had a lot of command experience, but I always worried about how well I would do each time I assumed a new command, and it made no difference how high-ranking I got. The longer you are away from troops, the tighter that knot in the stomach. Don't worry about all your uncertainties or the soldiers' reactions to your queries and comments. Once you learn that the soldiers do not expect you to know everything and that you can learn a lot from them, it is easier to force yourself into an environment that you should know more about. Remember that you must have something to offer, or you would not have been given a command. It is how you use your talents that counts. As you advance in grade it is essential that you learn more and more about soldiers, equipment, and the conditions under which they operate. Because command billets are limited and field-grade officers have to serve in a wide variety of assignments, the opportunities to be in a troop unit are few and far between. So make the most of the troop assignments you have.

The lieutenant colonel, returning as a battalion commander after a long absence from troop assignments, may have a slight problem, but if he learned his trade well at the company level he is at least on familiar ground. For the brigade commander who suddenly finds himself in command of units of several different arms the task is not so easy, but there are a lot of troops who can help him. He would do well to ask a warrant officer or noncommissioned officer to guide him along a line of bulldozers, howitzers, missiles, or radios and point out the things that create maintenance and safety problems if neglected. He could with equal profit ask to be shown the indicators that will help him recognize whether the driver or crew has been properly checking the equipment. Then he should check similar equipment to determine if he has learned his lesson well. Checking vehicles is a good way to start such training because there are so many, and the maintenance of wheels and tracks is one of a commander's greatest concerns.

As a general officer, I had occasion to ask for this kind of help frequently. It was always an education. I learned what to look for and I believe it gave the warrant officer or noncommissioned officer a sense of his importance and special knowledge. You will not only learn to recognize what is wrong this way, but you will also learn to see what is right. So much can go wrong in a military organization, where you have responsibility twenty-four hours a day, that it is good to be able to tell a commander and his chain of command that things are going well.

On occasion you will encounter an individual who talks a good game but does not know his job. But if you have consulted the manuals over the years, you will learn to recognize things that do not sound right. It does not hurt to be skeptical on occasion, because sometimes you can get bad information. Get a technical manual from the shop or vehicle when something doesn't make sense to you. Looking it up and talking it out will help clear the air.

The burden of care and maintenance of equipment weighs heavily on commanders and in this area it is easy to give specific examples of things to look for, but the same approach applies to other areas as well, such as tactics. Examples of proper positioning of weapons and what causes stoppages are in the manuals. Study the pictures on emplacement and the principles of employment for the weapons in your unit. Make it a point to observe the weapons positions. If one does not look right, talk to the crew. Get behind the weapon and check the sight picture. Ask the noncommissioned officer or the crew members if they consider their position good and why. Ask if they can see a better one. Ask what immediate action they would take to clear a stoppage.

As you go to the local training area or are just driving about the post, inspect each knoll, clump of woods, crossroads, or old shack with the eyes of a tactician. Could you have a small-unit problem there? What type: Attack? Defense? Withdrawal? Where would the enemy be? How would the friendly troops approach the objective? If you are armor would you want some infantry, or vice versa? If you are artillery, where do you think the supporting fires would be most effective? If the battery had to go into position there, where would be the best place for the guns? The fire direction center? Would it be a good spot for a night problem? Why? By asking such questions you will be on the way to becoming a sound tactician and good trainer because you will be looking at weapons and terrain with the eye of a professional. Gradually, and almost without realizing it, you will begin to see training opportunities in areas that were not previously considered for training and you will be able to visualize a variety of specific tactical situations.

Above all, when you get to the local training area learn to look closely at the troops. Do they have all their equipment? Is it in good condition? Are they interested in what is going on? Disinterested? If so, why? Are they confident? Do they work as a team? Do they care about what they are doing? Once you take an interest in them as individuals and as members of a unit, you'll be able to answer these questions at a glance.

But enough of examples. Learning to see is a capability that can be developed. Start early in your military service and be alert and observant, and you will be pleasantly surprised at the knowledge and perception of your profession that you will acquire. But you will need all the powers of observation you develop. Land warfare and the operations of army forces are far more complex and difficult than most people ever realize—and "most people" includes some military professionals. As responsibility increases, developing the capability to see helps to put things in perspective. That alone sets one on the road to becoming a good trainer—and a better commander.

WHAT ELSE TO LOOK FOR

So far the emphasis has been on the operational side of training—equipment, tactics, and troops. Read what General Patton wrote about another side:

> *Administrative discipline is the index of combat discipline. Any commander who is unwilling or unable to enforce administrative discipline, will be incapable of enforcing combat discipline. An experienced officer can tell, by a very cursory administrative inspection of any unit, the caliber of its commanding officer.*[3]

---

[3]George S. Patton, Jr., *War As I Knew It* (Boston: Houghton Mifflin, 1947), p. 350.

General Patton's comment highlights administrative discipline. Too few company and field-grade officers appreciate its importance and its bearing on training, especially the training of the chain of command.

It is often hard for a commander to accept it when a visitor finds a lot wrong in his unit in a short time. But in a unit with poor administrative discipline, the signs are obvious to the true professional as soon as he steps into the unit area. Battalion and brigade commanders can teach their subordinate commanders where and how to look for indications of lax standards. A quick walk-through of a unit's living, working, or recreation areas is a good teaching device. Not much time has to be spent, and not everything needs scrutinizing. Twenty to thirty minutes with a subordinate commander on any given day should be enough.

Teach commanders to look at the close-in areas and those just off the beaten path for what is wrong, and also for what is a high standard. If the first few areas checked look good, chances are the rest of the unit will be in good order and you can infer that the chain of command in that unit is working. Come back in a week and look at a different administrative area. If on one of these visits to a unit the first few areas do not look good, give the commander a chance to redeem himself and check a few more. If they are all bad, you know you have some teaching to do. Go back at the first opportunity to see if corrections have been made. That is how young officers and noncommissioned officers learn to raise their standards.

The areas listed below are examples of places to look at and things to look for. Checking them will provide a picture of administrative discipline and the effectiveness of the chain of command.

Barracks

Check the nonliving areas of barracks—attics, siderooms, classrooms, under stairwells; these are sometimes disorderly and littered with odds and ends of broken furniture. Look at a few of the rooms or bays in the living quarters. If you are in the barracks during prime training time, take special note of the number of troops not at training. Glance alongside the entrances for cigarette tips and other small items of debris; look up for bottles, cans and other items on the window sills.

Dining halls

Note the quality and appearance of the food, the general cleanliness of the facility, and the appearance of cooks. How long is the line? Check on a day when it is raining, to see if the troops have to stand outside in the rain. It happens. Is there self-imposed segregation of minority groups? Is it enforced? By whom? Naturally, this is not easy to find out, but the NCOs ought to know. Are soldiers wearing caps at the tables? You can learn a lot about a unit by a few quick trips to the dining hall.

Motor pools

Sometimes in maintenance shops heavy films of oil and water form on the floor, and tools, nuts, bolts, and parts are scattered about. These are safety hazards. Other signs of poor housekeeping are tires, batteries, canvas, and other items, that perhaps should be turned in, piled against the walls. Ask a few questions about them. Also, latrines in isolated areas, especially in motor pools, are often neglected. Walk along a line of vehicles and look into a few cabs and the beds of trucks or trailers. It takes only a sampling to tell you what you need to know. The quickest tip-off to poor maintenance is a dirty windshield. When you see that, you know the operator did not complete his after-operations check. Look at a few other items on those vehicles, and I predict your batting average for picking out vehicles that need attention will be high. All motor pools require close scrutiny. The ability to detect careless and disorderly procedures will not only improve administrative discipline, but it will also improve the overall maintenance effort. The motor pool is a magnificent classroom for teaching subordinates "how to see."

Gymnasiums, bowling alleys, post exchanges

In checking places of recreation pay special attention to the troops. Note their appearance and manner; observe the service they get or the equipment that is available for them. If it is during duty hours, ask a few soldiers why they are there and who gave them the time off. Make a mental note to spotcheck with a few commanders to see if they knew the men had been excused. This should not be an inspection in depth, just the type of quick check you must train yourself to make and ask questions about.

Fringes and fencelines

The fencelines of installations and motor pools, especially where service activities border the fence, will give you a quick fix on how effective the noncommissioned officers are in an organization, and how well the entire chain of command observes conditions in and around their units.

Off-limits signs on latrines

Walk through the barracks during breakfast some morning. Are signs posted on the latrines saying that they are off limits from 0700 to 0800 or some similar morning hour? Initially, you will be surprised at how often you find them. Consider the soldier who lives in the barracks; the commander who allowed those signs to go up did not. Making a latrine off limits in the early morning hours is unrealistic, given the breakfast hour, normal body functions, and the need to be clean for the start of the day. Would it not be better to keep the latrines open and allow the cleanup detail to report for duty—and even training—a few minutes late? Troops must cultivate an appreciation for one another and an understanding of cooperation for the common good required by communal living. Encouraging soldiers to keep latrines and washrooms clean as they use them is part of their training. Just think what would happen in your household if someone put the bathroom off limits at 0700 each morning.

This matter of observing posted signs may seem a bit offbeat and unrelated to training, but it is related to your concern for your troops. It is amazing what signs some barracks tyrants put up. Too often commanders making an inspection pass those signs and they do not register. Young officers must be encouraged to ask grizzled NCOs, "Why is that sign there?" A particularly common answer is, "It has always been that way." Signs prohibiting this or that are the little irritants that influence troop attitude and start the administrative discipline sliding downhill, because the soldiers begin to think no one cares.

Early-morning inspections

The meaning of "in addition to your other duties" and the value of early-morning inspections came clear to me from encounters with my first company commander. Within a week of my arrival he had assigned me several additional duties, one of which was mess officer. On one point he was most specific. He said, "The cooks get up about four o'clock to start breakfast. In some outfits the first thing they do is start brewing the coffee so the kitchen crew can have an early cup; by the time the troops come in for breakfast, the coffee is like mud." He told me to be sure the mess sergeant had a coffeepot to make an early cup of coffee for the kitchen crew, and to be certain the coffee for breakfast was freshly made.

I never liked getting up early in the morning, which is quite a cross for a soldier to bear, but I did get up to make my checks. In M Company of the 13th Infantry, the mess sergeant knew the "old man" and the troops got fresh coffee at breakfast. But as I went on to other units, I continued my early-morning checks and found that some kitchen crews did indeed start brewing the coffee at about four A.M., and it was mighty strong by breakfast. More important, I learned you can find out about things that go on in a unit in those early morning hours that affect the attitude of the troops—perhaps more than those that occur at other times of the day. I recommend that early morning check once in a while when you are commanding a unit. On the way back from the dining hall, check a guard post, walk through the motor pool or perhaps one of the barracks. You may find some real eyeopeners.

Once officers and NCOs learn the fundamentals of their trade and begin to recognize discrepancies and correct them in their own unit, training will get better and problems will be fewer. But "learning to see" takes training. Learn to look at every feature of your organization's activity to insure that unit training covers all the unit's tasks.

RECOGNIZING RELATIONSHIPS BETWEEN TRAINING AND THE WORK AT HAND

Another quality that contributes to competence as a commander and trainer is the ability to recognize the significance of what is observed and what transpires in a military unit, and to relate it to daily training. Consider first a few ideas on preventive training. Commanders responsible for men and equipment know that some sudden and unexpected accidents will occur no matter what. But when accidents and what appears to be hard luck persist, the commander had better start thinking about the training that might keep down the incident rate.

Serious-incident reports (SIR) often indicate training deficiencies in a unit. I want to emphasize that I am not encouraging senior commanders to use serious-incident reports as statistical evidence of incompetence. Rather, I wish to stress the need for company-level commanders to analyze their own, or someone else's, serious incidents in order to determine what training might curtail similar incidents. Reports of vehicle accidents, such as the following two, when thoroughly analyzed, are excellent sources of ideas for training a unit.

SIR on fatal traffic accident, 1830 hours, 16 FEB 73.
Report stated that a tank retriever pulled out of a parking area onto a freeway and was struck from the rear by a truck and trailer. Involved in the collision were four other civilian vehicles and a quarter-ton army vehicle. Several serious injuries, one fatal.

SIR on traffic accident, 1340 hours, 28 MAY 71.
Report stated that a 5-ton truck was towing another 5-ton truck in a northerly direction. The tow bar connected to the towed vehicle came

loose on the right side, causing both vehicles to go out of control. Both vehicles skidded through the center guard rail and into the path of a vehicle, which was traveling in a southerly direction. Driver of southbound vehicle was admitted to the hospital in serious condition.

Recovery of heavy vehicles with transporters and the towing of vehicles require skill, a thorough check of the details, and supervision. In a military community with thousands of vehicles, these accidents are not infrequent. Learn to drop into the headquarters office where the reports on vehicles are kept and read them from time to time. Compare what you read with similar operations that your unit carries out and ponder on the training of drivers and recovery crews. It is surprising, when you check up on most of these accidents, to find how little training the troops involved had on the details of the specific operations they were performing. Ask questions. How well trained are wrecker operators? Who is in charge of recovery operations? If he is a noncommissioned officer has he been trained in the complexity of recovery operations? Or is he sent out just because he is an E–6, E–7 or E–8? Have drivers and supervisors been taught to consider added momentum created by towed vehicles? Do they tow vehicles down a steep incline when a safer route might have been taken? Do they know how to secure a towbar? If the towbar was defective, why was the defect not spotted on the last equipment check? Do the warning devices work? Did the recovery crew have them at the time of the accident you are reading about? How good was the first aid training of the soldiers involved in the accident? How were their map-reading techniques? Did they get lost looking for the vehicle, delaying the recovery effort until after dark?

These are some of the questions that should come to a commander's mind when he reads about one of these accidents. The answers will generally indicate some voids in the training that should have been given to drivers and recovery crews. Most recovery operations are more complex than they appear on the surface and these fundamentals are often neglected in training. Every driver in the Army should be trained in the fundamentals of towing another vehicle in an emergency. In a well-trained unit, a recovery operation is just like a mission for one of the tactical elements. It requires coordination, timing, organization, and supervision, and troops can find the exercise interesting if they are taught to do it properly. Good recovery training is also a part of your safety program.

Serious-incident reports that pertain to wounds and death tell a lot about the quality of training and effectiveness of the chain of command in a unit. How many soldiers have been killed or wounded by weapons that had been "cleared" at the end of a firing exercise or by ammunition that had been "turned in"? This too is part of your safety program. I emphasize this point because many commanders who complain that they have too much to do cite "safety" as one of the straws that breaks the commander's back and keeps him from getting essential training done. Higher staffs and safety officers frequently give guidance on safety because the Army has equipment purposely designed to deal out violence. It must therefore be handled with care and good judgment.

A good trainer will not merely set aside a number of hours to talk about "safety"; he will integrate the safety into every-day training and use of the equipment. Here again seeing is important: A commander must be able to recognize when troops are not handling equipment or situations with intelligence and care. And this is where understanding the relationship between what is observable and what is possible comes in. The commander must visualize what can go wrong in a given situation when the troops do not follow proper guidelines. Generally, the guidelines for preventing serious incidents are neither complex nor mysterious; they are as simple as clearing the weapons, or turning in used ammunition. But when they are neglected in training, future problems are in the making.

Some reports are instructive as to the performance of guard duty too— those that tell of weapons and ammunition stolen from arms rooms or of vehicles and equipment stolen from motor parks. Does this sort of thievery reflect a laxness and indifference that could be disastrous in a combat situation? Reports of this type indicate, at the very least, that security is poor, that there is little regard for government property, and that the chain of command is not effective.

Endless examples of the relationship between training and the actual job at hand could be cited for every aspect of Army life. All too often discussions on training seem to apply only to tactical units, but the same principles apply to the support activities. Military Police, Finance, Adjutant General, and direct and general support maintenance units, to name a few, all need training and supervision. All troops must be trained in the use of individual weapons, gas masks, first aid, and other basic subjects. In the support activities, special skills and knowledge are required for the work at hand, and since the skill is most often developed at a special MOS course or school, supervising the job itself may be the most important aspect of training in support units. Commanders of support units should leave the office or the desk frequently to check on the supervision.

If equipment is being serviced, check both arriving and departing loads to see whether the equipment is properly packed for shipment. Visit the units you support and ask what they think of the support your unit is giving them. Quite often, you will learn of areas of dissatisfaction or misunderstanding that will suggest changes in training procedures and the need to talk with your supervisors. If your unit handles personnel problems, walk around the building to where the soldiers or families who come for help are entering and leaving. Glance at how long the line is. How does the organization of that activity strike you now that you are looking at it from the front door rather than from your office? Are chairs provided for the mothers with youngsters who have to wait their turn? Be sure to ask several of the soldiers coming out if their problems were solved. If someone says no, ask him if he knows why? If he does not, return with him to the section that handled the case. Determine whether something could have been done for that soldier. If not, be sure his or her unit gets the word on what has to be done. A soldier will not forget that kind of interest.

The foregoing suggestions are addressed primarily to support-activity commanders, since they offer a means of seeing and recognizing deficiencies in their own units. But they also point to a desirable course of action for officers reaching the rank of full colonel and general officer. In the higher ranks, you must be catholic in your interests and look at every element that influences the attitude and morale of your command because those two items are going to affect how well you train and operate. Too often as a general officer I found conditions that should have been corrected by the unit commander or someone in the immediate chain of command far below me. One example should suffice.

Once as I was dropping in to observe a Finance Office I stopped a staff sergeant who was coming out. I asked if his problem had been taken care of. "No, Sir!" he answered. A few questions and answers revealed that his visit pertained to an authorization for separate rations published eight months earlier. This was his third trip to the Finance Office, which was an hour and a half drive—one way—from his unit. Think how much training he was missing! I suggested that we return to the office together and talk with the officer in charge. Radios were blaring loudly in the Finance Office (I have found this distraction to be quite common in administrative offices). The sergeant and I stood quietly in the background and listened to an interchange between a soldier and a Finance clerk. It was difficult to hear the clerk's questions and the soldier's replies with all the noise. The noise alone suggested to me the need for better supervision, particularly since numerous pay errors were being made here every month. We then moved on to ask about the sergeant's problem. It developed that it could have been resolved easily. The signed statement from the company commander was a legitimate basis for payment. However, because the staff sergeant insisted that the Finance Office had lost his paperwork, the Finance noncommissioned officer refused to make the pay adjustment.

It is amazing how many petty bureaucrats our administrative systems can support. A good commander will recognize that such things happen and ferret them out. It works both ways; sometimes a unit blames the support activities for all the unit's problems when the unit is at fault. Learn to detect these problems and track them down as far as is necessary through the chain of command to get them corrected. Show up in some of these support activities, ask the troops what is going on, and take it from there. But do not get indignant—though on occasion you would like to in some of these forays, because with shifting responsibilities for support you might be in someone else's chain of command. Still, if a lapse affects your unit or troops, it is your business. Get the facts, talk to the senior member of the chain of command present, and then get back up or down the chain of command to get problems corrected—or someone commended, when he is doing a good job.

In some staff assignments, you can look at a unit's problems a little more objectively and with a little broader vision than when you are a member of a unit. Study the problems that develop in different units and try to determine what created the problems as you look for the best solutions. Decide how the problem could have been prevented and how it might be avoided in the future. Discuss your ideas with those involved—after giving them all the help you can. These ideas filed away will be a great help to you when you are in command and you can relate what you learned on a staff to the problems confronting you in a unit.

If you learn how to see and to recognize the relationships between what you see and what occurs each day in your unit, you will be well on your way to becoming an outstanding commander and trainer. At that time you will understand the phrase "training is all-encompassing" and your training will begin to reflect that understanding. From then on, training will become meaningful, interesting, and stimulating to the soldier. In addition, there will be great pleasure in a command assignment, *if* you have developed the capabilities described above in the chain of command. Being able to do things yourself is one thing, but the real art of training is teaching what you know to your subordinates—your chain of command.

PUTTING IT ALL TOGETHER
THROUGH THE CHAIN OF COMMAND

Army Regulation 600-20 states that the "chain of command is the most fundamental and important organizational technique used by the Army." There are individual acts of bravery and there are gifted individual leaders, but I know of no exception to the rule that successful military operations depend on a well-trained chain of command. "Learning to see" and "recognizing relationships" have been addressed sequentially in this chapter, but they reinforce and enhance one another in teaching and application. Developing these capabilities in the chain of command is of utmost importance to a commander or trainer. The face-to-face interchange possible in a unit school or between a commander and his subordinates as he observes their day-to-day activities provides superb opportunities to develop the powers of observation and the ability to recognize relationships, in junior officers and noncommissioned officers. Did they see the track vehicles fishtail when the tank trails were muddy and slippery? Do they think the track commander noticed it? What might happen if the cause is not corrected?

A good commander and trainer never misses an opportunity to teach all those in a position of responsibility, especially the noncommissioned officers and junior officers, what to look for, how to correct the deficiencies they detect, and why it is important to do so. Through such teaching, commanders at every level can stress the development of an effective chain of command in training.

In training, I always think in terms of the chain of command. To differentiate between the noncommissioned officer's responsibility and the officer's is a difficult task. The question is, "Who is in charge?" More often than not, it is a noncommissioned officer. With respect to training, if there is any difference at all between the officer and NCO, the officer has to be more aware of his responsibility to teach his subordinates how to be effective in getting the job done. As the officer gains a little experience, he can do much to improve the chain of command by showing noncommissioned officers what to look for and where to look for it. In recent years I have heard many officers and noncommissioned officers complain, "They have taken my authority away!" Those who complain were not quite sure who "they" were but it was always someone higher ranking. Yet all about them were deficiencies that they, the noncommissioned officers and officers, did not see or did not heed. From my observations, they themselves were giving their authority away by failing to correct deficiencies and establish standards. I contend that there are innumerable opportunities in the every-day life of a unit to improve the chain of command. A few examples of where to look for such opportunities follow. They generally fall in areas of responsibility of the noncommissioned officer, but in any of these situations, not far up the chain of command is an officer who is responsible too.

Formations

Troops get instructions at innumerable formations. Occasionally it is a good idea to saunter up to the back of one of these formations to learn what kind of direction the troops are getting. I have often been struck by how little can be heard in the rear of a formation. Trucks are often passing or track vehicles are revving up in a nearby motorpool. Add to this handicap the fact that the troops probably don't want to hear a lot of the guidance, since it involves work details and other negative matters. Small wonder that a lot of minor violations and failures crop up in a unit. Teach the chain of command to post a senior noncommissioned officer in the rear of these formations to call out "Sound Off," whenever the speaker cannot be heard clearly.

Occasional visits to these formations also reveal the amount of negative information the soldier is subjected to. At these formations he seldom hears he has done a good job; he most always hears what he did wrong. In most cases one, two, or three individuals in the group did not perform properly—for example, their rooms were untidy, they needed haircuts, or they failed to turn in a required form. Nevertheless the troops are invariably told, "The rooms were all in a mess," "You all need haircuts," or "Nobody turned in the forms." The chain of command must be trained to pin the shortcoming on the people who actually fail to comply or do not measure up. Too often the entire unit is blamed for the failings of a few. It is no wonder that soldiers sometimes don't care or fail to try. How can they put forth their best effort, if criticism is their daily lot?

Maintenance turn-in and pick-up points

A bit of training that will help in the maintenance area pertains to the part of the chain of command that supervises pick-up and turn-in points for items that are turned in for repair and are then picked up by the unit supply section. Generally there is a schedule for these turn-ins and pick-ups. As you move around your unit, don't neglect the training of the people involved in this activity. How is the equipment packed? Is there padding in the bed of the truck? Items are too often placed on the bed of the pickup vehicles negligently. They slide back and forth bending sights or breaking off knobs, antenna attachments or other important parts of communications equipment, weapons, and spare parts. Training each individual in the chain of command responsible for this operation will save unit funds and prevent many maintenance problems.

Police formations

The troops' time is wasted in many ways, but there is probably no greater waste of time than what occurs at police call almost every day. Drop around any unit during police call on any given day. If you want to see it at its worst, take a look on one of those dark, cold mornings in winter. The roads and areas around barracks will be teeming with groups of three to five men shuffling along, hands in pockets, shoulders hunched, studiously looking at the ground. Every so often someone will bend down to pick something up, but if you follow behind there will still be plenty left for you. Then some loud voice will roar through the darkness and the troops will stream into barracks. These formations are a farce and a colossal waste of the troops' time.

One way to train the chain of command, and the best way to conduct police call, is to give a small element a large area of responsibility for a period of time, perhaps a week, and then hold the noncommissioned officer responsible for that area. A tank crew, infantry squad, or fire-team, a gun section, communication section, or administrative group, could be responsible for a company area and be given a certain time in which to do the job. If the work happened to run over into the training time—and it shouldn't if the responsible group goes about the job energetically—then they could report to training late, as a group, under their own chain of command.

If some such practice were followed police call would come around less often; the troops would have more time for their ablutions, breakfast, or just relaxing; and the chain of command would have a specific responsibility. Lax police calls are one of the old, unchallenged traditions. It is time commanders broke it. The troops are not impressed.

Loading vehicles

Take a look at your vehicles. Do you have loading plans? Are they being followed? In preparation for alerts or for moving to major training areas, units generally take all equipment and basic load ammunition. All this equipment will not fit into vehicles unless there is a good loading plan. Each vehicle should have a loading plan which indicates where equipment will be stored and where people will ride when moving out. The plan should actually be used by the vehicle commander, and not be simply a piece of paper to show to inspectors. When property is thrown into vehicles and crammed into trailers, the result is often damage and/or thievery. In day-to-day activities certain pieces of equipment may not be left on the vehicle. In that case there should be specific places for it—bins in the supply or arms room. This sort of planning is one of the many "little things" that is standard operating procedure in an effective professional army. Combine it with men in proper uniform and in proper position in the vehicle, and discipline, pride, and effectiveness will improve noticeably. There will be less equipment lost and damaged and fewer injuries to personnel riding in vehicles because the vehicle commanders in the chain of command, generally noncommissioned officers, are carrying out their responsibility.

Control of ammunition

This last example relates to safety, a daily concern for every leader. On a field problem, at the range, or in any situation in which ammunition is issued, the noncommissioned officer in charge of each subordinate element should be the one to distribute the ammunition. He should check on its use by the members of his element, and insure that the ammunition is turned in or accounted for at the end of that phase of training. This accounting must include blanks and simulators, which can cause injury too. Noncommissioned officers in all units play a vital role in maintaining safety standards, and the procedures they use establish the importance of the chain of command. Each time a specific task or function is done properly, the sense of responsibility and quality of the chain of command goes up a notch, and that is what makes an army effective. In combat NCOs redistribute ammunition as a matter of course.

Learning to see, learning to connect what is seen with what happens in other on-going activities, and above all developing these capabilities in subordinates so that they are inherent in the functioning of the chain of command—such measures improve training so much it is a pleasure to observe it. But more important, they provide the basis for a force that will be ready to fight when the nation calls on it to do so.

When field-grade officers complain of the weaknesses of company-grade officers and noncommissioned officers, and in the next breath say they do not have time for unit schools, then something is amiss in their own education.

Unit Schools

The importance of schools in the training of an army cannot be overstated.[1] Unit schools are the bedrock for the improvement of individual development and improvement of unit training. Unit schools meet several needs; two are worth noting. First, a commander communicates his standards for training to his chain of command in unit schools. Second, the schools develop the capability of the trainer, enabling him to do a better job every day when he trains his squad, crew, platoon, or whatever his subordinate unit. It is in unit schools that noncommissioned officers refine the knowledge on which the individual training of their subordinates is based.

If young officers are properly prepared for troop duty in the basic and advanced courses of the service schools, they should be able to solve most of their local training problems with a vigorous unit school program, *but only provided* that field-grade officers have learned in the C&GSC and the War College that unit schools are an essential part of a unit training program. When field-grade officers complain of the weaknesses of company-grade officers and noncommissioned officers, and in the next breath say they do not have time for unit schools, then something is amiss in their own education.

I might do well to describe what I mean by unit schools, because somewhere along the line we lost our innocence and forgot all about them. Unit

---

[1]Trends in the senior service schools and advance courses were discussed in Chapter 3 above, pp. 14-16. Correction of the adverse trends is under way and going in the right direction.

schools are organized and operated at home stations to meet local training requirements. The most important are the company officer schools conducted by battalion and NCO schools run by company. The company- and battalion-level schools do not drain troops and equipment from the operational units. Units use their own equipment; the troops live in their own barracks; at the end of class, equipment is returned to the units responsible for its care. Other schools are normally operated for a limited period of time and for a restricted number of troops whose training requires special knowledge, techniques, facilities, or equipment. Cooks, mechanics, and communicators are examples of the personnel who may need to have their individual skills honed. Generally, these schools are best conducted by brigade or division. A little personal history might give a clearer picture of the unit school's place in training.

Soon after reporting to my first unit in 1938 I found myself attending a unit school for company officers one afternoon a week. The subjects were varied, but right down to earth: sand-table problems on tactics; how to run a mess and keep the ration records; how to pack a machine gun; how to run a range and qualify the gunners with a series of drills designed to save scarce ammunition. Schools also operated for NCOs one afternoon a week. I did not know then that most of the NCOs took correspondence courses on their own and many had reserve commissions. As a young officer I was learning early how much I did not know.

At each regiment I went to thereafter, the same routine was followed. The battalion commander conducted a unit school one afternoon a week for company-level officers. On rare occasions all officers would gather for a class by the regimental commander, a rather exalted figure in those days. One rule was understood by all: You just did not miss school. If you were on leave or in the hospital, it was OK, but any other reason better have been a good one.

When World War II came, the unit schools continued and picked up in frequency. Classes were held at night and my regimental commander had sand-table problems two nights a week for all the field-grade officers and senior captains who were soon to be battalion commanders or occupy other responsible field-grade positions. Those of us who were battalion commanders then conducted classes for our company officers. The company commanders conducted classes in turn for the NCOs. The classes dwelt on fundamentals—squad as a flank patrol, platoon as advance guard, use of supporting weapons, adjustment of artillery fire. On Saturdays, which were generally reserved for inspections by company commanders, there were tactical walks for the battalion commanders and discussions on how to teach most effectively with the least amount of ammunition. This was the period when the Germans and Japanese were winning on every front, U-boat sinkings were high, and ammunition was in short supply.

These personal remembrances may seem irrelevant now, but they are useful for conveying how important these unit schools were in the training of officers and NCOs both before and in the early days of World War II. The contribution of the schools became evident later, when the corporals and sergeants became lieutenants and captains and went on to field-officer rank. And we lieutenants were prepared so that we could command battalions and regiments with three to six years service. A little research will reveal that a large number of young officers who were outstanding battalion and regimental commanders were not yet thirty years old. My experience in World War II left no doubt in my mind that with proper training, most of it done right in the unit, competent young officers and noncommissioned officers would quickly emerge to fill the leadership positions normally filled by those well beyond them in years. The weekly classes brought people together who shared responsibility for making a military organization function. This helped develop a camaraderie in the units, which is so important in a military organization.

If training is to be worthwhile and interesting to the troops, today's commanders had better learn the importance of unit schools. The schools went into a gradual decline beginning in the late 1950s, and from 1965 on they were all but forgotten because of the instability created by the war in Vietnam. Now they are almost a lost art. In the early 1970s, the Army had many problems that unit schools would have helped alleviate, yet I do not recall finding one worthy of the name.

When I asked brigade and battalion commanders about their unit schools several months after their importance had been stressed to an entire army, the conversation went something like this:

"Do you have a unit school?"
"Yes sir."
"What's the subject for this week's class?"
"I haven't decided yet."
"When do you have the class and what do you cover?
"We have a class about once a week at an early breakfast. We talk about some of the problems we are having in maintenance or training, what we'll do next week and things like that."

That is not a unit school, at least not in my book. That is a commanders meeting or coffee call.

HOW TO CONDUCT UNIT SCHOOLS

Reinstitute the practice.

Battalion commanders should schedule company-officer courses as a part of the training program; they should be there and personally conduct some of the classes. This is an incentive for company-grade officers to be present.

Company/battery/troop commanders should conduct NCO classes for their own NCOs. Platoon leaders and NCOs should assist in giving classes, but company commanders should be present.

Specialist schools of short duration in communications, supply control, administration, and other subjects as needed should be conducted when there is a need. Brigade and division resources should assist with the best qualified instructors.

Classes should be one to two hours long, depending on the subject and place. Conduct training classes that get everyone involved—for example, sand-table problems, tactical walks, and maintenance-system checks in the motor pool. No lectures.

In developing the program, commanders at battalion and company level should look two to three months ahead to determine what subjects will be best for the unit. Develop a comprehensive outline of what is to be taught and how it is to be taught. Consider "How to run a range," "How to conduct rifle marksmanship," "How to check maintenance," "How to adjust supporting fires" (get some help from the artillery), "River crossing" (be sure you get some engineers involved), "Tank and infantry platoons in reverse slope defense." You can think of a hundred others. The most important point is to select subjects that will help your unit. Sit down with company officers to get their ideas. NCOs will have good ideas too. Then publish a schedule for eight to ten weeks designating subjects and instructors. Gear the classes to specific problems in the units, training, or other activities that lie ahead.

Schools should be conducted one afternoon a week for officers and NCOs. Forget the evenings, Saturdays, and after-duty hours. People assigned to units work hard all the time, and unit schools should not add to their burden. Time is available for classes during the training day in other than prime training time.

Officer and NCO classes should be held on different days of the week to insure that some part of the chain of command is available to supervise other activities. This flexibility will be a great help in developing the chain of command.

Generally, classes should be scheduled for the same day and same time every week—for example, officers on Tuesday; NCOs on Thursday. This way people will know when classes are scheduled. If day and time changes frequently people will forget; they are mighty busy in a unit.

Finally, brigade commanders and general officers should take an interest. Drop in occasionally, even if only for a short time. When visiting a unit ask the junior officers and NCOs what the subject for the unit school will be for that week or the next week. If they do not know start checking; the unit probably does not have a good unit school program. If the commander has not made up his mind what the class will be for the next week, the gathering will wind up being a meeting to discuss local problems or operations that are pending. That is part of the day-to-day operations of a unit, not a unit school.

There is no end to the need or the opportunity for this sort of training. Unit schools used to be standard operating procedure in the Army during the late 1930s and World War II. We should reinstitute that tradition because it is a commander's job to develop his subordinates. Numerous references have been made in this book to the chain of command. Nothing will draw a chain of command together more quickly than good unit schools.

Sudden situations do not require written plans or check lists. If there is a need for either, start thinking and doing some homework—because the conditions you want to check on should be in your mind, not on paper.

Situational Training

"What is situational training?" This is a legitimate question. "Situational training" may not be the best name, but the term describes a training technique developed to a fine art by General Hamilton H. Howze, one of the Army's most distinguished trainers. It is performance-oriented training applied for a brief period, from five minutes to half an hour, for a specific purpose. It consists of impromptu exercises developed by the commander to test a single aspect of training.

Applying situational training is quite simple once you learn the rudiments. The more you think about it—an essential first step in developing this training technique—and the longer you practice it, the easier it is for you and the more interesting it is for your troops. But situational training is not as easy as it looks. Anyone using it must know the capabilities of a unit and how it functions as well as what he wants to find out about the troops' state of training. Developing a variety of training situations to be executed over a period of time will give you an excellent picture of the state of training and readiness of a military unit. At the same time subordinates will learn to do the unexpected, which is desirable training for combat commanders.

It is useful to repeat here that training has four requirements: soldiers, their equipment, a place in which to conduct the training, and knowledge about unit capabilities. Situational training combines the four in a performance-oriented situation that requires action by the troops involved. Emphasize *action*. These sudden situations do not require written plans or checklists. If you need either one, back off and reexamine what you are doing. Start thinking and doing some homework, because the conditions you want to check on should be in your mind, not on paper. When you create situations for the troops to respond to, keep in mind the state of training of the unit, equipment capabilities, and the items to be checked in that particular situation.

Figure 9.1 is a guideline to situational training for battalion, squadron, and brigade commanders. It is intended to be cryptic. The major point is, never let the troops talk about the situation, make them do it and keep the situation brief. The approach to be taken here is giving examples of typical situations. The teaching would be much easier though, if it were conducted around a sand table or along a trail in a local training area. That's the way to teach officers how to develop this skill and to teach noncommissioned officers how to react to these situations.

FIGURE 9.1

SITUATIONAL TRAINING

REQUIREMENTS (The Four Ingredients):

1. Men assigned to unit. You have them. Don't complain about the men you don't have. Ask, "What can I do with the men I do have?"

2. Authorized Equipment. You have it in abundance — in fact, too much. Some of it probably has not seen the light of day in the last year.

3. A place to train. Street of installation, motor pool, local training area, orderly room, supply room — just about anywhere, if you have enough of the fourth ingredient in abundance.

4. Knowledge of unit's missions and your own imagination. This is all mental: what you have learned about your unit, what you know of its capabilities, how much you have studied terrain — it's all in the mind. This knowledge, in conjunction with a little imagination, is the critical ingredient in situational training.

OBJECTIVES:

1. To determine how well your troops can function in a given situation.

2. To evaluate individual or unit reactions to specific situations.

3. To check several aspects of a unit's operations. This can be done in depth. (In most situations, a dozen or more items can be checked. However, only check three to five at any one time.)

CAUTIONS:

1. Make it impromptu — but don't inject situational training if unit is headed for a range, has to cross IP, or has other commitments where time is critical.

2. Keep it brief; most situations can be accomplished in five to thirty minutes.

3. The training should not necessarily be tactical — test maintenance, supply, or leadership.

4. No special equipment is required; use what is proper for the mission.

5. Have only three to five specific objectives in mind. The soldier will be better able to focus on a few objectives and learn from them.

6. Keep it simple at first. Short, simple situations can be created daily.

7. By the time you become a battalion commander, learn to develop a whole series of situations for a company or platoon that will keep them busy all day and through the night. Such a series is a graduation exercise and is not impromptu. It will take some effort by you and the battalion staff. You should schedule it well ahead and tell unit that that is "your day," thus avoiding changes to training schedule. This continuous series of situations should be used no more often than about once a quarter for a given unit.

Most often situational training is injected into whatever activity is going on. It is performance oriented training applied for a brief period, from five minutes to a half hour, for a specific purpose. In day-to-day training, always be on the lookout for a training gem that is small and compact and valuable: the tactical situation, crew function, traffic condition, or maintenance situation that requires execution and action on the part of the individual crew or element that has been given the situation. It can be as simple as telling a track commander that there is an enemy foot column about a mile down the road coming toward him. His mission: "Delay it. Make them deploy." What action does he take? Does he select a good delaying position? Are fire teams set up off the road? How are machine guns employed? Does someone man the .50 caliber on the track to cover fire teams going into position? Does the track commander ask for artillery support? If he does, you can say, "I'm your forward observer; ask me for any fire support you want." As soon as the action has been completed, hold a critique on the ground and let those involved discuss what happened—or should have happened. For example, should the fire teams have been sent to the knolls 100 meters off the road or to the draw 50 meters to the right, or should they have stayed with the track?

Here is another possibility. Tell the track commander that the .50 caliber machine gun barrel is burned out and must be replaced. Then pick a man at random from the crew to replace it. Does he know what the proper headspace is and how to check it? Does the crew have the spare .50 caliber barrel?

In the maintenance shop, ask what causes most of the deadlines in the unit. Do the mechanics know? Ask the maintenance clerk to check on the requisitions for the parts needed to correct those deficiencies. If requisitioned, have they come in? When? Where are they?

While at motor stables, ask a driver if his vehicle has a trailer, If it does, tell him to hook it up. How efficiently does the driver go about it? Are the air hoses properly connected? Many accidents and maintenance problems will not occur if drivers know how to couple trailers properly.

Remember, these situations are in the mind. They pertain to what you want to know about your unit. When the right combinations of terrain, troops, and time occur, apply situational training in impromptu fashion. A good commander and trainer will be able to visualize innumerable opportunities for this type of training. Imagination and knowledge of the men, equipment, and tactics will help in developing the technique. Everything depends on the commander's knowledge of the fundamentals. Learn about the equipment that enables your unit to accomplish its missions. Learn how one function relates to another. Be aware of unit weaknesses in maintenance, administration, and operations. When you know these things, situational training will come easy.

For more examples of impromptu situations, see Situational Training Ideas 1 through 8, following the next section.

GRADUATION EXERCISE

In addition to the short training situations, situational training also encompasses "graduation exercises" for platoon- or company-size units. A platoon exercise lasts eight to twelve hours and a company exercise twenty-four to forty-eight hours. These exercises are best conducted by battalion or brigade commanders or assistant division commanders, since these officers have staffs to send out alert messages, reserve ranges or training areas, or call on other troops to participate. Some advance planning is required, but the simpler the better. An example of a company-size exercise follows.

A company-size unit is alerted to move from home station for a minimum period of 48 hours for a field firing exercise. All personnel present for duty will participate; all weapons and ammunition will be carried. The alert message is delivered 4 to 8 hours before the expected time of departure, providing the commander with an opportunity to check unit alert procedures. Have an artillery forward observer along and mortars or anti-tank weapons to be sure it is a combined arms operation.

Have a brief inspection of the unit to check on the number and condition of troops available and the equipment. Vehicles that can't move don't move; those repaired before the end of exercise will join the unit in the field.

Give the march order with a route map and coordinates of an objective area. Enroute to the objective area, the unit will encounter a number of independent situations designed by you to give a picture of unit's operational readiness:

Clear a mine field.

Repair a broken track. This operation includes dropping the track and repairing it with the sections that are part of the On Vehicle Maintenance equipment. This type of action is timed.

Stage a gas attack—requiring movement or activity while wearing gas masks.

Assess casualties with use of moulage; check on first aid and evacuation procedure.

Have the platoon attack an enemy strong point in "those farm buildings."

Have the platoon defend "that bridge."

Have the platoon man an outpost or any other tactical mission.

In some phase of the exercise the coordinates of an objective and a range should coincide so that weapons can be fired.

Require the kitchen crew to rendezvous at assembly areas and feed a hot meal or deliver hot food at appropriate times.

Have the power packs replaced; any breakdown calls for maintenance support starting with the company back through battalion, and brigade or division if required.

Have a night laager, night attack, or night movement; a river or stream crossing, or if not possible, passage of some obstacle.

With a tank company, at some time during the period have it rendezvous with an infantry unit for an armor-infantry problem. With an infantry company, rendezvous with an armor unit for same reason.

This rundown is enough to give you the idea. The terrain for each situation should be well chosen. No company should be given all the situations, but each one should be given enough to keep it busy. Performance and speed of execution should influence which company gets what assignment. If ranges are available, companies/batteries should fire all weapons. Only a few rounds are needed to demonstrate effective weapons firing. For missiles, use simulators.

By the time a company or battery goes through twenty-four to forty-eight hours of this kind of drill, its members know how well-trained they are and what needs attention. If they have executed their tasks well they will be proud of their achievements.

Directing such exercises requires thought and tactical reconnaissance by the commander. He should use his staff and resources to back up the maintenance and supply support, for reservation of ranges and training areas, and for whatever other advance planning is necessary. This graduation exercise is ideal for a "battalion commander's day" as discussed in "Situational Training," Fig. 9.1, pp. 80-81. It is also the type of operational readiness check that should replace some of those inspections which have been perverted and raise havoc with training (see Chapter 16).

SAMPLES OF SITUATIONAL TRAINING IDEAS

Situational training idea 1

TYPE UNIT: Cavalry platoon

OBJECTIVE: Check communications, crew duties, and fire control equipment

SITUATION: Limited space and time available

LOCATION: Track vehicle park or open space nearby

This exercise requires space enough to traverse and elevate the main gun of the Sheridan, and that's not much space.

Open the platoon radio net.

Using the platoon radio net, the platoon leader directs his platoon to place the fire control systems into operation.

Several orders should be given to elevate, depress, and traverse the main gun, both in manual and power modes, in order to check the capabilities of the Sheridans to take enemy forces under fire from any direction.

At each step, the platoon leader or the platoon sergeant can check procedures. This technique enables the platoon leader to check his platoon on their communications equipment, crew duties, and fire control equipment. If some turrets are not working, check on turret maintenance.

NOTE: The individual in charge should be alert for any failure to respond to specific orders.

Situational training idea 2

TYPE UNIT: Tank platoon

OBJECTIVE: Check communications, tool availability, technical
               knowledge, and maintenance

SITUATION: Platoon enroute to local training area

LOCATION: Area that permits a tank platoon to be halted in place on or
               off to side of road

The company commander (or any higher commander in the chain of command) sees one of his tank platoons enroute to local training area. He observes the interval between tanks. Company commander calls the platoon leader and directs him to halt at a certain point and then directs that turrets be rotated in one or two directions. After observing the response to his orders, he tells the platoon leader to remove bore evacuators.

This exercise enables the company commander to check march discipline and communications, and to determine whether each tank crew has the required tools and knowledge to perform assigned tasks properly. In addition, the bore evacuator can be checked to see that it is properly greased and maintained.

Company commander should know the tools required for removing the bore evacuator, should permit no running between tanks to borrow tools, and should check the time it takes each tank to complete removal and report that it is ready for inspection.

Situational training idea 3

TYPE UNIT: Medical platoon

OBJECTIVE: Check unit responsiveness, map reading, availability of
               medical equipment, and knowledge of corpsmen

SITUATION: Unit engaged in either tactical training or daily routine

LOCATION: Training area or home station

A commander calls the medical platoon and reports that there has been a medical emergency at designated coordinates. He directs that the unit respond with an ambulance and corpsmen. At the location to which the medical personnel are directed to report, a medical emergency is simulated with moulages and troops in the area who have been designated as casualties.

Medical personnel are required to take appropriate action upon arrival.

This exercise assesses the medical unit's ability to respond quickly to an emergency, checks its knowledge of map reading, and indicates how well or how poorly the individual corpsmen take care of a given medical emergency.

Further, the battery, oil, and other required operator-maintenance items on the ambulance can be examined.

While the medical element is present, this training could be extended to have corpsmen work with small groups of soldiers to have them demonstrate knowledge of first aid.

Situational training idea 4

TYPE UNIT: Mechanized infantry platoon

OBJECTIVE: Check teamwork, small-unit training, mine-probing techniques, security

SITUATION: Platoon engaged in tactical training

LOCATION: Assigned tactical training area

The commander stops an infantry platoon coming down a trail and tells the platoon leader that there is a mine field to his front which the platoon cannot go around. The platoon leader gives order to clear the mine field.

Several points can be observed: the way squad leaders carry out assigned missions, the use of security to protect carriers and men while halted, platoon's understanding and application of mine-probing techniques, reporting procedures, and several other tactical activities.

Following the exercise, a thorough critique should be conducted during which each squad discusses what has taken place.

NOTE: The commander must know how to select a likely mine-field location to avoid ease of bypass and should know what actions are required of squad leaders and men. Ninety percent of the critique should be done by the men; the commander should be merely the catalyst for questions or points to be discussed.

Situational training idea 5

TYPE UNIT: Any unit possessing wheeled vehicles

OBJECTIVE: Check safety, driver knowledge, and supply discipline

86

SITUATION: Unit engaged in routine daily activities

LOCATION: Home station

A commander sees one of his wheeled vehicles driving down the road on the post; he flags down the vehicle and tells the driver that the vehicle has just broken down. The driver is then directed to take appropriate action.

The driver is observed on actions taken when a vehicle breaks down on the highway. Is there a warning device in the vehicle? Is it put out? How far? Does the vehicle have the required equipment? Does the driver make a go, no-go check to the limit of his capability?

NOTE: This simple situation lets a commander know something about the little things that cause accidents. If he wants to check on maintenance, the commander could check on the air filter to engine, oil level, or some other indicator of state of maintenance. All units have vehicles and they can be a real problem. This type of on-the-spot observation will keep drivers, dispatchers, and the chain of command alert to their responsibilities.

Situational training idea 6

TYPE UNIT: Any unit

OBJECTIVE: Check communications, knowledge of guard duties, and reaction time of guard element

SITUATION: Guard on duty

LOCATION: Any guard post

A commander observes a guard on post and notices that there is a field phone on the fence nearby. The commander tells the guard to use the phone to call the guard house. Do the communications work? Does anyone respond to the communications check? Sometimes there is a radio as an alternate means of communication; if so, the commander should check that out too.

After checking communications the guard should be ordered to call the sergeant of the guard and request help or relief. How long before help arrives?

NOTE: Some people might argue that an action like this will confuse a guard. If a guard is confused, as he sometimes may be, he should know enough to call for the sergeant of the guard. That is positive action. Also, some sensitive posts have to be approached with care, but a unit commander must know how well-trained his guards are and he should think up some real-life situations to determine how well the guard has been prepared for his post. Guard duty needs much attention and improvement.

Situational training idea 7

TYPE UNIT: Mechanized infantry platoon

OBJECTIVE: Check unit physical condition, control by squad leader/fire team leader, and responsiveness to platoon leader

SITUATION: Platoon engaged in tactical training

LOCATION: Any track vehicle training area

The battalion commander is observing a mechanized infantry platoon. He tells the platoon leader to order his squads to dismount and move to a pre-selected objective some two to three hundred meters away. Speed of movement is paramount, and movement should be by small groups controlled by squad leader or fire team leader. Movement should be at double time by bounds, using available terrain for cover and concealment. The battalion commander tells the platoon leader to accompany him to the objective to observe how well squad leaders and men use terrain and to check the physical condition of the men when they arrive on objective.

Situational training idea 8

TYPE UNIT: Combat engineer platoon

OBJECTIVE: Check supply discipline, care of equipment, safety, and capability to execute demolition missions

SITUATION: Platoon in bivouac area or enroute to training area

LOCATION: Most anywhere

Company commander visits one of his platoons in the field and tells platoon leader to have squads lay out pioneer set and demolition kit and stand by their dump trucks.

Platoon leader is directed to have drivers lift truck beds and check the chains which set tailgate for spreading load. Results will indicate the state of maintenance and the drivers' ability to do a job properly.

One man should be selected to start the chainsaw in each squad. Do all saws operate? Are safety procedures observed in starting and handling saws?

Point out a culvert, tree, or other object that could be used to create obstacles. Direct platoon leader to have squad leaders rig them for demolition. It is worth checking to see if squad leaders have demolition cards. Are galvanometers and blasting machines working? What is condition of blasting wire?

A check of these items and reactions of squad members will tell much about state of training in a combat engineer unit.

88

 *The poorest trainers seem to be the ones who enthusiastically latch onto the latest training fad. In the process they neglect the day-to-day work necessary to prepare their units for their missions.*

Training Tips

Training tips encompass a broad range of activities. They include techniques and procedures which, when properly understood, pursued, and expanded on, will add new dimensions to the trainer's outlook and the quality of training. There is no end to training tips—everyone of us has his own. These apply across the board to most branches and functions. A few will imply the need for study and debate within the Army:

Battle Drill
Catchwords and Slogans
Checklists
Correction in the Presence of Senior Officer or Visitor
Critiques
Estimate of Training Situation and Training Plateaus
Firing Range as an Indicator of Readiness
Guard Duty as an Important Training Device
Live Fire
Mechanic/Clerk/Cook of the Month Program
Motor-Pool Syndrome
Movement vs. Fundamentals of Tactics
Night Training
Nuclear Weapons Training
Responsibility Training
Safety

Sand Table
Standards
Time
Training Anathemas
Training Films and Progressive Training
Training Noncommissioned Officer in a Unit
Training Notes
Tying Units Together—In More Ways Than One

BATTLE DRILL

Both unwelcome surprises and unexpected opportunities confront units in combat. Success or failure frequently depends on immediate action. Battle drill teaches small units to react quickly and with some semblance of order without lengthy instructions. The leader makes a rapid estimate of the situation and arrives at an immediate decision.

General Howze defined battle drill as "formation practice—quick change from one formation to another, over varied terrain—plus the practice of those elements of tactical movement which will permit a commander to launch his force into the starting phase of attack or defense by command, without benefit of assembly of his subordinate commanders or, of long, complicated instruction."[1]

Battle drill familiarizes soldiers with the mechanics of satisfactory solutions to types of situations frequently encountered in combat. The objectives are speed and coordination. Combat units must be able to apply power quickly. Battle drill helps them to do so.

Battle drill will not solve all battle problems. When a formation has been ordered and taken, it may and frequently should be modified to meet the special situation. But even if modified, the commander's decision has been quickly converted into action by battle drill. Rapid and forceful action will often surprise an enemy and throw him off balance. Quick reaction, the ability to accomplish tactical jobs quickly, is often the key to local success and local survival.

Training in battle drill should be conducted at a fairly fast tempo. Interest is sustained by rapid changes in formation and changes in pace, and much may be accomplished in a short period of time. Training should be lively and spirited, but never haphazard. The quickest and easiest way to learn battle drill is by *doing* after a brief explanation.

---

[1]*Howze on Training* (Ft. Benning, Ga., 1971), p. 3.

CATCHWORDS AND SLOGANS

Because Americans are great on catchwords and slogans, the United States Army comes by their use naturally. But don't believe training will be better with a Madison Avenue approach and the use of "buzz" words. During the period when training in the Army was the poorest in my memory, fancy terms abounded: "Dynamic Training," "Adventure Training," "Energized Training," to mention a few. They didn't make the training any better.

I can recall visiting any number of units in which the commander was caught up in the current training fad. Adventure training was one of the best examples. Elaborate plans, special equipment, and devoted attention were given to adventure training, and the battalion commander wanted to talk about these things during my visits. Yet, as we walked around the unit the on-going training did not measure up to standard. The ranges were poorly run, the tactical training amounted to a walk in the woods, maintenance proved inadequate, and often some scheduled training was not going on at all.

The poorest trainers seem to be the ones who enthusiastically latch onto the latest training fad. In the process they neglect the day-to-day work necessary to prepare their units for their missions. So watch the catchwords and the slogans. Generally, if highly charged words are needed to describe your training, or anything else you are doing, you are probably not doing a very good job.

CHECKLISTS

All units have to undergo tests from time to time and it is proper that they should. Too often, training is oriented toward the checklist and the actions of the umpire rather than being sure the soldier knows how to do his job right.

In the conduct of training tests, no sight is more unsettling to a young commander than a controller with a clip board and three or four checksheets with entries from top to bottom. These are the final words of a commander I heard briefing his platoons just before a training test: "OK, do your best to remember all those points on the ATT checklist. If you have the opportunity to do something that you know will be graded, make sure a controller sees you. And you squad leaders—watch the grader! If his eyes brighten and you see him act as though he has noticed something is wrong, move out—get ahead of him and correct it before he gets there."

I waited hopefully for the battalion and brigade commander, both of whom were present, to get things in perspective, but it was not to be. So I asked the platoon leaders how the squad leaders would know what the grader had seen, and wondered if the grader's eyes might brighten if he noted something well done. I did not wait for an answer because the platoon leaders were under enough pressure taking the test, without all that brass standing by. On departing I suggested to the platoons that they forget about the checklists, and depend on the training that they had been given to make them look good.

It is obvious that the major concern of that commander was not how well his platoons executed the missions; it was how they scored out on the checklists. Look around the next training test you observe. How many people are carrying a clipboard with long checklists on it? You don't carry clipboards in combat, so don't depend on them in training. If you must have checklists make them as inconspicuous as possible. Teach the umpires to make brief notes on mission performance in a pocket notebook instead of checking off a list of detailed procedures or separate steps in an action. We have passed through an era when the checklist was considered the answer to all leadership problems. Get it in the head or the notebook.

Commanders must get used to the pressure that comes from someone checking on their units. In the past decade, however, commanders seemed to consider the score awarded more important than how the unit did the job. Perhaps the schools can suggest how to correct this attitude, since most of those who are under the gun as commanders or who act as umpires go to the basic and advanced courses. They should have some ideas.

CORRECTION IN THE PRESENCE OF A SENIOR OFFICER OR VISITOR

While visiting various units, I have often been struck by the number of glaring deficiencies apparent that no one took action to correct in my presence. Generally I would wait a while before commenting, hoping that someone in the chain of command would spot a deficiency and correct it. But the spotting was generally left for me. I have asked many officers why this happens. Some say the commanders do not want to embarrass their subordinates by correcting them in the presence of a senior visitor; some say the commander intends to correct the deficiency after the senior officer leaves. These are not good reasons for failing to correct an error. The question that always came to my mind was this: Does the immediate commander, or any other member of the chain of command present, recognize what appears to be a serious deficiency to me? I was always concerned that, if I made no comment, those present might think everything was just fine.

As for not embarrassing a subordinate, some of the finest commanders I know have a knack for asking a private, noncommissioned officer, or officer a few questions about something that does not seem right. These questions get the corrective action under way. A really good trainer can always make a correction in a constructive and teaching fashion. That is what training is all about.

On several occasions while visiting the French, British, and German armies I noted things that didn't look right. In almost every case before a word was said by anyone in the visiting party a member of the unit quietly went over, had a few words with a noncommissioned officer or an individual soldier, and some corrective action got under way. Sometimes the senior officer escorting me called attention to a lapse and the local commander had it corrected.

On a visit I made to a German unit on a field exercise, the corps commander, who was accompanying me, saw a vehicle on a knoll with the windshield reflecting the sun's rays. He started towards the vehicle while pointing at it, and within seconds the unit exploded into action. An NCO or officer ran toward the area, a driver ran for the vehicle, and by the time we had walked the one hundred meters up the hill the vehicle was down in the brush with its windshield covered and was as hard to spot as the other vehicles in the area.

I asked the corps commander what German leaders did about errors noted when a senior officer or visitor happened to be present. He said he felt strongly on the subject and believed his fellow officers did likewise. When he visited a unit and found errors that were not corrected the only conclusion he could come to was that the commander did not recognize the deficiencies and was therefore not competent to command. The corps commander said that occasional errors would slip by, such as the vehicle we had just seen, but that they should be rare exceptions and that the chain of command in the unit should be making corrections before he had to.

Because the reluctance to correct deficiencies in front of a senior officer is so widespread in the U.S. Army, it should be a special subject for discussion in the leadership training in the military school system. In military operations people get killed or wounded when mistakes are made. It follows that a military error observed must always be taken notice of. There is a continuous need to teach young officers and noncommissioned officers how to instruct those under them. Correction of error in training is good instruction for all.

CRITIQUES

At a critique of a platoon exercise I attended the division commander observed to me that he learned a lot about his officers by listening to their critiques. He said he could tell what they had not observed in the course of the exercise by their failure to cover it in their oral assessment. To him this was a clear indication of their command capability. I agree. You have to know your business to be able to make a critical assessment of any exercise; to do it well is an art.

How many effective tactical training critiques have you heard? How often do you hear the officer conducting the critique do all the talking? In conducting a critique, your main job is to do everything possible to get the troops involved. At the end of a problem, position the men at a vantage point where they can see the area over which the action took place. You can then explain good and bad points in terms of the actual terrain. Sometimes, on a live firing range, this may not be practicable. In that case, it's a good idea to have a sketch or terrain board of the area. Be sure the sketch is good enough to improve the troops' map reading. The soldiers must be able to see the relationship between the map and the terrain over which they have just been operating.

In covering each of the points that are to be emphasized, do not continually repeat, "You should have done this" or "You should have done that." It is far better to pose questions that involve the troops: "When you arrived at the ford and you had to cross the stream, what action was taken?" "What do you think of that now, Sergeant?" "How about it, Private Ramsey, what do you think?" "Sergeant Brooks, what did you think of the action that was taken? Did you send any security? Do you think it was necessary?"

By a series of questions and probings, draw the men who were involved in the action into the discussion. They all have ideas. More important, eliciting their contributions is essential to the learning process. Once they begin to debate with one another you will know you are conducting a successful critique. All you have to do is to keep it moving in a positive direction. After a brief discussion of one point, move on to the next point to be emphasized. If you find yourself doing all the talking during a critique, you are probably making a poor critique and the troops will lose interest.

ESTIMATE OF TRAINING SITUATION AND TRAINING PLATEAUS

Whenever you take command of a unit, make an immediate assessment of the state of training. Avoid pronouncements on how good or bad things are until you have taken a comprehensive look. Even then, do not announce what you are going to do for the command, especially if you believe the unit is poorly trained and has a long way to go to meet your standards. Generally such pronouncements backfire or cause antagonism. Members of the unit will seldom share your view that they are not up to par.

If much is to be done, seek to make improvements that will establish a higher plateau; once that level is reached provide another set of goals to help attain a higher standard of excellence.

Start trying to identify the weak spots. Is it administrative discipline that needs attention? What are the weaknesses in the chain of command? Do commanders know what to look for? Try to clarify in your own mind what it is that is wrong and what techniques can raise unit standards. If you keep in mind that training is all-encompassing, you should be able, after identifying the weakspots, to decide what training is most appropriate for the unit and the chain of command to get things on the track.

Have patience. You can't get there all at once.

FIRING RANGE AS AN INDICATOR OF READINESS

What better way for a commander to check the state of training, discipline, and organization of his command—or his subordinate commands—than to be at the range himself at the time firing is scheduled to start? There he can gather the answers to many questions first-hand. Were range guards posted? Did transportation pick up troops on schedule? Was the proper ammunition available? How was the range organized? Was hot soup in back of the firing line in winter? Or a Lister bag in summer? Was there a meaningful review of preliminary marksmanship instruction and zeroing of weapons? Did the troops know the causes and remedies for stoppages and misfires? Was there concurrent training? Was the best use being made of the fewest possible rounds? Did the range communications work? Did the food arrive as planned? Above all, did that first round go down range on schedule? If not, why not? The range is a place where you have to put it all together.

No readiness report will tell a commander as much about his unit as personal observation of that unit on the range. Such on-site observation is particularly important for armor-unit commanders during tank-crew qualification. Tank gunnery requires efficient use of range facilities and good coordination of elements within a tank company and battalion. Armor commanders recognize this and their constant presence on the range is reflected in the efficient manner in which armor ranges are run.

Time on the firing range is precious, both in terms of cost and training benefit. Each commander must ensure that range training is conducted in a manner that reflects thorough preparation and demonstrated knowledge on the part of those in charge of the firing. Further, completing the training should give the soldier a sense of accomplishment. He should see the results of his efforts. Post the scores where all the personnel in a company-level unit can see them. *That* is healthy competition.

GUARD DUTY AS AN IMPORTANT TRAINING DEVICE

In recent years the pressure of time and the less formal style that has come into vogue have curtailed the formality of guard mount. This relaxation can be accepted. Along with it, however, the actual performance of guard duty has deteriorated, but this *cannot* be accepted. During this same period commanders have grown reluctant to give guards ammunition, possibly for fear that accidents may occur. As a result, men who are supposed to be professionals in the use of weapons fail to learn to respect the danger of improperly handling firearms. All these factors contribute to poor performance of guard duty. No army can tolerate low standards in guard performance, nor should our Army accept the premise that soldiers cannot learn to handle weapons and ammunition properly.

Every commander has to instill in all members of his command a proper respect for weapons and ammunition and an appreciation of their responsibility both to the government and to their fellow soldiers when they are performing guard duty. Whenever a man goes on guard duty, he should be part of a formation which is properly instructed and posted. When he comes off guard duty, his weapon should be cleared and he should be debriefed. Even if ammunition is not used by the guard, the noncommissioned officer responsible for each guard relief should inspect to see that the weapons are cleared. Training in proper clearing of weapons will reduce the number of tragic accidents that take place in all commands each year. Now, such training is basic, but how well is it being conducted in your outfit?

The following report indicates that in some units guard duty is not performed well:

> *"X" reported to military police that an M–88 track vehicle, USA number xxxx, an M–728 track vehicle, USA number xxxx, and one trailer, USA number unknown were discovered broken into at Tank Park Number Two at 0800 hours 12 September 1972. Further investigation revealed that four CVC helmets, valued at $140, two boxes of tools valued at $391, three bags of TA/50 gear valued at $528, one set tie-down equipment value unknown, one signal light value unknown, two burner cook stoves value*

unknown, and one headset valued at $25 had been removed from the M–88 track vehicle. Also one OVE set valued at $400 had been removed from the M–728 track vehicle. One M–32C sight valued at $110, one M–321R sight valued at $300, and one one-inch hose value unknown was removed from the trailer. "X" stated that the vehicles had been secured by padlocks at 1130 hours, 9 September 1972. The padlocks had been forcibly removed. The security of the above location is unknown. Investigation continues.

What had the guards in that unit been doing while all this was happening? Certainly they had not been alert. Lax guards are responsible for loss of property in peacetime. In time of war they are responsible for loss of life as well.

The security failure described here is particularly noteworthy because the unit involved was at a major training area, where units supposedly operate under field conditions. Were this unit engaged in combat, it would be responsible for its own security on a twenty-four-hour basis. The guards would pull their time on the perimeter or in the night laager and be prepared to go on fighting the next day. Each unit is responsible for securing its own equipment, whether it be against an enemy infiltrator or a vandal. We do a poor job of guarding our own equipment. Removing on-vehicle equipment (OVE) to some secure supply room is not the answer. The true objective is the proper training of the soldier on guard duty stressing the responsibility of all for safeguarding equipment.

LIVE FIRE

Live-fire exercises are clear indicators of the state of readiness of a unit. They are the climax of small-unit training, and the platoon-size problem is without doubt the most practical limit. Live-fire problems at company level and above begin to pose control and space difficulties in a peacetime environment, but an occasional company or battalion live-fire demonstration is desirable to show the variety of weapons in a unit and the effect of supporting weapons. For a unit scheduled for deployment to an active combat theater, live-fire problems at both company and battalion level are an essential part of training.

Deficiencies in live-fire training become most apparent in field exercises during the latter stages of the training. The most obvious are troops or firing elements being kept in straight lines and firing groups being kept in positions from which they can see one another for safety purposes—in such positions the troops would be decimated by enemy tanks, artillery, and mortars in combat. Movement and firing are closely controlled, so by the time a live-fire exercise has inched its way to a conclusion the troops have not learned much about how to operate and survive in combat. The excuse given for such unrealistic training is almost always the same: Safety regulations prescribe the procedures followed.

The importance of continuity in training with respect to firing weapons is sometimes overlooked. Reviewing the sequence of the firing of weapons and suggestions that might lead to more realistic live-fire problems is warranted. A fairly normal sequence follows.

First is the firing of weapons or weapons systems on a known distance range.

Next come live-fire problems. A firing problem is a situation that a commander might give to fire teams of an infantry squad, a mortar squad, a tank crew, and similar small element. A firing problem generally terminates when effective fire has been placed on the target, or when the target has been bracketed.

A live-fire exercise is conducted when a unit is in the field, and in the course of the training live ammunition is used. Such an exercise almost always involves the maneuvering of elements of the exercise unit and the firing of several different weapons systems to emphasize supporting fires and provide for combined-arms training.

The above definitions are not intended to be arbitrary. Throughout my service the terms "live-fire problem" and "live-fire exercise" have been used interchangeably. For purposes of clarity, however, it pays to make a distinction.

The first essential step leading to realistic live-fire exercises is teaching each soldier to provide for his own safety and that of his comrades by recognizing the danger inherent in weapons and handling his individual weapon accordingly. Everyone must carry out his responsibility in training those under him, controlling the fire of weapons, correcting the careless, and calling "cease fire" if he believes a dangerous situation has arisen. This habit requires initiative and confidence throughout the chain of command.

An example of realism that should start commanders thinking right at the start of weapons training has to do with the rapid reloading phase of marksmanship training. To develop speed in reloading some weapons, the individual fires one round and then reloads with another magazine containing one round. In some units the magazine is placed in front of the firer so that he can reload more quickly and improve his score. But in fact the magazine should be placed in the magazine pouch where it will be carried in combat. This is a small point, but the attitudes on live fire are influenced by each phase of training. Look for the opportunities to put realism into weapons training and the safety requirements will begin to fall into place.

Keep live-fire exercises short. Safety requirements dictate the use of shorter problems because they require less rigid control, and there is less interference with the conduct of the exercise.

Make live-fire training progressive. After individual firing, move to teams of three or four men going down lanes in the woods with pop-up and other surprise targets. The men in front will gain confidence as the men behind them fire. And the men in the rear will realize the importance of firing directly at a selected target; they will learn to avoid pointing their weapons carelessly in the direction of the soldiers in front of them. Build up to the squad and platoon, or with armor to three tank crews. Supporting weapons should be brought into the firing as early as possible—certainly by the time platoon problems are introduced.

Watch the rate of fire. Firing weapons on full automatic, Hollywood style, wastes ammunition, causes barrels to overheat, and results in inaccuracy that can contribute to the safety hazard in live-fire exercises. Those who fire automatic weapons, particularly the hand-held variety, should be taught to fire in short bursts. A training exercise might be conducted in which a given amount of ammunition is fired full automatic, semi-automatic, and single shot. The superior accuracy and economy of ammunition resulting from the lower rates of fire would be apparent to the participants and to the soldiers observing the exercise.

Some of the most realistic and effective live-fire problems I have seen were put on by the British Army. On several different occasions platoons took part in attack situations which looked like the real thing. There were no white tapes to mark the firing lines and lanes, and few if any controllers or safety officers were in evidence. The company commander seemed to have the whole job. He just stood on the hill and kept a close eye on everything going on. One element provided a base of fire, while another moved through a draw and woods and came right in on the objective. The element providing the base of fire shifted its fire ahead of the flanking force and started moving forward in small groups. The performance was perfect. My reaction was: That's the way I'd like my platoons to be trained if they had to fight tomorrow. Any commander conducting that type of training knows there are risks involved, but these are not great if all the participants are well trained. Our troops are seldom given an opportunity to train that realistically until they are on the verge of deployment to a combat environment. That's too late.

At this point, some people will no doubt observe defensively that the British Army problem was rehearsed. This may well have been true, but I have seen enough training to know when troops are well trained. I also know how bullets ricochet and accidents happen, and troops who can do what I saw those British soldiers do, even if their actions were rehearsed, are well-trained troops.

A senior French officer once described to me and others a live-fire problem he had observed the Russian Army put on. It was a battalion in the attack.

Someone in the group said that if the exercise had been as realistic as described it must have been well rehearsed. The French general was certain that it had been, but he added that if troops could use supporting weapons so close to their own forces, and if they maneuvered as well as he had seen them do, "they would be worthy opponents."

MECHANIC/CLERK/COOK OF THE MONTH PROGRAM

A check on these programs over a period of years indicates that the individuals nominated by company-level units appear before a battalion or a brigade board. Use the mechanics for example.

The board questions the mechanics and designates a mechanic of the month. It would be far better if the mechanic of the month were chosen by competition that involved evaluation of work on actual mechanical situations in the motor pool. The point is not to select "Mr. Personality" but to evaluate a mechanic's professional performance. The candidates could each be assigned a truck or parts that have similar deficiencies and be required to determine what was wrong and repair the deficiency. They could then be evaluated on how professionally they corrected the deficiencies within a certain time limit. This type of competition would be far more beneficial to the individuals and would also be a far more accurate evaluation of their ability than answering questions before a board.

Similar performance-oriented activity should be extended to other competitions whenever possible. Cooks could make cakes, rolls, or salads for certain meals. The food that disappeared first would be an indicator of who was the best cook—at least in the eyes of the troops.

Imagination and practical application are all that is needed.

MOTOR-POOL SYNDROME

This tip is most applicable to commanders of mechanized battalions, cavalry squadrons, tank battalions, engineer, and artillery battalions, but it is important to all commanders. Take a good look at what goes on in your motor pool because a lot of valuable training time is wasted there. Are men standing around just going through the motions of doing things?

Too many soldiers say that much of the time spent in the motor pool is wasted. Drivers and crews can do only so much in checking their vehicles. A period of up to about one hour per day should be allotted for motor stables, and it should not be in prime time. The motor-pool syndrome is evident when troops spend the major part of the working week in the motor pool and do little or no training while there. I have asked soldiers who went to the motor pool after the first morning formation what their program was for the day. It was "maintenance." When I asked what their program of the previous day was, they replied "maintenance." The vehicles had not left the motor pool in the interim period. Part of the disenchantment and boredom some of our soldiers suffer stems from this practice of using "maintenance" as a substitute for a training program.

If a soldier or a crew can take care of a vehicle in fifteen minutes, let the sergeant or the platoon leader check it and then turn the men loose. Don't insist that all drivers remain in the motor pool for a prescribed length of time, and don't delay the release of the soldiers who do their work promptly until the last laggard finishes his chores.

Keep in mind that maintenance is a function or duty to be performed by skilled mechanics. It is also training for raising the skill level of individuals who perform that function, and for teaching those who use equipment how to care for it so that the maintenance burden is kept to a minimum.

MOVEMENT VS.
FUNDAMENTALS OF TACTICS

Company and troop commanders spend a lot of time maneuvering their units all over the countryside. Generally this movement takes place in tracks, and commanders are involved with tactics and goose eggs on the map at the expense of getting some real training done. Looked at closely, some of this training shows commanders getting so involved with maneuver that they don't take the time to check other equally important activities. Some of the questions they could be asking are: How well are the tracks tactically positioned? How are squads and individual riflemen disposed in their positions? What are their fields of fire? Do they have security to the rear? Is the TOW in position that restricts the effective range to 60 meters instead of the 2500-meter range that is more appropriate? How is the camouflage? How often are the company commanders, platoon leaders, NCOs—or just maybe, the battalion commanders—lying down behind the machine gun to see if it has a field of fire? And how often are these others putting on the tank commander's helmet to see if orders can be transmitted to the whole crew?

On several occasions I have seen a battalion or brigade commander enthusiastically pointing out the splendid training going on as track vehicles moved all about the terrain to our front. The praise, like the activity, went on and on. As battle drill, this activity would have been all right if the training period had been short and snappy, but the periods were to go on for several hours. For a mechanized infantry unit this demonstration was particularly bad. Eventually in such situations I would have to ask, "When are they going to do something?" Too often the shocked reply was, "Sir, they are! They're maneuvering." What a waste of troop time, engine time, and fuel!

Unit commanders must be taught that just maneuvering about doesn't win the fight. It helps, but it is well-trained troops—each one doing his individual part as well as possible—that make the team function efficiently and win the battle. Therefore, unit commanders must check their men for the basic skills necessary for accomplishing the unit's mission. Frequent orders to set up weapons, a situation requiring elements to take up precise tactical positions, to replace a track, or to tow a vehicle would make this type of training meaningful. In this type of operation, situational training can be inserted most effectively. Gunners, tankers, infantrymen, and above all commanders must learn the fundamentals of their business. Commanders must know what they are about and what they are trying to find out, or what they are trying to teach their subordinates, so that the gunners, tankers, and infantrymen are not wasting their training time.

Infantry units are the main offenders in this respect. Infantry units should leave the tracks at home more often. If they did, the maneuver area would be less torn up, and some honest infantry training for the troops would be possible. They don't need much training in how to ride.

NIGHT TRAINING

In combat, when the casualties begin to mount and when the going gets tough, commanders turn to night operations. Often an imbalance between the resources available to two adversaries impels the weaker force to use the dark in an effort to prevail. History provides innumerable examples of successful night operations, but they suffer neglect in peacetime training. Modern weapons are so lethal that commanders must train their troops to take maximum advantage of the hours of darkness.

Night training is not easy to check because visibility is poor and the troops are hard to find. However, soldiers are a splendid source of information on the quality of night training, and if a commander has the good sense to listen to them, he will learn what he can do to make night training more interesting. A common complaint of soldiers is that all too often they go out just before dark, set up, and then spend a cold, uncomfortable night on the ground. In summer the ordeal is a little less unpleasant, but there is so little to do that they consider night training to be a harassment. It really is not, since at least soldiers are learning what a lot of long, dark nights will be like if a war comes along. But, still, the quality of night training can be improved if company-level commanders use a little imagination and think in terms of small combined-arms teams. Thinking is the important part of the preparation.

A series of concise night-training activities will get the training off to a good start. Establish listening posts, teach troops the sights and sounds of the night, and use night observation devices. In the early and reinforcing stages of night training, schedule each step so that the troops know what they are seeing or hearing. Don't simply send out an aggressor force to act like clowns in order to draw attention to themselves. That device only teaches bad habits.

The best night training comes from using two opposing forces. One element can carry on normal operations with its own security and listening posts. The other element can be an infantry squad or a patrol sent to a set of coordinates occupied by an artillery battery, signal unit, or any other element out for its night training. Give the patrol the mission of finding out as much as it can about the "enemy" unit. The unit being reconnoitered will learn a little about security, and the patrol will benefit from the need to be stealthy and alert. Men must believe there is some objective to night training before they will consider it worthwhile. Prior thought and planning are most essential for successful night training. When you train at night, do it for a week or a month at a stretch.

A few random thoughts on night training:

Be sure the troops and commanders are allowed to rest during the day. Some overzealous commanders have been known to get troops out of bed and barracks so that a visitor would not think they were doing nothing.

Checking night training is much more difficult than conducting it. Visitors can't see much, they are not involved in what is going on, and since few troops will see or recognize them observing the training in the dark of night, it is easy to think up excuses not to go. With little hope for recognition, the only qualities that keep a senior commander in the chain of command out there at night is a sense of duty, dedication, and character. These are attributes of good leaders.

Impromptu and unannounced visits don't work at night. Tell the troops you are coming and arrange for a guide. Otherwise you'll get lost.

NUCLEAR WEAPONS TRAINING

Anyone who has been in a unit which has technical-proficiency inspections is no doubt looking for some words of wisdom on nuclear training. I don't have any that are helpful.

Observation of nuclear training impresses me with two things. First, the unit has to pass the technical-proficiency inspection (TPI). This should not be the first priority, but it is. Passing such a rigorous inspection is important, but when one reviews the reasons for failure over the years one wonders. The surety aspect, which is important, is sort of a chamber of horrors for commanders. For instance, a soldier uses drugs—a fact that is in records not available to the unit commander but open to the inspecting team—and so the unit fails. Such an ordeal is frustrating for commanders. Although this particular reason for failure has now been rectified, throughout the history of the nuclear-training program similar examples have been abundant. In many inspections a unit fails for some slight procedural oversight, but is then allowed to redo that step and is certified as passing. The failure, however, stays on the record. This practice gets a bit absurd, but protesting to the inspecting agencies has never been productive. They have good reason for being so precise and you can't argue with their reasons. This brings me to my second observation on nuclear training.

We cannot afford to have an accident with a nuclear weapon. This is paramount and the reasons are obvious. The technical-proficiency inspection must therefore insure that no margin for error or carelessness exists. Everything must be checked in the most minute detail in order to develop procedures that will preclude nuclear accidents.

The result is that most nuclear training is oriented to passing the inspection, not to the tactics and operations. Most of the training that I have seen is boring and a strain on everyone involved. Each inspection looms like a threatening storm to the commander whose unit must pass the test "or else." But those responsible for the inspections have told me that inspections are now conducted in a field environment, and the whole atmosphere has changed.

For senior commanders with considerable command experience who can take these tests in stride the atmosphere at these inspections has always been good, but I suspect that a poll of the field would reflect an opinion that there are few such commanders in command. Directives still offer repetitious courtesy inspections—which indicates there are some jumpy senior commanders. The view from the top staff and command levels has persistently been at odds with the views at the unit level. Only time will tell if the atmosphere has changed for the better.

Another feature of nuclear-weapons training is that the nuclear element, which comprises a small part of the unit's personnel and capability, gets an inordinate amount of the commander's time. Many commanders slight other training and put the best personnel and effort into the nuclear capability to be sure of passing the nuclear inspection. Commanders can hardly be faulted for this ordering of priorities given the pressures that are on them.

Under the present organizational structure and with present standards and methods of inspection, I have no practical recommendations that would help commanders in nuclear training and I have little hope for improvement. Underlying factors of organization and philosophy need close scrutiny but they do not pertain to training. I do hope that time will change the system now in being. If that happens a great burden will be lifted from commanders with a nuclear capability.

RESPONSIBILITY TRAINING

Many training directives recommend that one way to develop a sense of responsibility in a young officer is to let him take his small unit out on a training mission in a remote area for a period of three days to a week with "absolutely no supervision." Specific guidance is generally included that states there will be visits by "no one in the chain of command."

While recognizing the benefits and supporting the objectives of this idea, a word of caution is in order. Such a mission is not a back-to-nature movement and a time to relax all standards of appearance, discipline, and cleanliness. This type of training requires a strong leader and a well-disciplined unit. The leader must maintain the highest standards of appearance, sanitation, and control. If the leader does not demand high standards, the men exhibit a natural tendency to go slack.

Many commanders were pushing these programs in the early 1970s when the discipline in most units was poor and the young officers had not learned proper standards. I visited several of these groups and found that conditions were markedly unsatisfactory as to cleanliness, security, care of weapons, and other fundamental matters. The enthusiasm was great and the young officers thought they were doing a superb job. Unfortunately, they didn't know how much they didn't know, and since *no one* in the chain of command visited these sites they were not going to learn. For any unit contemplating these programs, therefore, I have this guidance: If a battalion or brigade commander believes his junior officers are ready for this type of exercise, fine—he is the commander. But I suggest that the division commander or corps commander occasionally drop in unannounced on these remote groups. If all is well, the field commanders will obviously have been doing a good job of training their subordinates. If standards are low, the young officers can be given a hint on how to get things in order and the senior commander can bore in on the field-grade commanders who had judged their subordinates' ability so poorly.

In the early 1970s, as we were trying to work out of serious command problems, a feeling prevailed among too many junior officers that being checked on reflected a lack of confidence in them on the part of their senior officers. This attitude is difficult for me to understand. Generally, if someone is older, higher ranking, and has had more experience, he should be expected to teach a subordinate what needs correction and what could be improved. There was some warped thinking in this period, and this attitude is one example of it. If a leader's mistakes are not corrected he is going to go on making them. And who suffers? The troops.

SAFETY

Observance of safety precautions is necessary to avoid accidents, and procedures toward that end are described in regulations and directives or dictated by plain common sense. They all add up to safety. Safety prevents troops from being unnecessarily injured, but it is not intended to be the overriding factor for all training. The Army should neither overemphasize safety so as to make realistic training impossible, nor throw caution to the winds, allowing accidents to become commonplace.

Safety derives from proper training of troops. Since the tools of the soldier's trade are inherently dangerous, personnel must be trained to use them properly and command supervision must be exercised at all times. This fact of life is important for noncommissioned officers, who are always in charge of the small groups doing whatever has to be done. Soldiers should not fear their equipment, but rather should respect it. Knowledge of and respect for dangerous equipment are the best safety measures that can be taken.

A highly organized and powerful safety bureaucracy sometimes fosters ridiculous extremes and makes training with lethal weapons and heavy equipment difficult. Every commander can help by keeping his eyes open and learning how to incorporate safety into training. For example, ask yourself such questions as the following: Are the tailgate chains on dump trucks properly secured? Same for all tailgates? How many drivers do you see drinking a can of soda while driving? How does the mortar crew store unused charges when firing a mission? How about artillery charges?

Do track commanders have someone in front or in back of their track vehicles when moving in a bivouac area? Are drivers aware of the need of a guide before they move the track only a few feet? Those short moves sometimes result in the loss of an arm, a leg, or a life when there is no guide. Making the drivers aware is part of safety training.

SAND TABLE

The sand table, which was a fixture in all units before and during World War II, had almost disappeared from the scene by the early 1970s. I do not know the reason, but I suspect that commanders had so many nagging problems that they did not believe the time spent at a sand table would contribute much to unit readiness.

The sand table can take many forms, the simplest of which is the impromptu scraping of the ground with the toe of a boot to give some picture of what lies ahead. More generally familiar is the box of sand of varying dimensions set on two saw-horses.

The sand table is economical and has the great advantage that a number of people can be grouped around it to learn from one another. All present can consider several courses of action in a specific situation; all can see the situation as depicted and hear the queries, comments, assessments, and orders from the commander, instructor, or other participants. Each onlooker can benefit from the ideas and thought processes of the others participating in the training. The sand table is a most valuable training aid in a unit, provided the unit commander knows how to use it as a teaching device.

The advantages of a sand table and methods for using one should be taught in all advance and basic courses. The schools should use a simple sand table similar to those available to the units. The sand tables should not be rigged with lights and other exotic devices.

As emphasis on unit training has grown in the past few years, sand tables have begun to come back into their own. Insist that they be used in unit training and in unit schools. Keep them simple and young officers and noncommissioned officers will learn how interesting and valuable using them can be. Much money will be saved and much will be learned. But now that we have rediscovered the sand table, don't be one of the extremists who say, "Every unit will take a sand table to the field." There is plenty of sand and dirt out there. The troops can scrape up a sand table whenever there is need for one.

One more caution: Don't let the sand table landscape become such a work of art that nobody wants to change the scene. That happens.

STANDARDS

High standards must be established and maintained in the most routine matters. Shaving, cleanliness, police of areas, and care of weapons may appear to be of minor importance, but laxness of standards in these and other routine matters invariably leads to a breakdown in control and discipline. These factors in turn will result in injuries to the troops and a decrease in efficiency that cannot be tolerated in a professional army. In time of war keeping standards up is even more important, because the result of laxness is reflected in the casualty figures. In peacetime maintaining high standards is particularly necessary for small units that are on independent missions away from their parent organizations.

Maintaining high standards requires persistent correction. In units that are weak or have problems, close scrutiny will usually show that the chain of command has lost the art of correcting the soldier. Either nothing is done, which is all too often the case, or it is done too aggressively to be constructive. High standards derive from teaching—from first showing soldiers how to do something right and then insisting that they do it properly. Any unit that can teach the chain of command what to do and then insists that it be done will show marked improvement quickly.

Often, when unit commanders discuss low standards with their bosses, their first remark is a complaint about the shortage of middle-level noncommissioned officers. Unit schools will raise the standards of all noncommissioned officers—and officers too—if unit commanders take the time to conduct the schools.

TIME

Simple addition and ordinary human experience make clear that the day has too few hours and the year too few days in which to accomplish the long list of training tasks prescribed by higher headquarters. But lack of time is not a valid excuse for poor training. It is, however, a common excuse of weak commanders who do not analyze the training situation confronting them, who do not think through courses of action for accomplishing their training mission, and who then take no action, ineffectually complaining about the higher commands. An account of my own approach to the time problem, both as a field-grade commander and as a general officer may be useful.

Before and during World War II, time did not surface as a grave problem in training. Days were full, we were busy, but I don't recall the anguished concern I sensed in battalion and brigade commanders who brought this problem up in the early 1970s. My first memory of time as a serious problem dates back to 1955-56, when I became a regimental commander. After taking command of the 10th Infantry I assessed the state of training in my unit and then looked at the mandatory training, list of field-training exercises, and whatever else had come down from above. There were not enough days in the year to accomplish them all. I made notes on what was most important—at least to me as the commander—then on what could be done concurrently—for instance, combining a hike to the range with familiarization firing. After doing my homework, I explained to the assistant division commander and the division commander that there was no way the regiment could do all that had been directed, outlined how I planned to train the 10th Infantry, and assured them that they would have a well-trained, disciplined regiment. They approved my plans and came around often to see how the regiment was doing. I always looked forward to their visits, and we had no major problems.

A few months later Lieutenant General Henry Hodes, the Seventh Army Commander, visited the regiment while we were at Hohenfels. He was told what training was scheduled for the day and asked what he wanted to see. It was soon apparent that he just wanted to saunter around and look at whatever caught his eye. We had hardly started when he asked, "What are your training problems and what's wrong with training in Seventh Army?" You know how you feel when you're a battalion or brigade commander and the army commander asks you a question like that. I told him the division commander had solved all my problems, but not wanting to miss the chance to help a lot of harassed commanders I added that training directives were causing serious problems. Commanders without much troop experience who were trying to do everything that had been directed could not train their units properly. He wanted specific examples, and because my homework had been done the examples were there for the telling. He spent most of the day with the regiment just wandering from kitchens, to motor pools, to ranges, to a critique. We talked a lot about training, commanders' problems, soldiers—and General Hodes knew the soldier. General Hodes had an armor background, and as we went about he talked about armor-infantry tactics and pointed out terrain ideal for small problems. We did not talk about mandatory training or directives after our early-morning discussion of the subject. He left about midafternoon; it had been a pleasant day and I had learned a lot.

Within a week, Seventh Army published a training directive rescinding all mandatory training directives. I could not claim credit for this needed change. It was obvious from the early-morning question that the army commander had already been aware of a problem that needed attention, and I happened to be one of the subordinate commanders he checked with.

The point here for field-grade commanders is that if your unit has a *time* problem you can do something about it. First do your homework: Analyze your time, decide what really needs to be done, and figure out how you can combine training requirements to do all you want to do and a little more besides. Then tell your division commander how you propose to get the job done. If the directives from higher headquarters are too unyielding, too restrictive, or too something, provide your boss with good examples and recommend that he take them up with corps, army, or whatever the next level might be.

As a division and higher commander I have at times been told by a field-grade commander that he did not have time to do all the training prescribed. I always asked that he lay out the problem for me and assured him that I would rescind any directive that my headquarters put out that created the position he claimed to be in. As a general rule, the longer the list the less valid was the claim. The lists I received showed duplications, the same activity under a different name, and seldom provided for concurrent training. Also, the level from which many of the directives had come was not known: According to the list "They" had done it, but on more than one occasion the directive had been put out by the commander's own staff. On only a few occasions a complaint about training time made to me by a battalion or brigade commander was valid, at least from my point of view. Complaints by company-level commanders were more valid because field-grade commanders had piled on one requirement after another without analyzing the total impact.

Whenever you plan to make a statement about lack of training time, first do your homework, be sure you are right, and then go back up the chain of command. If you are right someone will listen and, from my experience, he will do something about it.

TRAINING ANATHEMAS

I have mentioned a tendency for form over substance in training. Here are a few specific examples that are indicative of the charge.

"Spit-shined" boots

How often have you heard the term "spit-shined boots" extolled, and the soldier told to so shine his boots? Boots should be scraped or brushed to get off the mud and dirt, saddle-soaped to be softened, and treated with the latest issue of water-proofing solution. Time spent on "spit-shined" boots would be better spent cleaning a weapon, caring for some equipment, writing home, or just resting.

Starched fatigues

Starching fatigues is a waste of time and money. Fatigues should be clean and sewn if torn, but on any given day they are going to be soaked through with sweat and marked with dust, bits of oil, dirt, and mud, if the soldier—and that includes the officer—is going about a soldier's business. Some officers believe they must wear the starched fatigues to maintain their image. Those officers do look good, but they seldom train effectively; and they certainly don't train because they too would soon get dusty, dirty, and lose their starched appearance. Starched fatigues are the epitome of form over substance, except for one thing.

Fatigue shirt tucked in

Tucking in the fatigue shirt is considered important in the "looking smart" department. I have never yet seen engineers build a bridge quickly, infantrymen move over the ground the way they should, cannoneers firing the guns or "humping" ammunition, or tankers cleaning a tube or breaking track while keeping their shirttails tucked in. Fatigues are a functional uniform, and the shirt was made to be worn outside the trousers because the physical exertions demanded of a soldier are so great. When the fatigue shirt is worn inside the trousers, the training reflects it: Training is often neat, but rarely energetic.

Examples of form over substance abound. Start looking for them in your command and do something about them.

TRAINING FILMS AND PROGRESSIVE TRAINING

Visits to German Army units and training centers were always an education in proper training techniques. All armies use training films and follow progressive training procedures; however, the thoroughness with which the German Army approached them should suggest some ideas to commanders.

Training Films

At the German Infantry School I saw a method for use of training films guaranteed to keep everyone awake and to get the troops involved. A team of two or three people present a training film. Before doing so they preview the film and the field manual pertinent to the subject. They decide where they will stop the film and what questions on specific points in the film they will ask. The technique includes asking questions about something in the film that might not have been well done. The team quotes from the appropriate manuals as to weapons or other capabilities about which questions may arise in the discussion. One objective is to keep the group small when using training films; larger groups can be shown informational type films. I was struck by the participation and interest developed in these training sessions. You might try it.

Progressive training or putting it all together

When the Germans plan to conduct small-unit training they break the training into its component parts whenever possible. One sequence of training went something like this: The tactical problem to be conducted, after about a week of training that led up to it, was attack in a village. First there was a training film on attack in a built-up area, then a sand-table problem with a mock-up of the village and the approaches to it. The officers and NCOs spent considerable time on the sand table emphasizing use of supporting weapons and how one small element would assist another moving across streets and squares. Then came a series of brief actions that taught the troops the important points on fighting in a village—how to cross a street, how to clear a house, how to exit from a house, and several other individual steps. These segments of training took only a few minutes, but each individual or fire team went through the exercise depending on the points to be taught.

These individual parts of the training were well conducted, and with no wasted effort, since several stations were operating so that the groups could rotate through the stations. Finally it was all put together in an attack on a village by a company using plastic ammunition. The performance was impressive. But most impressive was the thoroughness of the training leading up to the final action in this training sequence.

TRAINING NONCOMMISSIONED OFFICER IN A UNIT

A recommendation I have made repeatedly throughout my military career is that a training noncommissioned officer not be assigned to each company-level unit. I have always been opposed to this practice. The main reason is that, invariably, as soon as a noncommissioned officer was assigned as training NCO the company-level commander shed his training responsibility. In some units the training NCO made out the training schedule and the company-level commander initialed it; often the company-level commander was only vaguely familiar with the training in progress. I used to see this happen so often that whenever subordinate commanders recommended that we use training NCOs my answer was always no.

In addition to the general neglect of training by those responsible for it, the practice engenders one other significant disadvantage. Since no space is provided for the position of training NCO, a fine platoon sergeant or some other top-quality NCO is designated for the job. Thus, some element of the unit is deprived of the leadership and supervision of its noncommissioned leader every day.

In fact, every noncommissioned officer in a leadership position is a training NCO. If only one gets the title, many of the other NCOs begin to get the idea that they don't have to worry about training any more; they begin to think that keeping track of training manuals, training aids, and other items pertinent to their area of responsibility can be left to the training NCO.

Designating a training NCO is a common practice, and all my experience tells me it is a bad practice. Make all noncommissioned officers aware that they are the training NCOs for the unit or group they supervise and training will get the attention it requires.

In spite of my strong prejudice on this point I might be wrong. No matter what the directives say, the training NCO reappears on the scene, so there must be another side of the subject that I obviously don't appreciate.

TRAINING NOTES

By now, I hope, the reader has been persuaded that a lot of paper is unnecessary for good training, but here is a recommendation that will require some. If you follow the guidance that has already been given, however, on no checklists, brief lesson plans, no training highlights, your outfit will have saved tons of paper and thousands of hours of typists' time, so the burden should be easily borne.

Each division should publish a series of training notes to provide helpful ideas for junior leaders in the conduct of training. Training can be the most interesting and stimulating part of a commander's effort, and the tradition of training notes will help make it so for several reasons. The notes will reflect the interest of the division commander and, more important, once he starts publishing them he just might begin to take the interest in the training that is required of senior commanders. Writing a few of the notes himself would be fine, but in any case he should check them all before publication. He would be well advised not to turn publication of the notes over to the G–3 on a weekly or monthly basis. Publish them only when someone has had a good idea that the commander feels ought to be passed on. And the notes should be brief, written in the soldier's language, and not a repetition of what is in the manuals. This is a good example of an old training note in my files:

MACHINE GUNNERY:

Machine gunners must constantly practice manipulation exercises. Fifteen minutes devoted to manipulation exercises just prior to any actual live firing will speed target engagement and increase accuracy. Manipulation should be second nature to a machine gunner.

One example of such exercise is for an NCO to give a series of commands, e.g., TRAVERSE LEFT, DEPRESS, ELEVATE, TRAVERSE RIGHT, ETC., which the gunners follow. Another method is for an NCO to move up and down the firing line with an ammunition box on which a target is placed (the flaming ordnance bomb can be used), planting the box at any desired spot and announcing "_____YARDS, LAY." The gunners immediately lay on the target and NCOs then check each gun for correct laying. A note of caution: Be positive that the guns are empty prior to running this exercise. NCOs (good ones, anyhow) are not expendable.

This was one of General Howze's notes: Pithy, to the point, imaginative, and in this case with a light touch.

Training notes should be the forum for a free and productive exchange of ideas on the conduct of training. They are intended for the small-unit leader. The units should be encouraged to send in any good ideas on training to be considered by division in publication of training notes. Brigade and battalion commanders are a good source of ideas because they should be visiting the troops in training every day and that is where the ideas come from. There are no hard and fast rules on items for training notes, except for the commandment, "Don't publish something that is already in the manuals." Look for ideas that save time and manpower, increase effectiveness, and generate interest and enthusiasm.

For ease of reference, training notes should be indexed under major headings and an index published periodically. A good way to check the administrative efficiency of the chain of command is to see if training notes are kept up to date. Examples of major headings for training notes are Tactics, Training Procedures, Leadership/Discipline, Gunner/Marksmanship, Communications/ Electronics, Logistics/Engineer, and Miscellaneous.

TYING UNITS TOGETHER—
IN MORE WAYS THAN ONE

Too much security in combat may be an impossible dream, but commanders must always seek ways to achieve it and at the same time build more confidence and esprit in their units. They can help realize the dream by emphasizing security and teamwork in training. One example will do for starters. When setting up a defensive position the responsible leaders should require that soldiers in each position contact the soldiers on their right and left to discuss fields of fire, mutual plans, and the signals they will use to get one another's attention. Squad and section leaders, platoon leaders, and company-level commanders should walk defensive positions before dark to insure that positions are prepared, tied in, and coordinated. As platoon leaders and company commanders check their portions of the position, they should make it a habit to contact the leaders of any support elements, such as engineer and artillery, to be sure they feel at home, know where they should be in the defensive position, and what they should do if the position is attacked.

Battalion commanders will not always have time to walk an entire defensive position before dark, but they should check the supporting fires on critical approaches, the gaps between elements, the flanks, and the trouble spots. As time permits, they should get around the entire position in order to know the terrain and get ideas on what they might do if the position is penetrated. Such effort will also provide the commander a good opportunity to see and talk with the men.

This advice may sound so basic that it appears unnecessary. Experience discloses, however, that security does not get the attention it warrants and is often overlooked in combat. This bit of guidance will give a needed assist to security consciousness and will give the men of any unit a feeling that someone cares.

11

Individual training is the foundation on which unit effectiveness is built. It is the source of a soldier's confidence and trust in the Army.

Individual Training in Units

Though each level of training contributes to a unit's capability to accomplish its missions, the key to all successful military training lies in raising the quality of individual and small-unit skills. These skills make the greatest contribution to an army's effectiveness and require the most attention and time.

The primary resources are time and those using it. Variations in local conditions and operational requirements make allotting a proportion of time to each level of training difficult, but since the allocation is so important, I do not hesitate to do so. Both long experience in training units and observation of training results have persuaded me that 75 to 80 percent of all training time should be devoted to systematic individual training and collective training of crews, sections, and small units below battalion level. In the vernacular of the day, that's where it is at.

Perhaps the most important observation one can make on individual training is that few leaders recognize how important it is. Individual training is the foundation on which unit effectiveness is built. It is the source of a soldier's confidence and trust in the Army. What the Army does for each soldier is reflected in that person's attitude toward the Army after separation from the service. Through the years, each veteran's service experience is a major source of civilian support, or lack of it, for the Army as an institution. A sound individual training program therefore involves much more than the development of military skills. The objective of individual training is to maximize the full potential of the soldier through mental, moral, and physical development. That part of a philosophy of training which holds "that training is all-encompassing" means that individual training is designed to improve the whole person.

Because of personnel turnovers there will always be different soldiers at different skill levels in units. Nobody gets a totally untrained soldier, however. Training centers turn out men prepared to go into squads, gun sections, tank crews, and support positions. The unit commander's job is to use these soldiers as they are assigned, and in the course of time upgrade their skills through systematic training that covers individual and unit requirements. The ideal program should provide opportunities for the chain of command, particularly the noncommissioned officers, to reinforce and sustain individual skills.

Important as individual training is, it does not get the attention it warrants in units. In the early 1970s a series of surveys on soldier attitudes indicated that when soldiers left the training centers their morale was high and they were impressed with the Army. A few months after they had joined units, their morale had dropped markedly. This trend does not speak well for training in units. I suspect some of the drop in morale stems from a lack of information on what is going on in the unit because training is more complex there than in a training center. A soldier needs to know what he will be taught and when, and he must have realistic goals and performance objectives to relate to. A good chain of command is invaluable in keeping him in the picture. Too often the chain of command does not recognize the importance of keeping the soldier informed on what will happen tomorrow, next week, and next month.

Perhaps some commanders gave individual training scant attention in the past because they thought it was so easy to do. Not so, says a new publication:

> *This is the toughest problem of all. The unit does not have just one problem here—it has a different problem for every man assigned. Some will have just come out of Training Centers and will know only the most basic jobs in the unit. Others will have come from other units, or from overseas, where they may have worked at very different tasks under different conditions from those they now face. Some will be willing, and some will be reluctant. And they will all be changing—moving in, moving up.*[1]

With this blunt statement of the problem there should be no excuse for slighting this phase of training in the future.

The lists of mandatory subjects constitute a perennial problem in individual training. These lists grow with each passing year until they are stifling to company-level commanders. With each renewed interest in training they are

---

[1] Training Circular 21-5-7, *Training Management in Battalions*, p. 24. The first two chapters, both through diagrams and in writing, give a good picture of the interrelationship of various levels of training.

swept away, only to start creeping back within a few weeks. One way to avoid this cycle is to respect the dedication and judgment of commanders as well as their professional estimate of the state of training in their units. Special-interest groups at Department of Defense and Department of Army level slip the mandatory training requirements into the directives. The Department of Army Staff must guard against this habit.

The important point for commanders and trainers about individual training is continuity. This training contributes to sustaining individual and unit effectiveness as well as reinforcing the individual soldier's confidence in his or her ability. The methods through which individual training should be accomplished are inherent in the discussions and suggestions throughout this volume. Certain facets of individual training that warrant special comment follow.

ON-THE-JOB TRAINING (OJT)

An important form of individual training is on-the-job training, which is defined as a training process whereby students or trainees acquire knowledge and skills through actual performance of duties, under competent supervision, in accordance with an approved planned program. Unfortunately, much on-the-job training does not conform to that definition.

Over the years I have asked thousands of soldiers what they were doing and the response was "OJT, Sir." My next question was invariably, "What kind of OJT?" Quite often the look on the soldier's face made it evident that the question was pretty stupid. Most often the reply was, "You know sir, whatever happens to come in," or, "Whatever has to be done." Some on-the-job training gives the impression that those responsible for it believe that the trainee need only be in the vicinity where the skill is being practiced and he will develop the skill—sort of like getting the measles. Soldiers might pick up a skill that way once in a while, but not often. Worthwhile on-the-job training does not just happen. It requires good planning, organization, and supervision. The essentials are spelled out in the soldiers manual for each military occupational specialty (MOS).

Every OJT program should be progressive and have a planned course of instruction. There should be starting and termination dates and check points in between. One or two precise hands-on jobs or techniques should be taught each day. The objective is to add to the skill and store of knowledge of the trainee each day by accomplishing specific steps in the qualification process. For example, in training mechanics a maintenance warrant officer or NCO should, during a one- to two-hour period, assemble his OJT mechanics around several pieces of equipment that require the same sort of repair. The on-the-job trainee then does the repair job, while each step from diagnosis to cleanup is explained by a qualified mechanic. Discussion is encouraged. At the end of that period of instruction each trainee will have learned one thing thoroughly. If the task is a time-consuming one, the period can be lengthened or continued the next day.

Flexibility and understanding by those running the program are needed. The trainee can then turn to other tasks in the daily routine. At the end of each week a performance-oriented test should be given to determine if the soldier has acquired the skills scheduled for that week. Evaluation and repetition are important steps in assuring that the individual attains the desired skill level.

If you follow such a program your unit will have qualified mechanics, or whatever the on-the-job training program is directed toward. Improvement in unit efficiency and job satisfaction on the part of the trainees will be added bonuses. Finally, the warrant officers and noncommissioned officers will learn how much they can contribute to the development of subordinates and how important they are to the organization.

To insure that the on-the-job training programs accomplish what they set out to do, senior officers must get down to specifics when they encounter a soldier who says he is on OJT. Ask him what he learned yesterday, today, and what he will learn tomorrow. If he is a cook, he should be able to talk about the salad he made yesterday, the biscuits he made today, and the roast he will cook tomorrow. Ask him when his on-the-job training program will be over and when he will get his military occupational specialty (MOS). If the trainee can not answer those questions, you had better ask the unit commander to show you the details of the unit's on-the-job programs.

A final note: Be sure that credit is given for successful completion of an on-the-job training program and that appropriate annotation is made in the personnel records.

RELATING THE INDIVIDUAL'S MILITARY TRAINING TO CIVILIAN LIFE

The British Army has splendid individual training and education programs that raise individual competence in the military fields and enhance opportunities for civilian employment when a soldier leaves the service. One notable feature of their individual training is the role of senior noncommissioned officers in teaching small groups of soldiers in afternoon schools or during other periods not devoted to unit training. These senior noncommissioned officers give thorough, comprehensive hands-on training that raises the skill level of individuals in their MOS fields. A soldier has to qualify at a new level in his field before he can be promoted or earn a pay raise. When a noncommissioned officer completes the training of his men the trainees are tested to see if they can qualify. Over a period of time the results make evident the noncommissioned officer's capability to teach his subordinates.

The training for specialties such as cook, heavy equipment operator, truck driver, and other jobs has a high degree of standardization that can be translated into civilian employment. The military qualification cards for these skills are accepted by the trade unions in England. This acceptance is an incentive to a soldier to improve himself in the service, since it will lead to job opportunities when he leaves. I dwell on this feature of British training because it reflects a highly professional attitude and is understood by all ranks. I believe this system of military education, which requires its soldiers to meet prescribed qualifications before advancement, is a major contributing factor to the high standards of the British Army.

The United States Army now requires a certain score on skill-qualification tests (SQT) before an individual can be promoted. A healthy feature of the current program is the emphasis on the soldier's manuals, with the noncommissioned officers responsible for maintaining the job-book as they keep the soldiers proficient in their skills. Charging the NCO with responsibility for training the young soldier builds a close relationship between the NCO and his subordinates. This kind of relationship is critical and vital in combat because the NCO learns about the capabilities of his subordinates and the subordinate develops a respect for the noncommissioned officer who has taught him so much. In recent years commanders have not demanded enough of the NCOs in training; the same can be said for junior officers. This laxity needs correcting so that the junior leaders can develop as individuals and their responsibility can be clearly defined. It has been my experience that, where high standards are established, the NCOs and junior officers will produce results if the senior commanders create the proper training atmosphere.

MEDICAL BADGE, EXPERT INFANTRY BADGE, AND OTHER INDIVIDUAL AWARDS

Fine programs lead to these recognitions of merit, but do they need to be so highly organized and time consuming? It is of course important to maintain high standards in order to keep the badges from losing their value. But in recent years too much of such training has been done by rote. Elaborate plans are made for the test days and often an entire battalion is tied up for the test period. Why not charge the noncommissioned officers with responsibility for determining when their subordinates are ready to pass certain phases of the qualification requirements? When a small group of men are ready, send them before knowledgeable and experienced evaluation groups. Such a procedure could be followed throughout the year. It would not have to be overorganized, and would indicate how well noncommissioned officers are training their subordinates and how high their standards are. When subordinates fail to qualify in the evaluation, the immediate chain of command—senior noncommissioned officers, platoon leaders, and company commanders—can start asking, "How come?" of the NCOs responsible for the training of those who failed. This is one way to stress the importance of the noncommissioned officer and raise both his standards and prestige.

FORMAL EDUCATION

Developing military skills and discipline is obviously essential for the soldier, but formal education is an important feature of a soldier's individual training in peacetime and is part of the Army's side of the contract made when the soldier enlists. Fulfilling the promises on education is a command responsibility, and commanders are expected to recognize the merits and contributions of the education program. But fulfilling this promise involves a built-in conflict. Quite often the demands of formal education create resentment and antagonism in young commanders, both officer and enlisted. The time devoted to formal education interferes with military training and creates problems for the company-level commander who is responsible for maintaining a high state of readiness. Some senior commanders build a reputation on an aggressive formal-education program that looks great in the reports and is acclaimed by civilians both in and out of the Defense Department. The young commanders not only lose troops to education programs, but the young officers sometimes feel they are pressured into contributing their own free time to these programs after duty hours. Free time for commanders in units is precious, and subordinate commanders often see themselves whipsawed between the conflict inherent in training to meet readiness standards and education quotas.

In defense of commanders, especially those in the combat arms, it is important to note that the Department of the Army creates the conditions that turn commanders against the education program. Too often education goals are prescribed that commanders cannot achieve without neglecting the training their units need to meet readiness criteria. Army regulations which prescribe as

121

a minimum goal that "every service member" will be provided an opportunity to qualify for a high school diploma in the first unit of assignment along with other educational requirements are no help to combat-arms commanders whose units contain high percentages of non-high-school graduates. At the same time, commanders are constrained to maintain a high standard of readiness.

Unrealistic goals place an excessive burden on company- and battalion-level commanders and create hostility for formal-education programs. Education is important to the soldier as an individual, to his contribution to the Army, and to his betterment for our society. Rather than setting unrealistic goals, the Department of the Army should provide the opportunity and let commanders achieve the goals at a pace they can accommodate. I always told company commanders to put three or four soldiers in these programs; consider them casualties as you would in combat, and let them finish their schooling. Replace the individual who does not try with one who is eager to get an education, because some soldiers prolong their formal education to avoid the rigors of field training.

Attaining a high school diploma or other recognized symbol of achievement should not be a free ticket. It is worth using some training time to help a soldier get a high school diploma if there is no other way to achieve that objective. However, the soldier should be required to do some of his schooling in after-duty hours, or report to a study hall for a certain number of hours of study each evening to help him progress more rapidly. People do not appreciate what they don't have to sacrifice for. If some of these approaches are taken, commanders will be for, rather than against, the education programs and the individuals in them will benefit. A better coordination and integration of general education development with individual training is essential.

BASIC AND ADVANCED INDIVIDUAL TRAINING IN UNITS

Basic and advanced individual training in units has not been common in the United States Army in recent years. But the lack of emphasis on this training in units does not imply that such training is not good or is impractical.

In today's volunteer army the basic and advanced individual training conducted at training centers is essential to the high state of readiness which everyone seeks. It is also efficient and well done. On at least three separate occasions in my career, however, I was confronted with a requirement to train a unit from the start. The men came from the reception stations, went into basic and advanced individual training in the unit, and proceeded through unit training preparatory to deployment overseas.

On the first two occasions I didn't know who made the decision. On the last occasion the Department of the Army informed me that the 4th Infantry Division was earmarked for Vietnam, and asked if I preferred to get replacements after basic or advanced training. My response was that if I had at least six months before deployment I would prefer to take the men directly from the reception stations and train them from the start. There are unparalleled opportunities to develop noncommissioned officers, junior officers, and the entire chain of command when a unit is available for a complete training cycle prior to deployment. A unit so trained can be at least two to three months ahead of a unit which gets its replacements after advanced individual training, because the individual training of members of the chain of command, which is so important in combat, is concurrent with the training of the unit. Thus, a complete training cycle in a unit has its place. In the future, budget decisions or emergencies might arise requiring a decision on this method of training. If you ever have the choice and the time, training the whole rather than the parts seems to me a good way to prepare a unit for combat.

12

Teaching officers how to conduct thorough and interesting crew training in units with equipment ordinarily available should be a prime objective in basic and advanced courses.

Crew Training

In the mid-1970s "collective training" emerged as a term to describe all training where a number of soldiers worked together to accomplish a task. Crew, small-unit, and large-unit training all fall under the heading of collective training. The first level of collective training—crew training—and some of the devices that make this training and individual training more effective and less costly are the focus of this chapter.

CREW TRAINING

Just as individual training develops the stamina, attitude, and fighting qualities of an army, crew training develops the teamwork without which no army can be effective. Most frequently, crew training is described in the context of the combat arms because an army exists to fight. Nevertheless, identical training principles apply to the crews of support activities. Without effective maintenance sections, armor and mechanized units could not fight long, and without well-trained signal sections the various crews and arms could not fight effectively as a team. Crew training develops the fighting capability of an army.

Speed and precision are vital to success in combat. Rapidity and accuracy of fire are key ingredients to survival and success in small-unit actions. Ask any tanker about the relative value of getting off the first round in a tank engagement. Crew training develops dexterity in setting up weapons or component parts of weapons systems, loading and unloading equipment, and camouflaging or concealing equipment or activity. When these talents combine with knowledge of immediate action and deftness in disassembling and assembling military equipment to rectify shortcomings, a crew is ready for any emergency. Stopwatches are important training aids in developing these capabilities, and a plentiful supply should be available to small-unit leaders. Crew training is the cement that binds an organization together; it also provides superb opportunities for developing the chain of command and identifying future leaders, especially noncommissioned officers.

CROSS-TRAINING OF CREWS

Cross-training within a crew—mortar squad, gun section, tank crew, or any section that works or fights together—is essential, especially in the combat arms where casualties are certain to occur. But the first objective is to train the individual to do his own job well. From time to time the suggestion is made that soldiers develop proficiency with weapons systems not common to their crew or function. This advice is seldom practical in the U.S. Army because of the turnover in personnel. In addition to the crew-served weapon a soldier services, he is also required to be proficient with his individual weapon, grenades, certain antitank weapons, and often a machine gun that is attached to his mode of transportation. Cross-training within a crew is a demanding training requirement; making a soldier a professional within his assigned crew takes time.

SELECTION OF CREW MEMBERS

In the operation of weapons systems, particularly in the role of the gunner or shooter, differences in vision, coordination, and steadiness make one person better qualified than another for a specific crew position. This fact has always been known, but perhaps the high turnover in personnel has not permitted the Army to acknowledge the importance of this fact in crew selection. In the era of the guided missile, when antitank rounds cost thousands of dollars, it became evident that efforts had to be made to examine training, doctrine, and weapons development to provide a reasonable cost-effectiveness ratio for some of the new weapons. In 1975, the Training and Doctrine Command (TRADOC) instituted a major program to analyze training effectiveness.

Commenting on past experience, TRADOC said, "By any standard, the use of research by Army trainers has been less than satisfactory. In far too many cases, we have failed to ask the right questions, failed to coordinate current research or to build upon previous research, and failed to monitor properly to insure that research met our specific needs."[1] There was also a failure to take a continuing look at the human characteristics that affect operation of the system and the training of the soldiers who would operate the systems.

Collective training in units, particularly crew training, is certain to benefit from the program of study now in effect. Perhaps the best current example is the result of evaluation of Dragon training,[2] which showed that experts would be consistently two or three times more effective than first-class gunners. This evaluation suggests that only those who can qualify as experts should fire the Dragon. In the past there has been a tendency to demand too much of a weapons system, which makes the weapons system expensive, while neglecting doctrine and training. The Training and Doctrine Command is giving weapons training a critical look to correct these basic weaknesses.

The studies and publications of TRADOC are all central to the improvement of training, but in the past the mass of such information did not appear to surface in training form at the unit level. Good ideas were translated into good training only where the commanders were specifically interested, and oases of good applied training sprang up in the training desert. Regrettably, improved training was a matter of personality and personal interest rather than institutional support.

The reasons are obvious: low priority for training and emphasis by service schools on the podium and the classroom as opposed to more practical work in the field. The most important reason for the void, which still exists, is the lack of knowledge of weapons systems among officers. Many officers have had so little opportunity for duty with troops that they don't know the weapons, the troops, or the training environment. Perhaps Morris Janowitz's thesis that military managers and technicians are taking over from the heroic leaders (solid soldiers would more nearly fit my description) might have validity. The question provides a good subject for debate at the Army's senior service schools, but it is not much help to the trainer at the unit level. Two examples may suffice to suggest the proper orientation that commanders must take toward the real world of weapons to conduct thorough crew training.

---

[1]TRADOC PAM 71-8, Headquarters United States Army Training and Doctrine Command; December 1, 1975, pp. 1-10.

[2]The Dragon is a medium-range antitank weapon.

First, consider the mortar, a simple weapon. Generally, mortar training is neglected, and this tendency reflects a typical lack of knowledge or even curiosity about primary weapons and systems. Yet accounts of any small-unit action will reveal that mortars cause a great many casualties and, when well used by the enemy, are of special concern whether you are attacking or defending. Nevertheless, mortar training is neglected because commanders lack comprehensive knowledge of the weapon. Mortar sections and squads are dispersed throughout the command structure, and the crews get a lot of odd jobs.

One indication of this general lack of knowledge is the men's ignorance about firing mortars during a heavy downpour. When did you last talk to the men in the mortar platoon or section on the problems of firing in the rain? Can you fire a mortar round with wet charges? What effect will rain have on the trajectory of the round? Can you fire on a rainy night when someone calls for mortar rounds on the final protective line? I have always been surprised at how many officers with mortars in their units did not know the answers to these questions.

Try this small training demonstration: Take a few rounds of mortar ammunition and the accompanying plastic charges ("swiss cheese"). Keep some dry, dampen some, and thoroughly soak some. Then use these charges to demonstrate what happens when the mortar rounds are fired. Good mortarmen will keep their charges dry, but crewmen should learn how effective their weapons systems will be under adverse conditions.

The demonstration should be well supervised to ensure that the men get the proper message: that is, always try to keep the charges dry, but if they do get wet they can still be fired to accomplish the mission. Arousing curiosity about a weapons system and ensuring that the troops know how to accomplish their mission under adverse conditions is an important part of crew training.

Satisfying this aroused curiosity with knowledge is especially important in training for complex weapons systems. The thorough approach of an armor commander I observed in Germany was impressive. His battalion developed a night-equipment proficiency test to evaluate the skill levels of tank crewmen using night-peculiar equipment as applicable.[3] The nine stations of the test ran the gamut of night equipment available to the tank battalion under TOE 17-37 in 1974. The stations were as follows:

Station 1: M18 Binoculars—place into operation, focus.
Station 2: M24 Periscope—mount and adjust.
Station 3: IR Headlight Operation—turn on, check operation.
Station 4: Night Sight Reticle—place into operation, check alignment.
Station 5: Lensatic Compass—set an azimuth and bezel ring operation.

---

[3]First Battalion, 68th Armor, 8th Infantry Division. From a training note of that unit.

Station 6: Flashlight Signal Operation Procedures.

Station 7: Operation of Xenon Searchlight—white light and IR mode.

Station 8: Range Cards—circular and sketch-type.

Station 9: Operation of night observation device and metascope to include setting up metascope for night ranging operation in conjunction with the coincidence range finder.

Naturally, any unit possessing night-peculiar equipment could conduct similar type of training after checking appropriate manuals.

The point that this training program makes clear is that a weapons system is not just a tank and a crew. A lot of subsystems influence the effective operation of a tank crew. Remember too that this is only one phase of training for a tank crew. At times commanders forget the complexity of the systems and the demands it imposes in crew training.

Since such a variety of equipment exists, there is no point in giving other examples. The key to filling the void described is the service school. Courses for officers and noncommissioned officers must be taught in a fashion that will excite their curiosity about weapons systems and equipment peculiar to their arm or service. Teaching officers how to conduct thorough and interesting crew training in units with the equipment ordinarily available in units should be a prime objective in basic and advanced courses. Training devices that permit repetitive drills are also available at low cost and are convenient for the units. The chain of command must learn how to take advantage of these devices, and this can be taught in unit schools.

AIDS TO INDIVIDUAL AND CREW TRAINING

Aids to training are available to solve some of the problems of cost, size of training areas, and wear and tear on equipment. They also add to realism and provide opportunities for exercising major parts of a weapons system. Three types of aids—subcaliber devices, turret trainers, and training simulators—make an important contribution to individual and crew training. The advantages and warning notes associated with this assortment of training aids can be related to other training aids.

Subcaliber devices

Ammunition costs a lot of money, and as the rounds get bigger they get more expensive. The training areas at which the weapons systems can be fired are often some distance from home station or are not available because the units wanting firing ranges outnumber the ranges. Subcaliber devices permit an individual or a crew to go through entire fire sequences at minimum cost. They also permit firing at reduced distances, and thus make checking all of the operations easy and the men enjoy using them. So use these devices as often as you can. They beat a lecture or a lot of talk, and the men will be out to prove they are better shots or better crews than their neighbors on the firing lines.

When you use subcaliber devices, exercise the whole system. If they are artillery subcaliber, get out the battery commander's scope, set up the fire direction center, and use your communications. If they are mortars, get out the plotting boards, the field glasses, and anything else used for a live-fire mission. In any fire mission the orders and procedures are all important to accuracy and speed. Use of subcaliber devices is especially helpful in improving these aspects of shooting.

If your units are not using subcaliber devices, start asking why not. Before complaining to higher headquarters that devices are not available, start searching. They are probably buried in some supply room long forgotten because "they won't work"—no one in the unit knows that the compressed air cylinders that are a part of the mortar simulation system have to be filled—and so these valuable training devices are relegated to the dark corners. Find them and start using them. NCOs and junior officers should be experts in their maintenance and the set-up of the small local ranges. If company-grade officers don't think to schedule their use, a few suggestions by crew chiefs and gunnery sergeants will help the "old man" train his company better.

The use of training devices was no mystery to the pre-World War II Army. That Army was poverty stricken by comparison with today's military, and it had not nearly the capability we take for granted today. But ingenuity was used to make subcaliber devices in local ordnance shops to save on cost of ammunition, which in the larger calibers was doled out a few rounds at a time. The training device "system" most frequently used was the .22 caliber rifle and landscape targets; calling it a system in those days would have raised a few eyebrows.

Turret trainers

My interest in turret trainers was renewed by noting the way the British and the Germans used them. Both armies had one or two turret trainers in the armored units and used them regularly to maintain crew proficiency. The time allotted for their use was much in demand by the company-level commanders and closely controlled at battalion level to ensure that this valuable training device was not sitting in some training shed forgotten and unused. Russian troops also use turret trainers and a variety of mock-ups of weapons platforms. The value of the turret trainers is three-fold: crew procedures can be practiced and checked out under close control; the trainers save fuel; and the devices cut down wear and tear on the engine, tracks, and other vehicle components.

The Germans emphasize the importance of acquiring the trainers in the same procurement package as the weapons system of which they are a part. The good sense of this practice was reinforced in my mind when I noted how often our turret trainers were in a state of disrepair and how few were with troop units. Generally our turret trainers were obtained as an afterthought or in separate procurement packages from the original equipment. There would be just enough difference in some of the spare parts and in the maintenance to make them a maintenance burden and soon they would be relegated to the back of some shed or assigned only to schools able to provide the maintenance backup no field unit could afford.

In discussing the use of turret trainers in the early 1970s, I found that most U.S. commanders believed that more could be accomplished by training in the assigned armor vehicles. The lack of covered space for a trainer has also been a drawback for U.S. armor units, particularly in Germany. The lack of space points up a basic difference in attitude. The Germans and the British plan on the use of trainers; we don't. As fuel costs go up and as money gets tighter, we may find trainers more attractive. Total systems development is supposed to close this gap.

Training simulators

Simulators are a special breed of cat and require a lot of study, particularly at the training command level. We have to be careful about them. In some places they are invaluable; in others they are a millstone around the neck of the unit commander. A few examples:

Aviation. No question about the value, given the cost of operating equipment, complexity of systems, safety, and other similar factors involved.

Missiles. Essential and without a substitute. Some rounds cost several thousand dollars each, and the Army cannot afford to develop proficiency by live firing. All steps in a firing sequence can be accomplished with simulators, and a good instructor can tell the firer where he went wrong. But the simulators must be dependable and in good working condition. The M551 (Sheridan) Simulator was more trouble to operate than the M551. All indications are that the Russians use simulators extensively to help identify which men will be most proficient and which men should not fire expensive missiles.

Dune Buggies. At schools like Fort Knox and Fort Benning, where they can be used by officers and noncommissioned officers to get ideas on tactics and formations, dune buggies are efficient and less expensive than tanks and armored personnel carriers. These schools also have a special maintenance capability and can have a direct line to the supplier. But out in a unit, once the initial novelty and enthusiasm wear off, dune buggies and similar substitute vehicles are a headache for a company commander. I have seen company sets of this equipment sitting in cavalry and armor unit track parks seldom used and most often inoperable. This was not the fault of the commanders. The parts were not in the normal supply system, and mechanics were not trained to care for them and had to keep the company equipment operating. Simulators impose additional burdens on already overburdened unit commanders. Also, though not the case with dune buggies, sometimes these simulators are highly sophisticated and then the support problems multiply. Alternatives are available. Substitution of jeeps for tanks or other armored vehicles might be a better solution than non-TOE equipment in a unit.

SCOPES and REALTRAIN

SCOPES is valuable in infantry training, as is REALTRAIN in armor and anti-armor training. These innovations brought realism and interest to infantry and armor training. When SCOPES first appeared it was relatively inexpensive, easy to operate, and a boon to the most difficult of all training—infantry training. SCOPES had hardly been tested and issued, on a most selective basis, when its proponents—with that enthusiasm so typical of our Army and project managers—were out promoting the second generation. This new generation was going to be much better, having laser devices that would light up, a vest to be worn by each man, and an adapter that would cost more than the rifle. REALTRAIN was going through a similar upgrading. But was this really progress?

Two points are worth making. Neither the schools nor the units had time to teach the chain of command how to get the most out of the first generation of these two contributions to improved training, let alone be ready to utilize the second generation. Second, potential problems with some of the new features such as the laser devices were not discussed sufficiently. Nowhere did I see an analysis of the trade-offs in equipment and spaces involved in introducing the new systems.

For the past two decades, the Army has failed to plan adequately for the development of subcaliber and simulation devices at the time of weapons-systems development. This failure is now getting attention by TRADOC. If these devices are simple, inexpensive, and do not require extensive maintenance, they will be a great help. As they become more complex and expensive, and some of them will—for example, simulators to train aviators and engagement simulators—a definite policy must be made at Department of Army level.

The policy decision must be based on the recognition that obtaining these devices means something is going to have to be given up—a certain number of tanks, trucks, helicopters, radios, or similar equipment. The trade-off is worth making as long as everyone realizes what the bill will be. The decision naturally involves consideration of the places for which the devices are best suited and how cost-effective they will be. Also needed are some hard-headed practitioners to insist that the devices to be issued to units are simple to operate and maintain, and are manageable. They should make a point of not overcomplicating accountability and storage procedures.

Wherever possible—and it will not be possible in all cases—simulation devices should be kept compatible with basic equipment. Spaces must be made available for a maintenance-training group at some level, possibly brigade or division, to keep these devices operational as they are passed from unit to unit in the battalion or brigade. For the long haul, reliability and utility should be prime requirements for these devices. Simulators will not be as cheap and easy to operate and maintain as the brochures on their use indicate. For this reason the basic and advanced courses must teach young officers how to operate and use these aids and devices. If not, their use in units will be limited.

In checking on subcaliber devices in units over the past fifteen years, I have found that many officers did not know what they were or where they were stored. Until our officers and NCOs—or perhaps I should say the Army—really get serious about training, the best simulators and devices will be relegated to the dark corners or the nonoperational junk heap. This problem is more a state of mind than a need for material. Due to the neglect of training devices in the past, a willingness to take some risks to catch up is appropriate. New programs will be helpful if the Army undertakes them with forethought and makes a deliberate policy decision that recognizes the trade-offs needed to maintain them. Serious management problems could arise from the variety and complexity of devices appearing on the scene, if the training program is not based on the cost in money and people.

 *Skillful senior commanders can bring their armies into battle under favorable conditions, but it is the small unit leaders who win the battle.*

Small-Unit Training

WHY SMALL-UNIT TRAINING IS VITAL

Small units are battalions and their subordinate elements. Because battalions are the basic fighting units, division commanders make their battle plans in terms of the types of combat power in the battalions available to them. Almost all the discussion that follows has to do with the subordinate elements of battalions: squads, sections, platoons, and the company-level units—companies, batteries, and troops. Defeats, collapses, and panics start with small units, and victories are determined by their measure of success. Skillful senior commanders can bring their armies into battle under favorable conditions, but the small-unit leaders at the company level are the ones who win the battle. Given anything like equal terms, the best-trained army will win. Even if the odds are markedly against an army which has well-trained small units and small-unit commanders, that army will often defeat a force superior in numbers and equipment. At a minimum, it will not be routed and will survive to fight on.

In studying combat performance and what motivates men to fight, sociologists stress the importance of the soldier's loyalty to his primary group. These primary groups are squads, sections, crews, platoons—elements of company-level units and below. The harder the fighting, the more important are primary-group ties in maintaining fighting effectiveness. The sociologists' conclusions are supported by many military writers, including General S. L. A. Marshall, who has made a major contribution to the study of small-unit combat actions and the reaction of individuals in combat. These writings from different disciplines suggest that small-unit training, which knits the primary groups closer together and provides training opportunities for small-unit leaders, is at the heart of an army's effectiveness.

The variety of branches in the Army and the diversity of missions for each branch of the service preclude any effort to give detailed small-unit training guidance. That is properly the province of commanders and branch schools. Certain principles, however, apply to most small-unit training; those that follow will inculcate good training habits. If larger units are composed of properly trained and disciplined smaller units, the higher commanders' main concerns will be the support and strategy needed for victory.

KEEPING TRAINING PROBLEMS SHORT

Too many small-unit problems, especially at the squad and platoon level, take much too long and go too deep. Problems that take several hours get boring and tiresome for the soldier. The critique cannot cover everything, and by the end of the problem the troops are tired, have stopped listening and often the umpires have forgotten what they have observed.

Combat usually consists of a series of short sharp actions for subordinate elements of companies. Squads and platoons are interested in what is in the next patch of woods, around the next bend, or over the next hill. Even armor and mechanized units, which can cover greater distances, are generally concerned about the next terrain feature because that is where the enemy may be waiting.

A series of four or five squad problems about 75 meters in depth for a dismounted squad and 150 to 300 meters in depth for a mounted squad provides a good morning's training. A platoon can execute two or three such problems in a morning. The same goes for armor units which would normally operate as a platoon, with the recognition that armor problems require more depth. Three hundred meters would be a short "bound" for an armor platoon.

KEEPING ORDERS AND INSTRUCTIONS BRIEF

When small units make contact, speed in execution is often decisive. Issue fragmentary orders, keep orders brief, and point out objectives and boundaries wherever possible. If a sketch is needed, keep it simple. I have heard squad and platoon leaders giving orders to their units that would have been better suited to a brigade or division. Most often test situations were the occasions, and the pressure from the assembled umpires and visitors was oppressive for the sergeant or lieutenant. Things happen fast in combat, and you see, hear, and sense things. Fast action is all a commander has to provide in training.

Coming down the road you can say, "A machine gun just fired from that (pointing) clump of bushes; Hernandez is wounded. Sergeant Kelly, knock it out." Or, "I can hear three or four tanks moving; sounds like they are just over that hill. Set up antitank weapons there, there, and there. Jessup, notify company commander; ask if we can get any artillery support."

When issuing orders, any commander up to company level should position himself so he can point to objectives or areas to be defended. There will be exceptions, but they should be rare. When you hear orders or situations in small-unit training that ramble on for fifteen minutes about identification of enemy units, adjacent units, supply, communications, and so on, it's time to call a halt and get back to the basics.

PACE OF TRAINING

Mind the clock, but don't hurry. Do not confuse speed in execution with racing through training. Units should not be rushed through a series of situations, particularly on live-firing problems. Haste most often occurs when small units—squads, tank crews, and gun sections—are going through a series of stations to test their knowledge or procedures. A series of brief situations is generally good training and the troops enjoy it, but avoid a schedule that is too tight. It may be necessary to have rest stations or hold some men inactive in order to provide extra time to properly conduct and critique the live-firing parts of the program. These are generally more complex and require more time than the training at other stations.

Sometimes too much is attempted in training. A less ambitious program carried out with a maximum of teaching is more valuable than hurrying through a number of situations with time so limited that the teaching opportunity is lost. Some types of problems, like the attack of a bunker, require detailed planning and thorough coordination with all those involved. Rushing headlong into these situations costs lives in combat, so do not rush through them in training. A good trainer develops a sense of pace through observation and experience. It is an art that can be developed in unit schools and by experienced battalion commanders as they watch day-to-day training and counsel young commanders.

SPECIFICITY AND ARMY TRAINING AND EVALUATION PROGRAMS (ARTEPS)

In small-unit training, remember specificity.[1] The Army Training and Evaluation Programs should help because they are specific as to unit missions. Commanders should use them in planning and executing their training, but with two cautions. First, some commanders will believe that the suggested support requirements for evaluation are necessary for the training. It will help to have all the support requirements available for the evaluation, but the training can be done without the extras if the commanders use a little imagination and ingenuity.

Second, we must avoid the bad habits of the past. If practices of recent years are followed, the ARTEPs will hardly have gone through their first cycle before all the emphasis will be on the evaluation rather than training. I suspect there are already some who call the ARTEPs *test* and evaluation programs rather than *training* programs. Some commanders conduct rehearsals for the evaluation rather than training their units how best to accomplish the mission. The objective should be to avoid a stereotyped routine exercise that the troops know by heart, because the evaluation can and should be valuable training as well as an evaluation. No document and nothing written here will keep ARTEPs from going the sorry way of earlier training tests unless commanders place the emphasis on *training* and *mission performance* rather than focusing on often pointless competition to determine who is best. The mark of a good military unit is versatility in combat situations, not simply the ability to memorize and execute a set piece.

COMBINED-ARMS TRAINING

It is a rare mission that does not involve combined-arms effort, but too often commanders wait for major exercises to pull different combat capabilities together. Combat operations have always demonstrated the advantage of early integration of combat power; as a minimum, anyone in a fight wants artillery support. The Arab-Israeli war in October 1973 showed the lethality of modern weapons systems, particularly new antitank and antiair systems, and the absolute necessity for integration of combat capabilities. The same lesson was evident in World War II, Korea, and Vietnam, only now the weapons are more accurate and deadly. When a unit comes under fire, the faster it can bring to

---

[1]See above, p. 50.

bear its full firepower and the firepower of other arms on the enemy, the faster it will accomplish its mission and the fewer casualties it will sustain. Support by other arms is especially important to the infantry, which needs all the help it can get to accomplish its missions and keep casualties down.

Renewed emphasis on combined-arms training does not change the need for emphasis on small-unit training. It means that the combined-arms integration must come early in the training program and be evident and effective at lower levels of organization. The training does not have to be complicated. It can be as rudimentary as teaching an infantryman how to use the external phone on a tank to indicate a target, teaching armor and infantry noncommissioned officers how to adjust artillery fire, or teaching small units what special support is available from the engineers. Simple training exercises that teach soldiers of different branches something about one another's tactics, weapons, and firepower are a good start for combined-arms training. Such training will save lives in combat.

On a sophisticated battlefield there is an effective counter for each modern weapons system. Training to achieve tactical superiority requires knowledge of weapons, coordination of their use, and a keen appreciation of terrain. Small combined-arms task forces consisting of an armor and infantry platoon, antitank and/or antiair sections, with an artillery forward observer, and a combat-engineer section might well be the model for some phases of small-unit training in the future.

A TRADOC bulletin commenting on the role of the leader on the modern battlefield noted that "morale and motivation must be backed up in weapons and tactical proficiency."[2] Weapons and tactical proficiency is what combined-arms and small-unit training is all about, and the content of this and other training bulletins in the series should excite the interest and ingenuity of a new generation of trainers. The bulletins and directives will not mean much, however, unless the schools teach the officers how to translate the ideas into training on the ground and at the unit level.

VARIETY IN SMALL-UNIT TRAINING

Short tactical problems ought to be varied to include other than routine attack or defense missions—for example, ambushes, destruction of a bridge behind enemy lines at night, infiltration, and river or stream crossings. Emphasize a few basic points with time for discussion and for doing the problem over if desired. Brevity combined with variation in small-unit training will stimulate

---

[2]TRADOC Bulletin No. 8, "Modern Weapons on the Modern Battlefield," December 31, 1975.

interest while providing drill in fundamental tactical principles. The mutual exchange between the commander and his troops often provides the opening for original ideas to creep in. Variation can be easy if commanders make the maximum use of any piece of terrain: attack it, defend it, traverse it, and above all, study it. Constant study of terrain and use of varied terrain will pay off in training and in combat.

Adherence to these principles—keep problems short, keep orders and instructions brief, proper pace, specificity, combined-arms emphasis, and variety—will raise the quality of small-unit training markedly. Each principle, however, is more than just an idea. The application of any one principle demands much thought and the incorporation of the other principles. One way to emphasize this point is to take the principle of *variety* and apply it to the training of an infantry battalion where variety is sorely needed, but has been notably lacking in recent years.

VARIETY IN TRAINING
AN INFANTRY BATTALION

A first step toward achieving variety is to discard the mechanized infantry squad problem, or any other single problem, as a device for rating units. Then the way will be clear to follow the sequence of events suggested below. With appropriate adjustments a similar sequence can be applied in the training of small units of several branches.

About two months before an infantry battalion is scheduled for a field-exercise period or a visit to a major training area, the battalion commander discusses with his company commanders the type of squad and platoon problems they want for their units. Nine to twelve squad problems and four to six platoon problems would be good numbers to emerge from this interchange. Battalion and company commanders then visit the training area to check on the terrain and ranges that will be available, and go on a terrain walk to talk about the type of problems they want to conduct. If funds or time preclude a visit, aerial photos will provide valuable experience in terrain study to the commanders.

The battalion commander assigns each rifle company responsibility for three or four squad problems and one platoon problem. Requirements are established for problems for TOW, REDEYE, and other supporting weapons in the battalion. Headquarters and support elements help with appropriate problems.

General guidance, as in the following examples, should be given by the battalion commander. Primary emphasis is on short, quick, tactically sound missions, of the type infantry units are called upon to execute frequently in combat.

Squad problems—two hours total time—include issuing order, execution, critique, and possibly repeating some part or parts.

Hasty defense or patrol problems might be longer—three- to four-hour limit.

X number of live-fire problems; Y number of night problems.

Once the squad problems are agreed on, platoon leaders work up the details, since they generally will conduct them.

Every squad in the battalion will run through each of the problems, which should include squad ambush, attack of a bunker, and squad patrol (each battalion commander can set out minimum requirements for his battalion).

Each day a squad goes through two or three of the nine to twelve problems. When the problems are completed, each company commander can compile the results from all the squad problems and designate the best squad in the company in that series of problems. The competition need go no higher.

A similar arrangement can be made for the platoon problems, which are conducted after the squad problems are finished and the platoon leaders are available to command their own platoons. Rather than having one long, continuous platoon problem, it is far better to have four to six good platoon problems, stressing use of supporting weapons and working with tanks or other weapons systems in the battalion and brigade. If each platoon goes through two problems in a twenty-four-hour period, ample time will be available for critique, discussion, and repetition if necessary. If the battalion commander desires, he can use his staff to set up the platoon problems. This will take some load off the company commanders, but the company commanders ought to be asked for ideas; they will undoubtedly have some. If you don't ask, they'll stop having ideas.

There is merit in having each company commander conduct one of the platoon problems. Commanders develop ideas on training and learn about the quality of their training by conducting exercises for their own elements and elements of other units. The details are better left to local commanders, but however the training is organized the commanders of the squads and platoons should command their own elements in each exercise.

A battalion with such a series of problems can set up and operate almost as if it were in combat. By having a specified time for each problem, transportation for moving elements to the problem areas, ammunition distributed to the ranges, hot meals, plus a communications net that is certain to be kept busy by special requests and reports, the whole battalion will experience good training. If problems start on schedule and if umpires, range guards, ammunition, food, and transportation all arrive at the right times and places, all the support elements in the battalion and the entire chain of command will be soundly tested. When all of these things are working well, the battalion is ready for

139

anything, and that includes fighting tomorrow.

This variety will start infantry training moving in the right direction, but the training in general will still have a long way to go. The following elaboration on the principle of variety demonstrates that thinking about what is to be done in training is vital to the art.

Troop leading: Cross-country movement

An exercise of great benefit is the process of cross country movement on a wide front. This may be practiced a whole company at a time not in attack but in a situation presumed to be dangerous, or as an approach movement. Platoon and squad formations are changed as required by the commanders thereof. This is, so to speak, a tactical "gymnastic" rather than a tactical problem: a company is simply started from one position to get to another, platoons abreast, squads sometimes abreast and sometimes in column, but all units properly dispersed and under good control, seeking to keep under best possible cover. It is also manifestly important that a small covering force precede the unit, as security. This simple exercise, repeated frequently on different terrain, occasionally at night, will greatly improve troop leading procedures.[3]

The "orders group"

The task of command can be simplified a bit by use of the term "Orders Group," the group being composed of subordinate commanders, including the FO, if any, and attached unit commanders. An infantry company commander desiring to assemble his key personnel simply says, "Orders Group on me," or, if applicable, "Orders Group, 1700 at point 16." Each commander, on an exercise or in operations, should specify who he wants in his orders group.

It is also helpful to have each key subordinate located in the same relative position during the issuance of orders or other instruction by the unit commander; e.g., the rifle platoon leaders of an infantry company should be located with the 1st platoon leader at the company commander's left, and the other rifle platoon leaders positioned clockwise in numerical order—the weapons platoon leader and any attached or supporting unit leaders being located at the right.

---

[3]This extract and the one following are from *Howze on Training* (Fort Benning, Ga., November 1971). They are included for two reasons. First, troop-leading procedures are pertinent to small-unit training. More important is the desire to call attention to this small pamphlet crammed with superb training guidance. All officers interested in troops and training should get a copy for frequent perusal.

Wearing equipment

Leaving equipment in the barracks is the sign of a lazy, slovenly unit whose men will not last long in combat. Certain levels of equipment are appropriate for different phases of training—full pack for a twenty-five-mile hike, strip pack for a forced march, combat pack for live-fire exercise, or whatever is prescribed by the local commander. All soldiers, however, must wear an essential minimum of equipment when they go to the field for training.

I have seen parachutists jumping from planes or helicopters with no equipment other than the regular and reserve parachutes, soldiers exiting from helicopters without individual weapons, officers with their platoons in the field without field glasses, compass, and other items of equipment essential to their mission. Each time I saw these and similar operations, I asked the commander what the unit was doing, and the reply was often "tactical training." It didn't look tactical to me.

Whenever military parachutists exit from an aircraft in training, a tactical situation should confront them when they hit the ground and they should have their individual weapons and combat gear with them. The same goes for troops lifted in helicopters or trucks. Transportation just gets the soldier to where he can start going about his business.

British and German units always have impressed me in this regard. Each individual had the gear appropriate to his rank and mission. Every commander should look at the tables of organization and equipment and common table of allowances to determine the mission-essential items for each individual, and then see to it that they are taken to training and cared for. Not many entrenching tools are seen in the training areas, but soldiers had better get used to wearing them because they are handy items when the shooting starts. Small units properly equipped look like the combat units they are supposed to be, and this observation leads naturally to the following discussion of realism in training.

REALISM

Everybody agrees with the need for realism in training. Yet realism is often ignored when it is most easily achieved in training, and made absurd by efforts to create it where it is difficult to achieve. The paradox suggests that good judgment and balance are important ingredients in realistic training. In my experience, those who thought the most about training had the most realistic training, and this was most evident in their small-unit training. Individual, crew, and small-unit training lend themselves to realism. In large units the problems of control, space, and diversity of activity make realism harder to achieve except insofar as it is practiced in small units. Some observations on efforts to achieve realism in training at several different levels of reality may suggest parameters and provide some guidance.

Too often young officers tend to think that the best way to get realism is to use a lot of blanks, explosives, smoke, and other types of training munitions. These things help if used properly, but they are expensive, cannot be used everywhere, and often are not available. Thinking counts more than noise. Achieving realism means doing properly the jobs that must be done on the battlefield with respect to the siting of weapons, camouflage, security—everything the soldier faces in his moment of truth. Taking proper equipment to training is a first step toward creating a realistic mental attitude. An entrenching tool worn to training reminds a soldier that he may have to use one; an officer wearing his field glasses is likely to scan the terrain ahead much more realistically than if he left them in barracks.

Major General Frank Mahin, who commanded the 33rd Division for a short time in WWII, taught that innumerable opportunities for realism exist in daily training. His guidance was, "Realism is to be sought by every practical means." Company officers crossing an open area in some small-unit problem were often surprised—shocked is a better word—to see a figure emerge from the woods at one side of the clearing and hear the command, "Freeze the unit in place." General Mahin would then conduct a critique on the spot, asking the troops where they thought the enemy would be to defend that clearing or assessing a number of casualties, which invariably included the leader who had been foolish enough to place his men in the open without proper reconnaissance. That was realism, and the lessons were learned.

This is an abbreviated extract from one of General Mahin's bits of guidance for battalion commanders.

Realism can be achieved by assessing several casualties, including the leader, when a group leaves cover without first studying the terrain. The action should be an exclamation: "Blast of machine gun fire from left front. You, you, and you are casualties." Let the casualties follow and observe. See what the second in command does. At the first reasonable opportunity when he has exposed himself, say: "A sniper over there has hit you as you stood there. You are severely wounded and unconscious." Then see what happens. Someone must take command. The private who does so without being told to is probably good NCO material. You can get realism by suddenly shouting: "Artillery shells!" Use your ingenuity and imagination. It will be worse than anything you can imagine the first time you are under real heavy fire.

General Mahin didn't say a word about blanks or simulators—they were in short supply at the time—but he did have ideas on how to inject realism into every phase of training. He emphasized the importance of speed of execution as a unit moved into contact and set up a demonstration to teach commanders how to train their units to resupply ammunition without delay to troops moving up for an attack. Thereafter resupply of ammunition was often practiced but seldom seen as units hiked down a road at night. The only sounds breaking the stillness would be the crunch of boots on gravel, the swish of fatigues, or a grunt as a pack was shifted. Suddenly a supply point at each side of the road would loom out of the darkness. As each man passed, a bandoleer of ammunition would be swung over his shoulders as he ducked his head. At the same moment he would reach out to take the grenades handed to him and pass full stride down the dark road. I have never seen any training more realistic. No noise, nothing flashy—just professionals at work.

Such is the way realism is injected into training. Put your thinking caps on. Realism in many aspects of training, especially small-unit training, can be achieved by troops doing correctly what they will have to do in combat to keep the casualties down—in using cover, concealment, and camouflage; selecting good firing positions; firing from defilade, or as much defilade as the weapons system will stand; avoiding straight lines and open areas; using fire and movement and supporting weapons to advance small groups of men; recognizing that the enemy will be hard to find and placing targets so that they will be hard to find in field firing exercises. Don't place targets in the open so the troops will get a lot of hits.

These are just a few out of hundreds of possible examples. Anyone who complains about not being able to make training realistic lacks the power of observation, tactical knowledge, or imagination. He may be deficient in all three areas—if so he should not be training troops. SCOPES, REALTRAIN, and other programs promoted by TRADOC in the mid-seventies will add to realism in training. When the time comes that the devices and support are not available, however, your imagination must go to work.

With respect to sound, realism can be introduced through the use of an infiltration course. The soldier who recognizes the crack of a bullet nearby and the sound of supporting fire overhead is better prepared to fight. When enemy weapons are available, soldiers can learn to distinguish between the sounds of their own weapons, especially small arms and machine guns, and those of the enemy. Important for soldiers who will be in forward positions, especially infantry, this bit of realism and education is worth the effort.

Nothing is more confusing and more likely to detract from realism than dividing field training into "tactical" and "administrative" groupings. Designating the company headquarters "administrative" while calling the platoons "tactical" doesn't make sense. Since front-line troops are rarely, if ever, administrative, field training should be tactical at all times. If administrative units have to participate in a field-training exercise, they should be separated from the tactical units.

During tests and field-training exercises, controllers, umpires, and observer personnel frequently drive through the tactical area at night with headlights on, build fires for warmth, and congregate in the open on a tactical position. Umpires and observers often park vehicles in the middle of a tactical position without camouflage, giving away the position to the opposing force. Such carelessness destroys realism for the individual soldier and reduces his enthusiasm. Controllers and visitors must strive to be as inconspicuous as possible while they are in a two-sided maneuver area.

At times, attempts are made to inject realism into training for which it is not appropriate. A prisoner-of-war situation cannot be made realistic in training because the atmosphere of prisoner-of-war camps is impossible to duplicate. Every attempt I have seen has been a fiasco. A lot of profanity, loud shouting, waving of clubs, and occasionally a little brutality seeping in constitute part of the act. The prisoners are only too happy to show their bravery and belligerence because they are quite certain the guards are not going to hurt them. Quiet reading of prisoner-of-war reports from World War II and the Korean and Vietnam conflicts and possibly the viewing of a documentary training film is the best way to prepare for a situation that no one wants to be in, but that does occur.

Basic schools and NCO academies conduct a Leader's Reaction Course to identify leadership strengths and weaknesses in students. One half the group performs tasks and the other half observes. The basic program is good, but a precedent of controlled harassment and heckling by the observers has developed to put pressure on the leader and team performing the tasks. Observation of this training indicates that the heckling tends to be extreme and that the exaggerated shouting and epithets detract from the training atmosphere. A French general officer who observed this training in a service school said the harassment made no sense to him. It does not add realism to the training.

My experience indicates that as a general rule efforts to inject realism into what is a state-of-mind situation often result in undesirable and unrealistic training. The fears and pressures of combat result only when one believes that life is at stake and the enemy is near. The objective of realism in training is not so much to create fear or pressure as it is to foster an understanding of the extreme mental and physical demands of combat. The objective should be to make a soldier realize, insofar as he can, what really happens when the shells start flying and to imbue him with the firm conviction that he can still function

144

effectively once the fighting begins. Commanders can inject realism most effectively into day-to-day training by insisting that the troops do correctly what they will have to do in combat. Only commanders who are observant, know tactics and weapons, have high standards, and know how to maintain them can attain the goal. This subject requires clear thinking and is a worthwhile subject for discussion and clarification at the service schools.

14

The benefits from a field training exercise extend to units two levels below the highest headquarters participating.

Large-Unit Training

Until the early 1970s, if anyone had asked me what was meant by large-unit training I would have answered, "Division and above." I would now place the brigade under the large-unit tent. The organizational trends in our own and other armies, the stationing of our forces in Germany, the operations in Vietnam, and the lethality of the modern battlefield as demonstrated in the 1973 Arab-Israeli War have all contributed to this change in view.

Throughout my service I have repeatedly observed that in a maneuver, or field-training exercise (FTX), which is the normal form of large-unit training, the higher the level of the participating units, the poorer the performance of the small units. Exceptions to this generalization were rare. Research indicates that this has been a consistent criticism of large-unit training since the Louisiana Maneuvers in 1941. In 1963 I was asked for my observations on large-unit maneuvers conducted by U.S. Strike Command. An extract from my notes follows:

> *One of the major weaknesses in the U.S. Army continues to be the small-unit training. It is not unusual to go along a road and see some men standing around near a crossroad with their 106s on the brow of a hill, their machine guns emplaced at the side of the road, their vehicles right beside them at the intersection and then find out from the company commander or the lieutenant in charge that he is conducting a delaying action. Non-commissioned officers just do not pick out good positions for their*

weapons. No one thinks of pulling vehicles back behind the brow of the next hill; men do not withdraw through the woods or over the best ground available while someone covers their withdrawal.

What's the reason for it? Well, there are many. One—that we are not placing the responsibility where it belongs and putting the pressure on the subordinate commanders. A second reason might be that too many people are flitting around in helicopters. You just don't see the spots on the leopard when you're 2-3000 feet up, or else you are reluctant to stop to correct what appear to be the little things, but which add up to be most important in developing well disciplined fighting units.

Similar weaknesses were evident in large-unit exercises in the 1970s. The problem is persistent.

Over the years, observing exercises has led me to the following rule of thumb: The benefits from a field-training exercise extend to units two levels below the highest headquarters participating. In a company-level exercise, the platoons, squads, tank crews, and gun sections derive the most benefit; a battalion exercise benefits the company and platoon level; a brigade exercise benefits the battalion and company level; and so on. If this is a sound rule of thumb, and if the training of individuals and small units is the real key to successful training, then field exercises above battalion level do not add much to the quality of training. The large-unit exercises consume time and resources that could be better used to improve individual and small-unit training, the foundations of unit readiness. Battalion-level exercises should not be held too often; once a year is enough. Other opportunities will certainly arise for battalions to go to the field in the joint exercise program and in operational-readiness tests.

Some will disagree strongly with this outlook on large-unit training, but there are good historical precedents to argue persuasively that full-scale division and brigade level FTXs are not essential to achieving a fully trained status. For World War II, the Japanese trained a formidable fighting force with no exercises above battalion level. The training of the *Wehrmacht* emphasized small-unit training and was done for the most part near home *kasernes* (barracks).

Corps, division, and brigade commanders will want to check communications and the training of their staffs and subordinate staffs through battalion level. They can do so through command-post exercises (CPXs). Map exercises provide good training for corps and division commanders and their staffs. Reduced-distance exercises for commanders and staff are valuable at brigade and battalion level. All these forms of training can be done without the cost and loss of troop time involved in large-unit field-training exercises.

Command-post exercises should be held at intervals so that commanders, staffs, and communications personnel can practice proper procedures. They should·be conducted in the field with realistic distances among participating headquarters in order to make a fair test of the communications and the command and control systems of the element involved. It does not take many CPXs and FTXs to develop battalion, brigade, and division teamwork, because commanders of these units have staff officers of considerable experience and background in military operations.

In times past I have questioned the value of holding CPXs at reduced distances because they tend to produce false impressions about the effectiveness of communications. With the increase in the cost of fuel, however, and the energy resources required to move all the communications elements to the field, the reduced-distance exercise might be a necessary alternative for the future. Recognizing the limitations, commanders must give thought to the tradeoffs in a reduced-distance CPX because there are benefits to be derived.

As a regimental commander, I conducted reduced-distance CPXs for my battalions and their companies when training funds were low. At regimental level we set up a small control headquarters of three or four staff members to help me out. The battalion headquarters were just over the hill, but out of sight. The company headquarters were similarly hidden from the battalion headquarters. The whole layout was not more than 500 to 800 yards in depth, and field phones provided the communications. This arrangement enabled me to walk from control headquarters to battalion or company level to see what was going on and to listen to the discussions on the situation. Also, it was easy for the battalion commanders to assemble their company commanders to discuss what was happening. And, not the least of the benefits, it provided a wonderful opportunity to get better acquainted with battalion and company commanders. The simplicity allowed for easy personal interchange between commanders and an opportunity to watch them in action. Although these exercises lasted only one day, all of us involved were a bit surprised at how much we had benefited from these very simple training exercises.

Despite the cited drawbacks of large-unit exercises, a certain number of them will be scheduled. One good reason is the need for joint training, and this can be provided through the joint-exercise program. Since large-unit exercises will continue, a few observations that merit commanders' consideration follow.

A large-unit exercise or maneuver is neither an operational-readiness test nor an Army Training Test, but too many commanders have come to look on them that way and conduct rehearsals. Every commander wants to do well on a maneuver, but several warm-up exercises should not be necessary. I have seen corps maneuvers in which the battalions, brigades, and divisions went out for a rehearsal in that order. By the time the big maneuver came around, the troops had spent too many days on exercises that deprived company-level commanders of time needed for small-unit training, which, as stated earlier, is just what gets neglected in the large-unit exercises.

Another problem for large-unit commanders is the operational-readiness report, which has been given so much emphasis and visibility in the past ten years. At the highest levels of Department of Defense or Department of the Army there is a tendency, especially among civilian secretaries, to expect all battalion-size units in the large units, like divisions, to reach peak proficiency at the same time and to maintain that peak. Because of the replacement training flow, availability of major training areas, and other factors that affect the state of training, different battalions and squadrons will be reaching peak proficiency at different times during the year. To accommodate reporting requirements, some large units designed programs that would, they hoped, bring subordinate units to the highest state of operational readiness just in time for the large-unit exercise programmed for that year.

The peaking of training for all battalion-size units in a division, brigade, or group is not practical in a peacetime environment. Training facilities, demands of National Guard and Reserve training programs, and a host of other day-to-day realities, like the personnel flow, will not permit all battalion-size units to reach a high state of readiness at the same time. Peaks and valleys in the state of training are inevitable. This fact of life should be accepted and training programs should be designed to make the best of it.

Study over a period of time indicates that proficiency for larger units deteriorates if the lower units do not have systematic measures to upgrade individual and small-unit training. If large units design a training program to sustain and reinforce individual and small-unit skills throughout the year, and if they conduct CPXs and space battalion tests evenly throughout the year, they can maintain the highest practicable state of combat readiness over the long haul.

During the past thirty years, being opposed to a large-unit exercise in the Army was akin to heresy. Recent publications of TRADOC and some other major commands indicate a renewed awareness of the crucial importance of field training exercises at battalion and lower unit levels, even at the expense of large-unit exercises.[1] I hope the heretics prevail.

---

[1]Par. 8a, FORSCOM FY 75 Training Objectives.

15

In any large-scale military organization, a relatively small number of men under arms personally experience combat.

Combat Arms Training

Direct your attention now to the quality of combat arms training, especially to infantry training, for it needs the most attention. Quality of personnel is a major factor in the quality of training, and the combat arms get short-changed in the personnel area. At the national level, there has been little effort to assure an equitable distribution of the talents to the respective services (see Chapter 19). The Army does have control of the distribution of personnel once they are in the Army, however, so any shortcomings on assignment of Army resources to the combat arms in general or the infantry in particular are an Army responsibility.

In any large-scale military organization, a relatively small number of men under arms personally experience combat.[1] This statement will continue to hold true in modern warfare, and the Army will be well served by seeing to it that the most competent and most intelligent men available are assigned to the combat arms. They have not been so assigned in the past, and they are not being so assigned now. But let us turn first to the low branch on the totem pole—the infantry.

---

[1]Charles C. Moskos, Jr., *The American Enlisted Man* (New York: Russell Sage Foundation, 1970), p. 138.

INFANTRY TRAINING

The Indian guide to statecraft, *Arthashastra*, written about 300 B.C., devoted a page of close print to the functions of elephants in an army and only one line to the functions of infantry: "At all times to carry weapons to all places and to fight."[2] Things haven't changed much in the last twenty-two hundred years with regard to slighting the infantry, but it would be hard to improve on that one-line quotation on the role of the infantry.

The poorest training in the United States Army is infantry training. The poor quality of the training is widespread, for several reasons. One is that a lot of people, including members of the military profession, think infantry training is relatively simple—just teach a man with a gun to either move forward to take a piece of ground or stay in a position to defend an area so small it can be of no great importance. Another reason is that only a few people are aware of how demanding and varied infantry training must be. Once combat is joined, the importance of the infantry becomes manifest. After the casualties mount up, the scramble to provide infantry units with replacements begins, but the infantry units are so low in the priority lists that they don't get the quality of personnel they need.

Too many of those responsible for training management and supervision do not think enough about when, where, and how the infantry fight. Over the years, I have listened to many lectures on the complexities of communications training, the precision of artillery training, or the importance of timing and teamwork in armor training. But few training managers recognize, let alone admit, that no training requires the variety and demands of infantry training. The infantryman must learn to execute more different missions than the soldiers of any other branch. He must accomplish the missions under the most adverse conditions of the combat environment, with all its hardships and hazards, for prolonged periods. Sustained combat is the role of the infantry. Ambushes, day and night patrols, city fighting, mountain warfare, attack and defense in a variety of forms, river crossings, amphibious landings—to name a few—all require special knowledge and additional training. In those situations, the fire missions for the artillery are much the same. The variety of missions are not all suited to armor. The most varied and difficult training confronting the combat-arms commander is infantry training. It should never be dull and uninteresting, but too often it is. We had better determine what the flaws in our thinking have been because, as a distinguished British general once wrote, "The whole alertness of a front, however wide, ultimately turns on the infantryman. By day or

---

[2]Quoted in Philip Mason, *A Matter of Honor* (New York: Holt, Rinehart, and Winston, 1974), p. 43.

night, in fog, in rain or in snow, it is he who stands sentry and guards the front. The front crumbles when infantry crumble. The front holds when infantry hold."[3]

History and tradition are partly responsible for the poor quality of infantry training. Historically, the infantry was the cannon fodder marching forward to the beat of the drum, in closed ranks, to charge the cannoneers. Even as late as the battle of Gettysburg massed infantry marched across open fields in the face of muskets and cannons. Over a hundred years later, in spite of all the advances in weaponry, one can still read in some periodical of the countless places in the infantry that can be filled by men with less than average intelligence. Unfortunately, too few combat infantrymen become writers and opinion makers on matters so vital to individual and national security.

The brigade organization has contributed to the deterioration of infantry training. A regimental commander, brought up in the infantry, was conversant with the complexity of infantry training. He was senior enough and confident enough to question directives from higher staffs which impeded training. He let each battalion commander manage the training of his battalion and pursue a training program which each one swore produced the "best battalion in the regiment," if not the Army. The regimental commander gave guidance during his visits and kept things in balance by suggesting ways for battalion commanders to do the job better. At the same time he knew which was the best battalion in the regiment and why it was best.

In the brigade organization the brigade commander is often from a different branch of the service. The difference doesn't cause much of a problem in combat, but it does create problems when units are training. The brigade commander may be a splendid commander from another combat-arms branch —but few from other branches know enough about the full range of infantry missions to be good infantry trainers. The same thing can be said for officers of other branches who become general officers and wind up in the training chain of command. They frequently impose requirements in the training of infantry that are not realistic, given the multitude of tasks for which an infantry unit must be trained.

Many aspects of artillery and armor training lend themselves to quantification and statistical comparisons; complex scoring and procedures evolve that are manageable burdens in specific phases of training. However, applying similar statistical indexes to infantry training is absurd. Who knows what each individual will do in an infantry squad of nine to twelve men? How each man will use the ground? Whom he will shoot at? Where he will move to next? An infantry squad is not like a gun section setting, laying, and firing a gun, or like a tank crew working as a team to take under fire the target the tank commander has designated. A good infantry squad will act as a team, but there will be so

---

[3]Sir Richard N. Gale, "Infantry Today and Tomorrow," *Army* (March 1957), p. 51.

many opportunities for independent action in a close infantry engagement that no one can really be certain which individuals will act, and which action will be vital in each of the numerous, small, sudden encounters that are typical of infantry action in close combat.

The battlefield is a very lonesome place for the infantryman. Even though a member of a squad, he is not confined to a precise role as is a member of a helicopter or tank crew, nor can he see the gun which is the object of all the artilleryman's attention. If the infantryman is lucky, he might be able to see the man on his right or his left, but even that view is everchanging. So infantry training does not lend itself to some of the more precise gunnery situations that artillery and armor commanders can use for crew training and small-unit training.

Worse than imposing requirements that are not helpful in training is the practice of placing infantry battalions in support roles in order to allow the more technically oriented units to accomplish their "complex" training. Too often brigade commanders lack the confidence to request a change when instructions coming from corps or division on infantry training do not make sense. Some brigade commanders just let the instructions stand, and a frustrated infantry battalion commander tries to attain the higher levels of training prescribed so that the high-level units can participate in the big field exercises. The result is neglect of the individual and small-unit training so important to the infantry. When the big FTX comes along, therefore, the infantry units are usually just out for a walk or a ride, but they are far enough off the road so that they are seldom seen and their poor performance goes unnoticed.

My intention is not to criticize artillery or armor commanders. Infantry brigade commanders lack the detailed knowledge to train well the battalions of the other arms. They are prone to stay away from the armor and artillery battalions and cavalry squadrons because they don't know much about them, and they leave the training to the respective commanders. To compensate they tend to hover over the infantry battalions giving the infantry battalion commanders more attention than they want. It is not easy to develop the expertise to train troops well in several arms of the service. An occasional officer can do it, but he is a rare bird and is just about extinct. There are too few troop-assignment opportunities for gaining the basic knowledge required at the company and battalion level for all the arms. Further, many of our brigade commanders lack the experience with troops that would make them good trainers even in their own branch. But this lack accentuates the need for all commanders, regardless of background, to recognize how much is involved in training infantry units and not brush the job off as something anyone can do. Though commanders can be faulted on this attitude, the policies of the Army as a whole and the failure of the school systems to emphasize training contribute significantly to the distorted picture some commanders have.

What are some of the manifestations of neglect that stem from Army policies? The quality of personnel assigned to the infantry is one. Just check the distribution of talents for almost any period in the last fifty years. Do some decision makers believe that because infantry casualties are so high there is no point to risking the lives of the more intelligent citizens who are called to the defense of their country in the infantry? Past practice of assigning a high percentage of low-quality personnel to the Army is also pertinent in a period of an all-volunteer force. The volunteer situation results in the Army's getting a lower percentage of individuals in the higher mental categories. This result is felt thoughout the Army; thus, the combat arms get a higher percentage of those in the lower mental categories and the infantry gets the highest percentage of those scoring lowest in the classification tests. In a volunteer force the infantry gets the individuals who are left, the ones who are not in a position to exercise some other choice.

This situation in the distribution of individuals also contributes to the large number of infantry casualties. In peacetime the noncommissioned officers in the infantry come from the ranks of soldiers who start out as infantry privates. In time of war the same will be true for the junior officers as well. Some resourceful and fine leaders will emerge, but on the whole the higher the mental category in any group, the more competent will be the individual members of that group. No branch of the Army is more in need of intelligent, capable leaders than the infantry. A leader will accomplish his training and missions better if he has a little more grey matter than the leader who has not been so well endowed by his creator. Not only would training be better, but I believe the number of casualties in combat would be reduced if the infantry got a better slice of the higher category soldier. In time fairer apportionment would produce better leadership and better chances for survival in the branch that has traditionally taken more than 75 percent of the casualties in combat.

Army policy contributes to the poor quality of infantry training when it condones such directives in training guidelines that say, "Fill of tank battalions should take precedence over fill of infantry battalions." Such guidance, common in the U.S. Army, leads some commanders to think tank training is more important or more complex than infantry training, which it is not. Once this attitude has been created—and it has been in some commands—the next step is to have the infantry battalions support the tank battalions while the armor units are at major training areas. I recall visiting brigades at major training areas where the infantry battalions were providing support for the armor battalions that were going through their tank-gunnery programs. In one extreme case, an infantry battalion spent twenty-two out of thirty days at the major training areas supporting the armor battalions. The last eight days had been made available to the infantry battalion for conducting squad and platoon problems and finishing up its field firing. As you can imagine, the performance was below par, and the infantry soldiers and commanders were neither happy nor impressed with the importance of infantry training. I can only conclude that a lot of other senior commanders did not consider infantry training important, since no one from the corps commander through the brigade commander had stopped what was going on. Surely one of them, the division commander above all, should have noted and corrected this gross abuse of proper training management.

There is no need to continue to cite examples of the poor quality of infantry training. Suffice it to say that those already cited are not isolated instances. In some units the neglect of infantry training has been going on for several years. My purpose is to make you aware of this situation. It is time it was recognized and corrected.

I could be accused of branch bias since I am an infantryman. But I believe that one can look objectively at training deficiencies, since the fundamental weaknesses stretch across the board. What saddens me is that so many of our senior commanders do not recognize how poor our infantry training is, or if they do they don't know what to do about it. Sadder still, infantry commanders with such a variety of types of training to teach their men miss the opportunity to provide the genuine satisfaction that comes from demanding, thought-provoking, interesting training which will give the infantry soldier the pride and ability his combat role demands.

The basic message in this chapter is that infantry training has been thrust into the background. This situation may have resulted from guidelines that give other elements in the Army priority in numbers and quality, but whatever the reasons, no army with poor infantry is going to win a war. The good army will train all elements to perform their respective missions as part of a combined-arms group, all working together to accomplish the mission with a minimum of casualties. This is the true measure of a fighting force.

Since it appears that the brigade organization is here to stay, and since the brigade organization does provide more opportunities for combined-arms training, the Army had better give special attention to infantry training. The service schools, to include the Command and General Staff College and the Army War College, could help by insuring that officers of all arms gain a better appreciation of the complexity and demands of infantry training. An encouraging sign is an Annex to a Division Training Directive, contained in a 1975 course of the Command and General Staff College. The Annex, entitled Training of Infantry, covers the subject so well it is included here (Figure 15.1, see p. 159).

The following extracts from a fine book on infantry training written in 1917 might help young officers, and older ones too, to turn their thoughts to the demands of infantry training and the command of infantry units:

Let us remember the great part that is played by the infantry soldier in war. The artillery help us, the cavalry help us, and the engineers are there to confirm our success and overcome obstacles, but it is the infantry soldier, officer and man, who must bear the great stress of battle. He has no immovable gun to serve, and no horse to carry him forward; of his own initiative he advances against the enemy's position with a fixed determination to drive him back and defeat him. It is not generally considered that he requires any very high training, and yet his training in the correct use of ground and of his rifle, in the dire stress of battle, is more complicated and more difficult than that of any other arm of the service. He is more influenced than any other soldier by those characteristics of the human mind which are adverse to success; ground is never the same and can never be treated in the same way, and therefore we can give no fixed rules to work by.[4]

* * * *

The training of an infantry company for war, considered by the uninitiated as one of the simplest things in the world, is in reality the most complex; it is one constant struggle against human nature, and incessant variations of the tactical situation and of the ground, to say nothing of the frequent changes in the company as regards the junior officers and noncommissioned officers.[5]

ARTILLERY TRAINING

In my experience, whenever a piece of equipment is vital to the mission accomplishment of some arm or service, a special advantage accrues to the organizations both in training and the development of esprit. Whether cannon, tank, aircraft, or bulldozer, as long as it takes a crew to operate and maintain it a special attachment develops between the crew and the piece of equipment. The more the mission demands of each member of the crew, the better the training and the higher the morale. Perhaps the best example of this phenomenon is the artillery. The training of U.S. Artillery in fire missions and in providing fire support is superb, and the artillery has a special esprit built around the cannon that helps maintain that "Redleg" tradition. In combat, I have never known a time when our infantry—or any other arm of service— lacked confidence in our artillery. But when the artillery turns to the common training not related to fire missions—training such as first aid, map reading, and the like—it is guilty of the poor training practices common to all branches; that is, too much talk and too little practical application. There is the occasional martinet who believes that nothing contributes more to artillery training than the

---

[4]R. C. B. Haking, *Company Training* (London: Hugh Rees, Ltd., 1917), pp. 105-6.
[5]*Ibid.*, pp. 461-62.

"cannoneers' hop." A few minutes of this exercise has some merit, but when it goes on and on, as it sometimes does, it is a waste of the cannoneers' time. It is also a sign of poor leadership.

ARMOR TRAINING

Armor training is strong in the same sense as artillery training. The tank in particular, and other armor vehicles in general, requires extensive crew training. The armor trooper feels about his tank just as the cannoneer feels about his gun. Crew training and qualification firing are highly systemized, easily scored, and well done. The tank crew qualification course (TCQC) is the climax of training for the tank crew. In the past, I believe, individual crew training has been emphasized too heavily and at the expense of platoon firing and tactics. Since combat experience shows that in an armor battle speed and accuracy of fire are vital to success, it is hard to fault stress on the tank-crew qualification course. Further, the firing fans required for a platoon of tanks in a live-fire exercise limit the use of the ranges, and anyone familiar with training knows what a critical commodity range space is. But individual tank crews will not win battles; tank platoons will. Tank platoon leaders need more opportunities to command a tank platoon acting as a unit in a live-fire exercise.

In this respect, the three-tank platoon used by the British, Israeli, German, and Russian armies has much to recommend it. For the armor commander who complains about not having enough men and too small a training area, a three-tank platoon would provide an opportunity to train tank platoon leaders and tank commanders to work together. Given the lethality of the modern battlefield, there may be an advantage in the smaller tank platoon. There would be more leadership up front, and additional units could be organized for battle while a unit that has been fighting is refitted.

Armor training, except for that which focuses on tank gunnery and other firing courses, suffers from the same lack of imagination as that for all other arms. One aspect of armor training needs to be brought into balance: maintenance, which at this time is a major deficiency. Mechanized vehicles do need detailed attention; they should have supervised operator and crew maintenance every day. The maintenance in recent years, however, has been translated into many hours of "Maintenance" on the training schedule, which is poorly organized, wastes time, and is boring to the troops. I am not talking here about a "Q Service," when an entire platoon goes to the tank maintenance area for a quarterly service. That is most proper. My complaint is with instances when one to three weeks of "Maintenance" appears on the training schedule for entire companies or battalions, and a visit to the track park discloses that only one or two members from each crew are present and that there is little or no supervision.

One of the great strengths of armor units is the interest of the officers in tank gunnery. These officers are dissatisfied when it is not good, and they are curious as to how they can make it better when it is good. Their attitude is conducive to good shooting and this in itself will result in improved performance. If this same interest can be generated in platoon tactics and the maintenance can be kept in balance, armor training will get high marks.

COMBAT ENGINEERS

The Corps of Engineers is designated as one of the combat arms, but only the combat engineers fulfill that role on a day-to-day basis. Combat engineers approach pioneer and demolition training, construction and clearance of obstacles, and attack of fortified positions with zest. Many engineer soldiers are drawn to that branch of the service because they are practical by nature and working with tools and heavy equipment appeals to them. Incorporation of small combat-engineer teams with infantry, armor, and artillery units at the company level provides good training opportunities for all.

Engineers provide river-crossing capabilities which are vital to an army. Opportunities to exercise this capability also test a commander's ingenuity. If a river is navigable, those who use the river do not want it closed to traffic. Practical work for these units requires thorough advance planning and imaginative commanders.

Combat-engineer units do their own specialties well. When it comes to the common subjects, however, training in engineer units can be as dull as that in all other branches, unless of course the unit is lucky enough to have a commander who is truly interested in training.

FIGURE 15.1.
ANNEX B. TRAINING OF INFANTRY*

DEPARTMENT OF THE ARMY

Headquarters_____and Fort_____

Fort_____ , _____ _____

1. The infantryman in combat has the most demanding job in the
   Army. His job requires an almost superhuman combination of
   skills, endurance, and acceptance of personal risk. Yet, his is a
   job that must be done by ordinary men. The task of infantry
   leaders is to make infantrymen out of ordinary men. Once this is
   done, these men are no longer ordinary; they are extraordinary
   — they are infantrymen. Yet, they are the same men.

2. The skill and training of infantrymen is of primary importance
   in the division. This annex deals only with the training of the
   infantryman in the rifle squad and rifle platoon. Training in
   weapon skills, land navigation, first aid, field craft, and the
   various other individual subjects that infantrymen must know
   well is covered elsewhere, as is the training of mortar crewmen,
   106-mm recoilless rifle teams, radio operators, and other
   infantrymen.

3. The rifle platoons and squads of the division are the cutting edge
   of the division. The rest of the division, with all its helicopters,
   artillery, logistics, communications, and other combat, combat
   support, and combat service support exists for only one reason
   — to assist, support, provide mobility for, and otherwise
   multiply the effectiveness of these rifle squads and platoons.
   The division can be no more effective than its rifle squads and
   platoons. These small units will bear the brunt of combat. Their
   performance will ultimately determine whether, and how well,
   the division performs its mission.

4. The basis of squad and platoon training and operations in the
   division is the booklet, "Handbook of Infantry Tactics,
   Division." All infantry leaders should study that handbook
   carefully and master its contents completely.

5. Infantry squad and platoon training is a matter of the following:
   a. Simple drills, repeated again and again.
   b. Intelligent tactical judgment by leaders, adapting these
      simple drills to the existing situation.
   c. Simple orders, using the chain of command. Orders are given
      by voice, by radio, by hand and arm signals, and by example
      ("follow me").

  d. Disciplined, responsive obedience to these orders.

  e. Initiative of infantrymen in doing what is right in the absence of orders.

  f. Discipline and adherence to basic standards.

6. The infantry leader at brigade, battalion, company, and platoon level must have a consuming devotion to maintaining the strength and integrity of the rifle squad. Leaders must take every possible measure to maintain their men's fitness, to keep the squad intact, and to train the squad as a team with all members present. The division should recruit enough infantry to fill every rifle squad to at least nine men assigned. Only as a last resort may men of two or more squads be combined into a single squad to make it "big enough." In general, when a squad trains as a team, no man should be absent without an overriding reason. This key principle must pervade the attitude of leaders to squad and platoon training. The squad operates as a team, trains as a team, works as a team, and lives as a team, so that when it goes into operation, it will function as a disciplined, confident, and competent team of highest quality.

7. Training of the infantry squad and platoon differs from other military training. It is not centered around an item of equipment, such as a tank or howitzer. It is built entirely around the idea of the team, which is only an idea in the minds of its members, agreed upon and accepted by them, and used by the leader directing the team.

8. Infantry tactics take place on the terrain, which, with its folds, vegetation, and relief, is the infantryman's best friend. The infantryman who can take advantage, will live longer and will accomplish his missions more quickly.

9. Infantry combat is against a live and thinking enemy. Battle on the smallest level is the interaction of the two opposing sides — each determined with deadly weapons to destroy the other. The mix of weapon capabilities, infantrymen's skills, terrain, and tactics is what finally determines the outcome of the battle. This outcome is affected directly by the tactical skill and determination of the leader.

10. An infantry training situation must be realistically portrayed to the troops (as to the weapons, the terrain, and the enemy) in such a way that the soldier can see in his mind what situation he is in. For the most part, our young infantry soldier has not seen combat. He must use his imagination to visualize what it will be like. Leaders must take time to set up the situation carefully and talk with their men about it at enough length so that the troops will understand what the specific exercise is all about.

11. Furthermore, in every instance in which training is conducted, the dispositions of the friendly force, its employment, and what it is expected to do must make sense in real terms. The thinking infantryman rapidly understands when these dispositions do not make sense. When he makes an unnecessary direct assault on a heavily defended position, his mind tells him that "something is wrong here." He resents the idea of his life being put at risk unnecessarily by leaders who do not take into consideration the realities of the situation as they move about accomplishing their mission. But when he realizes that his leaders are men of skill in whom he can have confidence, his loyalty and devotion are boundless.

12. In training, each leader must put himself both in the enemy's shoes and in the shoes of the thinking soldiers in his organization. In a pre-exercise "skull session" with his men, the leader should ask, "Is that really the way we should do this?" He should use the terrain — every fold, every ditch, every hill, every treeline; he should use his weapons to their best effects; he should use finesse, maneuver, and skill; he should use the darkness when he can; he should calculate his advantages and the enemy's disadvantages and then maximize his advantages against the enemy's disadvantages; he should recognize that sweat saves blood; he should make plans that conserve his ammunition and the strength of his men for the decisive attack or action. He should use the coordinated firepower of his own small arms, together with the supporting firepower of mortars, artillery, and air. He should put all of these factors together in the best combination to save his men's lives and to accomplish the mission. When the time comes, he may have to use the brute force of infantry in the assault, but this should be done under conditions of great advantage to his own unit and disadvantage to the enemy.

13. Any leader responsible for setting up a training exercise for a squad or platoon has to go through a certain sequence.

    a. First, he has to find a piece of ground — one which is reasonably realistic to the visualized unit mission and to the purpose of the training. This is usually not hard, because infantry operates everywhere.

    b. Then, he has to set up the exercise. What is the overall situation? Where is the enemy? What is the rest of the platoon doing? What is the mission of the squad? The situation has to be understood by the men. In battle, the soldier is fairly clear as to his own situation. He is in it and part of it. But, in training he has to take more time to absorb or understand the assumed situation he is being placed in.

He has to discuss the situation and have it clear in his mind before he goes any further. The squad leader must insure that his men understand "What is the situation in this particular training exercise?" and, "What is our mission?"

c. Next, the leader has to think out his own approach to the problem. Is it an attack problem? If so, he has to figure out his own organization, his formation, and his route of advance. Is it a defense problem? If so, he has to determine where his positions are, the locations of his crews and weapons, and the locations of his men's individual foxholes. If it is a delay problem, he has to figure out timing, the positions to be occupied, and the best use of the terrain. Whatever the problem, he has to think. Whether it be a squad as an antitank patrol, on a night raid, or on a security mission, he has to think the problem through (considering the terrain, the enemy, his own forces, and the mission) and come up with the best tactical plan that will accomplish the mission under the conditions that are established.

d. Infantry tactics have endless variation. No two situations are alike. There is no pat answer to every situation. At the same time, because of this great complexity and variety, it is most important that simplicity be the keynote of infantry operations. Simplicity, teamwork, discipline, and standard drills must be clear in the mind of the members and adapted to the situation by the leader, depending on the conditions that exist. A reasonable solution, well executed — this is what we seek.

e. Having done all this, the leader is then in a position to go out and train his men and do it right.

14. All of the above is only the prelude to this: Infantry training must be done right.

a. If the training exercise is not done right the first time, the unit should do it again — the same day, on the same ground — until it is done right. Leaders must understand and comply with this fundamental guidance.

b. Each leader in the field must insist that his men "do it right." Usually the men know what is right. It takes the strength of leaders to require that they do what is right, no matter how tired they are, how long they have been in combat or in the field, or that they have been under pressure. Doing what is right will save their lives.

c. Infantry troops tend to bunch up. Leaders must keep them spread out, for their own protection, to keep one high explosive round, one grenade, one booby trap, or one burst of fire from wiping out a group of men. How do leaders do this? They can stop and move each man, one at a time, if necessary. The division battle drill cry can be used.

d. Weapons on "safe," camouflage, personal hygiene, range cards, weapons cleaning, voice radio procedure, individual loads — these are only a few of the areas where leaders must insist on "doing it right."

e. And finally, when the squad or platoon is out there on the ground going through its exercise, the leader's watchful eye catches the unit or men that are not doing it right. The leader then corrects the error right there, on the spot. If necessary, the exercise is repeated until it is done right. Supervision is the key.

15. Leaders — do what we say in this annex and in the "Handbook on Infantry Tactics." Do it in a thinking, motivated, self-critical, and determined way. If you do, you — infantry leader — will have elite infantry. That is the standard of the division.

* Extract from Course 9005, Training, 1975, USA Command and General Staff College.

 *In spite of all that is written by its critics, the Army has always striven to maintain a high standard of honor and integrity.*

Competition, Testing, and Inspections

Americans are born competitors. The trait is most apparent among sports fans, whose desire to back the number one team is loudly and visibly displayed at a big game. The desire to be at the top is so much a part of the American way of life that it surfaces naturally in the Army, where it is reinforced by the élan and rivalry of military organizations. To want to do well is essential for success, but carried to extremes the determination to be first can be corrosive. When it occurs in the Army it can undermine integrity, and too much competition adversely affects training.

COMPETITION: INFLUENCE ON INTEGRITY

Consider the natural carry-over of the competitive spirit from the civilian athletic scene. Like the coaches who don't hestitate to violate the recruiting rules to get a good prospect, some officers in times past were known to manipulate the assignment system so that the best athletes would all be in one unit which would be sure to win the athletic trophy. It did not matter to the manipulators that other units did not get a fair share of the talent. Hopefully the current assignment system will make similar practices impossible, but the tendency to win at all costs is also found in range competitions. Qualification scores are important indexes of a unit's readiness and a commander's competence. Sometimes when the marksmanship in a unit is not very good an appropriate caliber pencil is used to puncture the target or a weak tank crew is reinforced by the unit's best gunner while the regular gunner hides out during the qualification run. When such habits begin to emerge, compromising integrity in military matters is on the march.

There is also the international competition in which a representative automatic-weapons crew or squad will compete. The senior generals are the first to say, "It's important to win, our national prestige is at stake," so the commander responsible screens the units for the best soldiers and the best weapons men. The "representative" squad is then placed in a special training detachment with several other squads so constituted, and those soldiers spend most of the year preparing for a brief competition of but a few days. The first thing you know, several hundred men are involved in the training of this "representative" squad. It is easy to rationalize such a practice. "They"—the other countries—do the same thing, and national prestige is worth the effort. But is it? These compromises of principle contribute to the erosion of integrity, as well as to the erosion of training that results when so many competent soldiers and their trainers are absent from their units.

Now add the ambitious commanders who make all men deposit a signed leave application with the first sergeant so that, if someone goes absent without leave for a few days, the fact does not show up in the adverse statistics. The pressure to look good mounts as fund drives get under way, and someone encourages the engineers to sell gravel from the river bed in order to make the unit contribution the biggest in the command. Again it is easy to rationalize; no one in the unit benefits and it is all for a worthy cause. Do the goal setters ever wonder what effect those actions have on the outlook of the soldier or the young officer?

In spite of all that is written by its critics, I believe the Army has always striven to maintain a high standard of honor and integrity. Given the national norms, I believe the Army has done pretty well in this regard, but it is important to do better. Too often today the reason given for doing something that is not appropriate is that "everyone else does it." All the more reason for commanders to set high standards. Some of the examples I have given are signals of wider contamination; commanders must be alert to stamp them out. Battalion and brigade commanders are on the front lines in the battle to eliminate the kind of practices cited. They know, or should learn to recognize, when such subterfuges are taking place. This is still another arena in which lieutenant colonels and colonels earn their pay, and where they also earn respect. Too many lack the confidence to stand up and be counted because of their limited experience with troops and because the competition for promotion and recognition is so pronounced.

General officers must recognize that they create the pressure to be "number one." Too many of them seek to load up their commands or staffs with the outstanding officers of the Army by requesting them by name; thus they demonstrate their lack of concern that many other commands don't get their share of the talent. General officers must be certain that they do not contribute to the shading of principle. The guidance, "Get it done and I don't care how you do it," can be an invitation to steal. When the thermometer and bar graph "fever charts" begin showing up like billboards at the entrance to installations with the start of some drive—they even stud the corridors of the Pentagon—the senior commanders should say, "Take them down!"

In every study on professionalism, in the comments of young officers resigning from the Army in the early 1970s, and in Department of the Army pamphlets on retention in that period, two conditions described by those involved, generally the junior officers, were cited often: that many lieutenant colonels and colonels did not know their jobs; and that excessive career competition prevailed among senior officers, who let their personal ambitions show through in their actions and decisions.

On the positive side, the problem was recognized by the Department of the Army in studies and reports. Recognizing a problem is always the first step toward correcting it. Maintaining integrity is an individual responsibility. Whatever your rank or position, you can influence those around you. The higher your rank, the greater the number you can influence for good or bad. If something is wrong, don't complain about it at every gathering of peers and, above all, don't complain about it to subordinates. Work up the chain of command and get it corrected. Write an article for *Army*, *Armor*, or the *Military Review*. If you are afraid to take that route, then there is always the Inspector General. Many things can be done if one just has the guts to do them.

In all my service I cannot recall ever being asked to do something improper by a superior. I can remember occasions when I was told to do something that I did not think was right. In those instances I got the facts and went back up the chain of command, and I was always supported. At times others disagreed with my judgment on tasks or missions or opinions, but never on a matter of principle; nor do I recall any recriminations being handed around. One always hears horror stories about how someone's career was ruined because he spoke up. The horror can happen, but if you are in the right, and present the case with reason and logic, I venture the judgment that you will do all right. So don't talk about what is wrong; do something about it.

INFLUENCE ON TRAINING

It is clear that competition, notably when it is covetous and spurred by excessive ambition, has a bad effect on individual ethics. Not so often noted is the effect competition has on training. Competition at the higher levels of organization induces practices that can be disastrous for training. Competition intended to make the statistics—and incidentally the commander—look good is to be guarded against and rooted out.

Consider those competitions that tend to erode integrity. A few examples were given above, and range seasons are something one can zero in on. Make the troops meet the standard. Learn enough about the weapons systems being fired so that marked variations from the norm catch the eye. The higher the rank the more the need to recognize when things don't ring true.

I would suggest this warning note for commanders: beware the 100 percenter. For every soldier in a rifle company to qualify with his individual weapon is rare. The same goes for all tank crews in a tank battalion, although since the number of crews is smaller the probability of success is higher. The individuals or crews might make it on a second or third try, but seldom will all of them qualify in a normal range season the first time around. When they do, take a close look. Perhaps the troops had superb training and their commander has ideas which can be passed on to other units. But look for ways to determine if they are really as good as the scores indicate.

Not long after I took command of a regiment, we had a range season. I informed commanders that statistics didn't interest me; I only cared about good shooting. In the range season several company-size units qualified 100 percent, and the scores in general were high. I thought some of the scores were suspect, because I'd been through enough range seasons to know that troops don't shoot that well unless the preliminary training is beyond compare. But even then, 100 percent? At the end of the range season I informed the battalion commanders that we were going to have a regimental match and that the twenty men from each battalion with the highest scores in the qualification season, supposedly all experts, would compete. The regimental executive officer was given responsibility for a well-supervised pit and scoring detail. It was no surprise to me that some of the men who had qualified as experts failed to qualify at all in this match. Now, an expert rifleman doesn't lose his form like that. He might have had a headache or even have been out all night before a match, but on his worst day on the range he would still be a high sharpshooter; bolo, never. Some battalion commanders had red faces because their 100-percent company-level units had the most men in the match who fired scores far below their original qualification scores. No soldier respects a commander who permits these things to happen. Sometimes commanders do not want to see the obvious; sometimes their desire to look good is overriding; and sometimes they use the old saw, "Everybody does it." The commander's sense of values is dulled by this rationalization. It is obvious that these practices are bad for training, and they are no help to the Army.

The bad influence competition has on training derives from honorable objectives, too, like keeping the competition "fair." That is a desirable objective,

167

but when you have to struggle to keep it so, take a close look at what fairness is doing to your training. In all units certain weapons-qualification courses or crew courses are run as part of the training program. In recent years commanders have tended to supervise the scoring closely in order to select the best crew or squad in a division, brigade, or battalion. There have even been some attempts to designate a number one crew in an entire command. For a crew to claim that it is the best is quite all right, but it is quite another thing to score training results so that the higher headquarters can make these pronouncements.

Competition is most damaging of all to infantry training when the problems are designed to allow for picking out the best infantry squad in a brigade or division. All squads must go through the same problems, and they are so controlled that those I have seen in recent years teach more bad practices than good. Further, the variety of tactical situations an infantry squad will be confronted with in training designed exclusively around competition is extremely limited.

One serious aspect of the competitive approach is the curtailment of the tactical development of intermediate commanders. In order to keep things fair in the selection of the best element in a division, the brigade commander who is an infantryman falls heir to the infantry squad problem. Then the brigade commander with an armor background runs the tank-crew qualification course and the other brigade commander is responsible for setting up tests for TOW squads, mortar crews, Redeye teams, or similar groups. When a division parcels out these assignments to brigades it stifles the ingenuity of battalion and company-level commanders, who should be setting up a variety of training situations for their own units. The greatest disadvantage of the centralized arrangement—all done in the name of fairness—is that it limits the smaller tactical elements to the same test for all squads or crews in a division or brigade. It is deadly for infantry training.

If each battalion commander is left to his own resources in developing tactical tests, many more situations and innovations will emerge than if the responsibility lies with the brigade commanders. Whenever a commander goes to the field to set up a tactical exercise accompanied by a few noncommissioned officers and junior officers, everyone benefits in terrain appreciation and tactical knowledge even though these benefits cannot be quantified.

The ultimate in folly in pursuing the will-o'-the-wisp of fairness is to deprive commanders of the opportunity to observe the tests of their units lest they influence the outcome. This restriction makes scoring and rating more important than the training, but it is applied in the name of fairness. Watching subordinate elements go through tests is one of the best ways for a commander to determine how well his subordinate commanders have trained their units. At times I have observed questionable tactical situations in which the junior officers running the problems either did not recognize or did not consider apparent errors, and the errors were repeated each time the problems were run. Battalion commanders should be in a position to see and correct these deficiencies as they occur.

Centralizing control above battalion for conducting tests to evaluate the tactical training of subordinate elements of company-level units—squad, tank crew, gun section, or platoon—reflects a lack of faith in battalion commanders. Who knows better the capabilities of the battalion's subordinate elements than the battalion commander? Or how to train them in the fundamentals? How important is it to have a relative score for all the squads, or even the companies, in a brigade or division? Competition is healthy and natural, but it must be kept in bounds. Here are a few suggestions to keep it so.

Limit the competition to the level of the commander of the competing elements. The tank crew that fires a TCQC on a raw, cold, overcast day in January has a much more difficult situation than the crew from another unit that fires on a clear, pleasant, warm day in June. The visibility alone makes a big difference, not to mention changing machine-gun barrels when fingers are numb. The elements of a company-level unit generally go through a test within a period of a few days. The chances are that the weather and other conditions will be fairly uniform for the elements of company-level units—squads, tank crews, gun sections, communication sections, and engineer sections. Also, the men in a company-size unit know pretty well which elements in their company or battery are consistently the best—outside of their own, of course. If competition is maintained at that level, even the elements in a company that do not place first might grudgingly concede that the winning group is the best. To eliminate any question about who is first and who last, post the scores on the range so that as individuals or crews come off the firing line they can see how they are doing. Those with low scores will no doubt have alibis, but they won't like the position they are in and will try harder.

As the designation of the "best" moves to battalion, brigade, and beyond, the credibility of the judgment declines in the eyes of the soldier, and he seizes on all sorts of reasons to explain why his crew or section did not win. Also, the reputation of the field-grade commander begins to get involved, and the competitive urge among field-grade officers is then added to their concerns.

Another disadvantage of selecting one element from many in a large organization is that all other accomplishments fade by comparison. Being best in a company-level unit doesn't mean much if the next step is to designate the best in brigade or division. If the designation of best for military accomplishments is limited to the company-level unit more soldiers get recognition for their accomplishments, the results have more credibility with the soldier, and an over-ambitious field-grade commander will not be tempted to stack the deck, or the crew, in favor of his battalion or brigade.

More fundamental is that the quality of training in any military element depends on the competence of the commander. If fairness is the objective, and of course it should be, compare tank crews, infantry squads, and various types of sections from the same company-level units, because the quality of their training will reflect the capability of their respective commanders. For a rule of thumb, keep competitions to the level of organization where there is a common commander; designate a best company or battery in a battalion, or a best battalion in a brigade or group. In that way the competing elements get their leadership and direction from the same commander.

Competition at the proper level is healthy. Soldiers enjoy it and strive to do their jobs better. Several stopwatches in every company-level unit would help noncommissioned officers and lieutenants to speed up the performance of their soldiers in the fundamental skills of their particular MOS or crew function. Stopwatches add to the competitive instinct in developing higher physical fitness standards. So keep up the competition at company level, keep it honest, and use a lot of stopwatches.

One last suggestion for field-grade commanders—in the form of an anecdote—when the competitive urge is strong. The 33rd Division was just about ready to go overseas during World War II. I had been commanding the 2nd Battalion of the 130th Infantry for about six months. During the first three or four months, it was a difficult and demanding command assignment, but gradually the battalion had become a jewel; at least I thought so. Whatever had to be done was done to perfection by a well-honed chain of command. It was sheer pleasure to command that battalion, and took little effort on my part.

It was no secret that our first battalion had problems, and I was thankful they were not mine. Late one afternoon I got a call from the regimental commander. When I reported to him, the conversation was brief and to the point: "Effective right now you are in command of the first battalion." He could not miss noting the look of dismay on my face and before I could open my mouth he said, "Young man, you might have the best battalion in the Army some day, but if you ever do, you can be sure of two things; it will be because you have the second best battalion on your right and the third best battalion on your left." I gulped; I'm sure I said, "Yes, Sir," and left in a state of shock, because I had some inkling of the difficult weeks and months ahead.

I never forgot those words and what they meant. They were a beacon to me throughout the rest of my service. In the military service where life is so often at hazard, the importance of all the units around you and those supporting you takes on special significance. When you feel the urge to be too competitive, when you want advantages for your unit at the expense of those around you, just remember the advice this sage old soldier gave to me. The high moral character and integrity of this regimental commander inspired all of us who served under him.

COMMAND MANAGEMENT MAINTENANCE INSPECTIONS (CMMIs) AND ANNUAL GENERAL INSPECTIONS (AGIs)

The reader might consider the title of this section out of date, since CMMIs no longer exist. Don't kid yourself. The CMMIs were replaced in the early 1970s by "maintenance assistance teams," which were just coming to help the commander. The intent was there, but not the will. In spite of all the guidance, by the time the assistance teams passed through two or three generations the old CMMI problems were back. The name was new, but that was all.

My first confrontation with a CMMI came about a week after I took command of a regiment in 1955. A battalion commander said his battalion was having a CMMI and he wanted to stop training for the next two weeks to prepare for the inspection. This was my first time back with a troop unit since 1946. Though I had heard of a CMMI, I did not know the full scope of the inspection, nor was I aware of the pressures to pass one. I refused permission and told the battalion commander that if every man in a unit did his job every day there was no need to stop training for two weeks to pass an inspection. He was shocked and explained that this had become standard practice. I told him it would not be standard practice in my outfit and the "no" policy was established in the regiment. Frankly, I don't recall whether or not the battalion passed the CMMI, but two weeks out of a training year just to pass an inspection made no sense at all to me.

By the late 1960s and early 1970s, a regular ritual was associated with inspections that no doubt derived from commanders' fear that if their units didn't pass they would be relieved or get terrible efficiency reports. Senior officers must have contributed to that state of mind, but they were not paying much attention to what was happening to training as a result. Units stopped training two to five weeks before the major inspections were to begin. The period varied in units and with the inspection. The first indication of an impending CMMI was a noticeable reduction in the number of vehicles dispatched for training. This provided an opportunity to catch up on maintenance, which was one of the biggest headaches for commanders. Then there were courtesy inspections—brigade would conduct one for battalion, the next week division would do the same, and in some cases corps would offer their good offices. The end result was that units were literally standing down from training for a month to prepare for the CMMI. The same sequence developed with the AGI.

I recall visiting one unit in which the training for all elements of the battalion was "Display of TA 50 equipment" from 0800 to 1200. No training whatsoever was going on. A talk with the commander and a few men about their activity made clear that they were getting ready for an AGI. I went back the next week: same thing on the training schedule. When asked "why" the commander explained that this was a courtesy inspection to help him prepare for the AGI. I asked for his training schedules for the past three weeks and for the coming week. One full morning every week was devoted to display of TA 50 and a follow-up to correct shortcomings in the TA 50 was scheduled on another day of each week. (In truth this is not training but something NCOs are responsible for.) The other days of the week were devoted to other aspects of the inspection —check of individual weapons, check of training or administrative records, and a host of similar entries. The battalion commander was determined to pass the AGI, and his senior commanders were giving him considerable support. No one seemed concerned that about a month of training time was being lost. The men, when asked how they felt about all the displays of equipment and preparation for inspection, answered "boring," "deadly," or words to that effect. Similar practices were going on in every type of unit and in every element of the command.

These derelictions must be stopped. They easily consume six to eight weeks of the training year when one considers time taken to prepare for all inspections. The Department of the Army puts out memorandums to stop them but the commanders don't appear to think that DA is serious. They are probably right, since senior officers not only let these bad habits persist in their units but contribute assistance. It would be nice to know that commanders had enough sense to stop this practice, but the evidence indicates otherwise. I therefore propose the following: a combined CMMI-AGI which would be the inspection for the year.

Call a unit between 0100 and 0300 and inform the charge of quarters that the unit is to be prepared to depart home station at 0800 the next morning for a field operation; tell him that a written or telegraphic message with more information will be delivered at 0500. This early warning will provide you with an opportunity to check alerting procedures in the unit. State in the message that all personnel present for duty will go, that weapons, ammunition, and rations will be taken, and that the unit is to be prepared for a field exercise up to seventy-two hours in length. Include in the written message coordinates of an objective or assembly area that happens to coincide with an available range. From there on, the requirements should be as outlined by the responsible headquarters—maybe division or corps—and should include as a minimum: firing of all weapons; notation of weapons that would not fire; a simplified range firing so that each individual could fire his weapon at a silhouette, or some suitable target; and the recording of hits. Check the number of unit vehicles able to depart home station and how many broke down enroute. Be sure the kitchen crew is instructed to serve a certain number of hot meals, not all of them C ration. Require layout of equipment at some field site. Have Finance and AG present to spot check a certain number of records for accuracy. Also talk to a cross-section of men to see if there are any pay or other personnel problems the unit has not acted on. Depending on the type of unit, assign a number of missions appropriate to the unit and see how the subordinate elements execute them.

At the end of forty-eight or seventy-two hours—or whatever time is required to carry out a reasonable program—give the unit a march order that will take it back to home station. Give the troops a day to clean up, an inspection in ranks by either the battalion or brigade commander, and a critique by the responsible headquarters. That should give a pretty good picture of the operational readiness of any unit on any given day. Then give the unit a day off. Adoption of this proposal would save the training time that is now lost in "preparing for inspections" and would by the very nature of the test or exercise provide some good training situations. It should be obvious that this is the Ph.D. phase of the "graduation exercise" in situational training described in Chapter 9. In fact, some enterprising corps commander should try to sell it as a test to see how it works.

I have made a strong point of "no changes to the training schedule," yet have extolled on occasion the merits of unannounced inspections. A good example is the proposed substitution of an unannounced operational-readiness test to take the place of both the command maintenance inspection, or its latest lineal descendant, and the annual general inspection. This substitution is certain to change some training already planned. I believe such a violation of the no-change principle is sound so long as it does not occur too often and commanders and staffs keep their thinking caps on.

The headquarters responsible for the readiness test should be familiar with unit training programs, and should not interfere with phases of training that require special facilities, such as annual qualification firing or field exercises. There are long periods when units are doing routine—that does not mean unimportant—training at home stations. The unannounced operational-readiness test should be scheduled during those periods. The senior officer should take enough interest in the tests to insure that good judgment is used in scheduling.

17

Total fitness for combat includes technical skill, mental and emotional stability, and physical endurance.

Physical Training and Sports Program

Development of stamina, heart, and muscle builds men's bodies, improves their physical well-being, and develops the physical strength and mental alertness needed to perform the strenuous and demanding duties of a soldier. Maintenance of men is as important as maintenance of machines. After all, who runs the machines? In the Army we talk a lot about our concern for people, but I have noticed that as commanders set priorities and allot time to take care of all their responsibilities the emphasis is on things rather than people. Look at your own training schedules and note how much time is scheduled for maintenance of things as opposed to maintenance of the soldier. And note what the Russians and Germans say:

> *Physical training and athletic competitions permit people to develop "endurance, self mastery, courage, and even competitive aggressiveness."*[1]

>   *   *   *   *

> *Sports are an indispensable element of training and education in the Bundeswehr.*[2]

---

[1] Herbert Goldhamer, *The Soviet Soldier* (New York: Crane, Russak and Co., 1975), p. 104.
[2] *German Army White Paper* 1971-72, p. 73.

It is the responsibility of the leaders of all units to insure that their men are physically fit. Even before Sparta's days of glory, nations recognized that the effectiveness of fighting men depends to a large degree upon their physical condition. Total fitness for combat includes technical skill, mental and emotional stability, and physical endurance.

War places a premium on the soldier's strength, stamina, agility, and co-ordination because victory and survival so often depend upon these factors. Combat is a grueling ordeal for soldiers and makes severe physical demands upon them. Marching long distances with full pack, weapons, and ammunition through rugged country, and fighting effectively upon arriving at the objective; driving fast-moving vehicles over rough terrain; running and crawling for long distances; jumping into and out of foxholes and craters; lifting and carrying heavy objects; and going through any or all of these activities for many hours without sleep is common in war and requires superbly conditioned troops. The facts that warfare has become mechanized and that we now stress continuous day-night operations accentuate rather than minimize the importance of phys-ical fitness. Soldiers must still perform arduous tasks, but they have less time to devote to pure physical conditioning.

Physical fitness is important from another point of view. There is a direct relationship between physical fitness, mental and emotional fitness, individual morale, and unit esprit. Fatigue, weakness of body and spirit, lack of stamina, and poor morale are usually found together. The rugged, tough, well-conditioned soldier has a feeling of fitness and confidence and is less susceptible to the factors that erode morale.

Physical fitness is too important to be an after-duty option. Schedule physical training and competition involving physical exercise as regularly as you schedule vehicular maintenance. Design your training exercises to be physically demanding and challenge your men to extend themselves to com-plete them.

Because the problem of extremes is pertinent to this activity, a few red flags should be waved. First, restrain the young commander who comes to a unit fresh from Ranger or airborne training and is determined that *everyone* in his outfit will be as fit as he is. In his enthusiasm, he tends to forget he has troops of all ages and levels of physical well-being, and he sets out on physical-fitness programs which do not adequately provide for these differences. Such ambitious programs are doomed to failure, and the young officer may create friction and misunderstanding that could have been avoided with a little mature thought.

Keep things in balance. Be sure you do not get carried away by the enthu-siasm and fitness of youth before you ascertain the level of fitness at which your outfit has been operating. Then, whatever program you set up, make sure it provides for two things: a gradual program to raise the physical conditioning of all and a program varied enough to allow for those who are in their forties, or those that have profiles resulting from wounds, injuries, or just plain lack of physical coordination. Don't let the fastest man in the unit lead the morning run.

Now a flag for the elders, who ought to know better but who let ambition get in the way of good judgment. They want to win no matter what the price. Unit pride is at stake, they believe, and generally they are thinking about the battalion, brigade, or division. Even though that higher level unit doesn't mean very much to the soldier in the company, battery, or troop, some senior commanders compromise a few principles by juggling men around to make sure that their battalion, brigade, or division will win a trophy. This kind of juggling causes all kinds of headaches for the company-level commander. It also accounts for the absence of many soldiers who ought to be present for training with their units. When commanders begin to think that being number one is the important point of the competitive side of the physical-readiness program, it is time to get things in balance. Don't encourage the win-at-any-price attitude. It harms your integrity as a commander.

A comprehensive and well-conducted physical-readiness training and sports program does several things in addition to conditioning a unit. It helps the Army's human relations problems by bringing people of different races together in an activity that forces them to know one another better and to respect individual talents and abilities. It also leads to more outside interests, and encourages soldiers to engage in physical activity on their own time. Teaching new sports is an important part of the program. Men who learn to play a sport better or can complete confidence courses and physical-fitness tests inevitably become more confident. This sort of satisfaction is important to the many young men who enter the service expecting the Army to do something for them. Next, a good program improves rapport among officers, noncommissioned officers, and the men—the "communications" that everyone talks about today. That "open door" is not as open as commanders like to think it is. Finally, a vigorous physical-readiness and sports program aids the drug- and alcohol-abuse programs because physical demands encourage men to stay in condition. Also, it provides an interest in sports that might fill some of the soldiers' lonely hours on weekends and evenings with activity and companions. And finally helps the commander identify abusers, since they are unable to keep up the pace. These are rather significant benefits.

A physical-training and sports program should consist of three elements: physical-fitness training; organized company athletics (an *on-duty* training program); and company-level sports (a *voluntary off-duty* program) (see Figure 17.1). Battalion-size units are ideal for all three elements. In separate companies or isolated detachments there will be exceptions. A company-level sports program will not be practical, but a vigorous sports program between sections in the unit can be conducted on-site along with the regular physical-fitness training.

PHYSICAL-FITNESS TRAINING

The morning run, jog, daily dozen, rifle drill, log exercise, grass drill, and all the other exercises in the manual add up to physical-fitness training. Those soldiers

FIGURE 17.1.

PHYSICAL TRAINING AND SPORTS PROGRAM, THREE ELEMENTS

PHYSICAL- FITNESS TRAINING	ORGANIZED COMPANY ATHLETICS	COMPANY- LEVEL SPORTS
Morning Run	Not Voluntary	Voluntary
Calisthenics	On-duty	Off-duty
Rifle Drill	Instructional	Competitive
Confidence Course	Unit Instructors	Players: source of instructors for
Tankers 600	Variety -	organized athletics
	Intramural	
Program for those with physical profiles	Program for those with physical profiles	
Exercises		
Therapy		
? Mile Walk		

A good physical-training and sports program will improve human relations, broaden horizons, suggest more outlets for free time, improve self-confidence of soldiers and their confidence in one another, improve rapport, open the "open door," help the drug- and alcohol-abuse program, and enhance team-work.

who have medical profiles which limit their physical activity should participate in this training.[3] They are a problem in our Army and one we don't do much about. Some of the troops with profiles are just "getting over" on the system and something should be done about them. Others have legitimate complaints. If a man's bugbear is poor legs, he should be doing some upper-extremity exercises. Or if his profile is for the upper extremities, maybe he should be going on a two-mile walk or jog, or whatever he can do in the time available. Perhaps he should be getting some therapy. Involving people who have medical profiles this way will give commanders a better check on them. The main point is not to neglect them, which there is a tendency to do. The frequency and duration of physical-fitness training depend on other elements of the training program. Certainly all personnel should be getting some type of exercise every day. The variety of programs and the small groups that may have to be organized, as with the profiles, provides wonderful leadership opportunities for NCOs and junior officers as they organize and conduct this training.

On visits to German Army units I observed several physical-fitness drills related to their equipment, which is another approach to be considered. One that stands out in my mind was a mechanized infantry squad drill supervised by the squad leader. The men had on sneakers instead of boots, they lined up about twenty yards in back of the carrier, and on the command "*Aufsitzen*" the first man ran forward and nimbly mounted the carrier and disappeared inside. Came another "*Aufsitzen*" and the next man followed, mounting the carrier in the same fashion. As he disappeared the next man followed just about the time the first man was appearing through the driver's escape hatch. Soon a moving line of soldiers was mounting, dismounting, and crawling out of and under their vehicle and re-forming in front of the NCO. As he left to follow the last man he turned the group over to the next in command, who gave the starting command in the same precisely timed sequence. The safety aspect was noticeable. Every man stepped up on the same part of the carrier, took the same handhold, and so on throughout the exercise. It was a short snappy drill, not too long to become a bore. It was physical fitness with a purpose and provided an opportunity for the NCO to control his men in a precise and disciplined physical drill. I am sure it contributed to the rapid and businesslike way I saw the men of this unit go into action in some field training later in the day.

Several U.S. armor commanders developed a similar drill for tank-crew members which was called the "Tankers 600." Developing physical-fitness drills and exercises that can be related to equipment is of great merit. Done with

---

[3]Profile: The physical profile is the estimate of the overall ability of an individual to perform military duties made on the basis of physical and mental condition. There are six factors; P—physical capacity or stamina; U—upper extremities; L—lower extremities; H—hearing; E—eyes; S—neuropsychiatric. Generally the first three—P, U, L—are the basis for profiles which exempt soldiers from certain physical activities.

speed and guidelines for safety they can add to a unit's proficiency. Drills can be done on equipment of all the branches. A little interest, imagination, and thought by the junior officers and NCOs are the only requirements.

ORGANIZED COMPANY ATHLETICS

An intramural company athletic program constitutes training, which is everybody's business. The development of greater endurance, improved agility, and coordination results in a better state of health and a better mental attitude. Commanders' reluctance to take the time to improve both physical conditioning and mental attitude through this program must be overcome. Too many of them wear blinders, particularly at battalion and brigade level.

Several features of this program require emphasis:

It is not voluntary.
It is training and is done during duty hours, even during prime training time.
It is instructional, and generally instructors should come from the unit.
It should contain a variety of sports.

When a unit falls in for organized company athletics the whole company, including the officers, noncommissioned officers, and the troops with profiles, should be there. The last category should get some special type of physical conditioning. Only someone to answer the phone and guard the barracks should be left behind. Headquarters and signal units pose problems, but with a little thought shifts can be worked out.

One of the major benefits to be derived from an organized company athletic program is better communications and rapport. The many letters requesting help in righting alleged or real injustices, misfortunes, and the like written to congressmen, the Chief of Staff, and the President take a great deal of a commander's time because they are bucked down to him to frame the answers. It is my judgment that 95 percent of those letters will not be written if a unit develops a good company athletics program—a program involving the whole company, including the company commander. When the commander is standing behind the backstop watching a soldier learn how to hit or standing on the sideline waiting to get into a flag football game, that's the time when a soldier who has a problem might edge up to him and say, "Sir, my wife is going to have a baby and we can't get any medical support." Maybe medical help is available but the soldier doesn't know. Some other soldier may not have been paid for four months or can't get leave and the company commander does not know about it. Most of the things that soldiers write to congressmen about could have been taken care of in the unit if someone had only listened. Fifty percent of the complaints that come to the Inspector General are justifiable. When a letter containing a reasonable complaint gets to a senior officer, he says, "How could they let it happen in that unit?" Too often, commanders at company level are not as accessible to their men as they think they are. A good company athletics program puts the company commander in close proximity to his men in an environment where he is more approachable.

Remember, such an effect is just a bonus. If a number of men approach you with problems in the athletic periods, start taking a close look at yourself and your unit. How often do you talk individually with the men in your unit? Is your executive officer or 1st Sergeant cutting you off from the men? Are they "protecting" you from things you "shouldn't be bothered with" but which can cause you a lot of trouble?

Planning and organization of the two on-duty elements of the overall program—the physical-fitness and the organized company athletics—take thought and effort, but they provide great training for lieutenants and NCOs. Just make sure that both elements are not scheduled on the same day. Organization for the instruction takes more effort. Check over your units for instructors. The company should be identifying those men who can instruct in basketball, volleyball, team handball, and so forth. Instruction is a most important element in your organized company athletics. Any sport can be broken down to a few basic fundamentals. Take basketball—what do you have to do to be able to play it? You have to be able to dribble, pass, shoot, put the skills all together, and know a little about the rules. That's what you should be teaching in organized company athletics. When your troops go out there for basketball, they are ripe for learning. Teach your men something about the sport. Break the company down into groups. Sports training gives you a good opportunity to take advantage of the special talents of some of your minority soldiers. In these programs the troops learn to respect one another for what each one can do.

All sports can be reduced to component parts that provide an opportunity for teaching, learning, and developing respect and confidence. The attitude and techniques of the instructor are most important. He is not out there to show the rest of the men in the company how good he is. He is out there to teach the fundamentals to men who do not know the game or have only a passing acquaintance with it. In handball, for instance, the simplest ways to play the game should be taught. The star handball player should not start teaching with a shot that bounces off two walls and the back of the court. Shots that destroy the confidence or interest of the one learning to play are no help at all. So keep the instruction simple and basic. Service schools could help this program by teaching young officers and NCOs practical methods for organizing a sports program. Only minimum skills are necessary for young officials in organized company athletics. Technical emphasis is out of place here. Remember that the objective is to teach soldiers how to play the game. As time goes on the games will be longer and will provide the participants some pleasant hours in any advanced training program.

Company athletic programs do not result in spectacular games by men who literally spend all their free time at athletics. They do not appeal to *Stars and Stripes* and the other news media. But more men are drawn to a physical fitness and sports environment than to any other competition for miles around. So once you have a good program going, try to get a little publicity or a few pictures in the local paper. The program may not be glamorous, but it will benefit everyone and some exposure will help. The unit or installation papers should give the program coverage.

Figure 17.2 shows one possible combination of sports. The important thing to keep in mind is that variety is desirable. Combinations will depend on facilities and the density of units at each facility. You should have three or four cycles a year. You have a lot of sports to teach your men, so you must consider when you are going to rotate them. Are you going to give them three weeks in basketball, two weeks in volleyball, one week each in wrestling, handball, and paddleball? Deciding this is part of your planning and organization. Look at the resources that are available and what you can do with them. One cardinal rule: Don't let the soldier determine what he will do. These sports activities are training. Time spent on them is in on-duty time. Make each soldier take a turn at all of the sports activities. If you can teach these men about several different sports, you can hope that in their free time on the weekends they might ask one of the other men, "How about going out and shooting a few baskets?" or "How about some volleyball?" The instruction is important because if it is well organized it will develop skills and generate interest.

Figure 17.3 shows one example of a formation for organized company athletics. Since this is an on-duty program, start with a formation. The company commander and 1st Sergeant should be there. After attendance is taken, the senior instructor for each group can march the group off to the exercise area. Don't let groups straggle out on their own, especially those with profiles. Too many men will find a way to avoid the exercise.

I have observed a lieutenant in charge of the training line the company up in the gym and say, "Who wants to play basketball?" A dozen hands go up. "Who wants to play volleyball?" A few more volunteers. "Can anyone play paddleball?" His final question was, "Who wants to go to the sauna?" This is not organized company athletics.

181

FIGURE 17.2.

POSSIBLE COMBINATION FOR A SPORTS PROGRAM

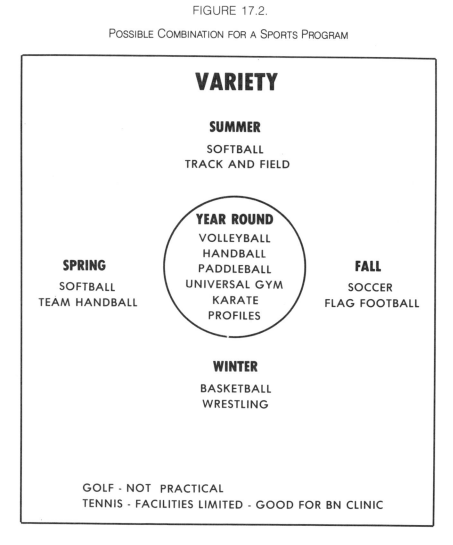

FIGURE 17.3.

FORMATION FOR ORGANIZED COMPANY ATHLETICS

EXAMPLE ONLY

CO CDR

SR INSTR	SR INSTR	SR INSTR	SR INSTR	SR INSTR
HEADQUARTERS PLATOON WEIGHTS ALL PURPOSE GYM PROFILES	PLATOON BASKETBALL	PLATOON HANDBALL PADDLEBALL	PLATOON VOLLEYBALL	PLATOON WRESTLING

NON SWIMMERS
SWIMMING

PRINCIPLES:

MAXIMUM PARTICIPATION—TO INCLUDE NCO'S AND OFFICERS; DON'T FORGET PROFILES.
UNIT INTEGRITY.
ROTATE EVENTS TO EXPOSE SOLDIERS TO ALL SPORTS.
SHORT COMPETITIVE GAMES AFTER TEACHING SESSION.
COMPETITIVE ROUND ROBIN AT END OF CYCLE.

In another unit I asked a clerk what he did that week in organized company athletics. "Sir, I played pool." "Played pool? Where?" "Up in the day room." "What are you going to do next week?" "Play pool, Sir, I like to play pool." Well, that's great if the soldier can get away with it. But it is an indication of a mighty weak commander. Incidentally, if you want to find out how effective training programs are in a unit just talk to the clerks and the personnel in the supply rooms or other administrative offices. The conversation may turn out to be very enlightening.

In still another unit I was pleased to see the number of men that turned out because it indicated that the commander was trying. About six volleyball teams were playing, but on one court both teams and all the cheering substitutes were Chicano—that is, of Latin American origin. The commander was trying but he wasn't thinking. Games between squads or gun sections would eliminate the tendency to segregate.

These examples all demonstrate what organized company athletics is not. They also exemplify weak leadership and poor supervision by battalion or brigade commanders, who should have been dropping around to those activities.

Certain questions come up all the time. For example, people often ask whether golf is appropriate for organized company athletics. I don't think golf is practical because finding a place to play is difficult and equipment is expensive and hard to come by. Tennis might be a little easier. But, again, facilities are limited and rackets and balls are expensive. If you have a good instructor, the teaching might work in the form of a battalion clinic. The same goes for skiing. If you have the facilities for the costly individual sports you are lucky, but don't be concerned about the skier, golfer, or tennis player. Each one will get out and play regardless. Further, Special Services has good programs and equipment for the soldiers in their free time. Your concern should be directed toward the youngster who doesn't want to do anything. Bowling is a great thing to develop an interest in recreational activity, but it is of no use as a physical conditioner. Further, the soldier has to pay to play, and you can't ask a soldier to pay in a training program. Bowling can be a good program for a unit clinic in off-duty hours, but it has no place as part of an organized company athletics program.

The dotted box about swimming on the far right of Figure 17.3 deserves a special comment. One of the overall objectives of the physical-fitness program is to develop the confidence of the individual soldier as well as his heart and lungs. When you teach a man how to swim, you have done something for him. That man might think a little more of the Army for having taught him this skill. Swimming has to be handled in small groups on a special basis. First, identify your qualified lifeguards. Then, take a small, well-disciplined group of non-swimmers down to the pool during the organized athletic periods with a good firm instructor. You must make it clear that the group at the pool is there to learn to swim and not to horse around. Most major installations have pools, but to

184

serve the community they will probably be used by several groups, so it helps a unit image to be all business in such a program. In Germany where we have a lot of troops there are few pools on the installations, but every German community has community swimming facilities and the local officials are most helpful in accommodating a request for a certain number of spaces.

At the first athletic formation after a man learns to swim, have him come front and center to get a swimming badge for his athletic uniform. It will give him a little more pride in himself. This is the type of thing that is beneficial for both man and unit.

Most of our gyms now have a piece of equipment called the Universal Gym. You can build a good company athletics program around that. You may only be able to train one gun section at a time, but the first priority in any case is to teach the men how to use the equipment without getting hernias or straining themselves. Then, at the end of the week when they have gone through all the exercises, have a little competition. Find out who can pull the most, push the most, or whatever the exercises require. The men like that kind of competition, and it's right down there in the squad, gun section, tank crew and platoon. Then, on the weekends, they'll use the equipment on their own.

At company-commander level the commander can use this program to increase the efficiency and teamwork of his unit by organizing the entire company into various teams for competition. A battalion-level commander may plan a battalion competition among the companies in his battalion at the end of each cycle, or once or twice a year. But don't let the competition go any higher. Within a battalion the schedule is easily handled because all the units are about the same size and a competition won't disrupt training programs. Set a day aside on the training schedule and have the companies/batteries/troops organize several different types of teams so that everyone gets in on the act and the battalion can have a great field day with families present.

The organized company athletic program should be the province of the battalion S–3 rather than an unauthorized athletic and recreation officer.

COMPANY-LEVEL SPORTS

And now to the third facet of the physical-fitness and sports program, and one about which there tends to be confusion: company-level sports. Although company-level sports and organized company athletics differ markedly, commanders tend to confuse them. The important things to note in a company-level sports program are that it is voluntary, an off-duty program, and competitive. The best athletes will be in the company-level program. In other words, the battery or company commander will want to beat everybody else. A Company will want to beat B and C. A unit in the 1-35th which plays a unit in the 1-14th will want to clobber them. So the best basketball players, the best volleyball players, or the best players in whatever the sport happens to be, will be the participants. In this off-duty program, the officers and noncommissioned officers who want to will coach and manage a team. The company-level program represents the professional side of company sports. The men do their own playing on weekends and evenings and arouse interest. The program is also a good way to get soldiers together to root for their outfit. And the interest is real because it is in behalf of their own company, battery, or troop. Someone on the battalion staff should be responsible for arranging the schedules to provide activity for the free time of the men in that unit. The installation commander also has a responsibility for coordinating the use of facilities in off-duty time.

In discussing the on-duty, organized company athletics I mentioned that the officiating could be marginal and not too technical. In the off-duty company level sports, however, you have to have well-trained officials. Poor officiating hurts a competitive program where skilled players, playing on their own time, want to win. It is important to recognize the difference.

The Army has always had a vigorous interunit sports program, so that need not be discussed here at length. But a few cautions with respect to interunit sports are in order. The first pertains to the level of competition. Keep it at the company/battery/troop level, and get the good athletes out at training just like everyone else in the company. As soon as you raise the level of competition to the battalion or brigade level, some fileboning colonel who wants to win the championship will start reassigning the good athletes so that he can have them all in one unit; or he will have them placed on some type of special-duty assignment so that they are not available to carry their share of the load in their units.

The second caution pertains to the level of the play-offs. Keep them at home, and the closer they can be to the basic unit the better. In my book, the battalion is the best level at which to terminate play-offs. The excitement is great, each unit knows the people in the next barracks pretty well—everyone is aware of the enthusiasm a battalion play-off can generate. The big advantage of keeping the play-offs at home is that all the men of the unit can enjoy it. When the play-offs move to brigade, division and higher levels, the cost of traveling uses up unit funds that should be spent on equipment for all the troops. And the higher the level, the longer the soldiers will be away from their units.

FACILITIES

Battalion- and brigade-level commanders should take a look around the athletic facilities whenever they visit units. Many installations do not have enough athletic facilities, and some that do exist are marginal. Look at the equipment. Determine whether you can use movable baskets and outside volleyball courts to get more playing space. Use imagination to lay out running or exercise courses similar to those professional football players use. These courses can be used in all three elements of the physical-fitness program. Brigade and battalion commanders must coordinate the use of indoor and outdoor athletic and recreation facilities to insure that they are available to and used by all units equally. This is particularly applicable for periods of bad weather. There are seldom enough athletic and recreation facilities to go around.

The Army has not done a very good job on our overall physical training and sports programs in the past. Strangely enough, it has done better in the off-duty program than in the on-duty one. Some commanders have always believed that they had no time for on-duty sports. Considering all the benefits that can be derived from the on-duty program, I don't know how they can afford not to have the time for it. We are going through a period in our history, in our society, and in our Army in which we have serious racial and human-relations problems. Drug and alcohol abuse is serious. We have produced a generation of young-sters who are soft and fat from overeating and watching TV. Many of these problems of our society can be helped by a good on-duty physical-fitness and sports program. All commanders had better think about it, along with shooting and maneuvers.

I may appear to have lingered too long on the subject of physical fitness. But the Army has given this type of program only lukewarm support in spite of its constant pronouncements on the necessity for physical conditioning. The Army starts on this cycle about every ten years and then drifts quickly back to the big teams, which contribute neither to the physical readiness nor to the combat readiness of the Army.

Comparisons with foreign armies make us look pretty sad. The British, French, and German armies all issue an athletic sweat suit to their men. We are the richest nation in the world—but we can't afford to issue sweat suits.[4] The Germans have an extensive schooling program for both officers and NCOs so that there are always several well-qualified officers and NCOs in the units to organize and run their athletic programs, which are first class. The British have NCO and officers' schools, and the quality of their on-duty athletic programs reflects the fact.

One problem in our Army has been the continual influence of a group of civilian sports advisors who have grown old with the division- and brigade-level programs so popular in the 1940s, 1950s, and 1960s. They didn't want to give up the brigade and division teams and gave little support to the new company-level programs. A number of these civilian sports advisors were over fifty-five

---

[4]As this book went to press the Army approved an athletic uniform. That's progress.

and some were over sixty. What we really need are young leaders with the capability to change with the times and to recognize the benefits of what is really an intramural program.

One comment the old timers always make is that this program won't provide an opportunity for a soldier to go to the Olympics with the intramural program. But few soldiers in a volunteer army are going to be good enough for the Olympics, and there is just too much money on the American sporting scene to give the Army much of a chance to enlist an Olympic prospect. Further, the Olympics are composed of for the most part individual sports, and anyone who comes close to meeting the Olympic criteria is well known. Any soldiers who were good enough for the Olympic team would come to the fore in service matches and training sessions. Holding out for possible Olympic-level sportsmen does not justify the failure to conduct a vigorous and worthwhile intramural program for all the soldiers. The teams that represent higher headquarters benefit only a few soldiers, and incidentally deprive them of the opportunity to do the type of training for which they were enlisted.

18

Reserve Component Training suffers from the Army's failure to make a realistic assessment of what the Army can expect from the Reserve Components in an emergency.

Reserve Component Training

For a variety of reasons, all subject to challenge and emotional debate, Reserve Component Training suffers from the Army's failure to make a realistic assessment of what can be expected from the Reserve Components in an emergency, and from the Reserve Components' promise of more than they can deliver. The reasons for the unrealistic assessments are complex; they relate to the historical, political, constitutional, and budgetary circumstances of a society which has an aversion to military service and gives primacy to individual freedom. Given the increasing importance of the Reserve Components and the resources now being invested in them, we have a need for more realistic appraisals of what can be expected of these forces in a national emergency.

Active Army officers and noncommissioned officers are being assigned to Army Readiness Regions and Readiness Groups in increasing numbers to provide training assistance to Reserve Component units. Because of the new emphasis on the Reserve Components' role and their greater likelihood of assignment in an advisory role, active component commanders should better understand the training environment of Reserve Component units. At the same time, Reserve Component commanders should have a good sense of the training standards their units will have to meet before they can be committed to combat.

Conditions that create an adverse training atmosphere for troops often have little to do with the training process itself. They derive from political and budgetary pressures, resulting in an overriding preoccupation with the ideal of readiness as opposed to the practicality of being as ready as one can be under the given circumstances. It may surprise Reserve Component commanders to learn that Active Army commanders are faced with a training atmosphere similar to their own, and that the emphasis on readiness as a reporting and measuring device is the cause of the common problem. For this reason much of the general guidance suggested throughout this book would be of help to Reserve Component commanders. But it must be noted that Reserve Component commanders carry two special burdens: the compression of time, and the conflicting demands on the civilian-soldier, who has to look to his civilian pursuits while he carries out his military commitment. These added burdens make training in the Reserve Components much more difficult than in the Active Army. An appraisal of the problems suggests the following basic guidelines for Reserve Component Training:

First, make the highest priority individual training. If individuals are well trained in their MOS they will be valuable wherever they go. MOS training is generally hands-on training and can be made interesting.

Next, emphasize the first collective training group in the unit's chain of command—the crew, squad, or section. Such an emphasis will minimize the Reserve Component problem of distance and space.

Concentrate on small-unit training at company level and below. The highest objective should be readiness at the company level and a confident sense of professional competence at all levels subordinate to the company, battery, or troop.

Utilize the NCOs and junior officers to the fullest measure of their potential at each level of training. You will thereby insure the development of the training potential of NCOs and junior officers. Over a period of time the company commander will thus have an opportunity to make training interesting.

Insure that there is a constant interchange between the chain of command and the troops. Ask for ideas on training. In a Reserve Component unit the educational level is generally high. The more education a soldier has, the more ideas he has and the more he wants to be involved. The more involvement, the less boredom.

Expand the affiliated unit program wherever possible.

Recognize the ongoing revolution in our society. An accelerated change in attitudes, with the emphasis on individual freedom and self-gratification, took place in the 1960s and 1970s. The tone of the revolution was antiestablishment and opposed to authority. Such changes in social outlook have posed a problem for all components, but they confront the Reserve Components directly and daily.

Let all those who inspect the Reserve Components heed the advice for generals on unannounced visits in Chapter 21. By dropping in informally, all commanders above the company-commander level should begin to set the right tone. Reserve Components have no time in the limited number of training days to get things in shape for a visitor, for an IG inspection, or for the statistics for readiness reports. They must devote the limited time available to training and let the technicians and record-keepers work on the reports. A visitor should check ongoing training and note whether it is on schedule, and if he finds the training uninteresting he should be ready to give some suggestions on how to make it better. But don't put on a show; emphasize the teaching. Since the Reserve Component training is concentrated into short periods, visitors are a source of distraction and the units are too often overwhelmed by the visitors and inspectors. It is essential that senior Reserve Component Officers and active-duty advisors make a concerted effort to improve the training atmosphere for the Reserve Components.

This ordering of priorities and emphasis stems from the training environment confronting Reserve Component commanders, especially those at battalion level and below. As always, the heaviest burdens are on the company-level commanders. Active-duty personnel tend to think that the problems of the Reserve Components and the Active Army are similar, but they are so only up to a point. One major difference is the company commander's time-consuming responsibility to recruit in his community, an essential ingredient in maintaining the strength of his unit.

Perhaps the greatest difference is the limited training time available to a National Guard or Army Reserve unit. Although thirty-eight days are provided for by directives, recent studies conclude that approximately twenty-four days are really available for training. Full-time technicians in Army Guard and USAR units devote considerable time to planning for and arranging necessary training for the unit. However, very little time is available for the trainers—the NCOs and junior officers—to prepare, rehearse, and conduct the necessary training.

Some combat-service support units have special training problems. A unit will often train for an optimum mission without specifically knowing of the unit's wartime mission. Maintenance units train in the repair of equipment at hand, not necessarily on items that would be supported after deployment. Often essential equipment such as computers for direct-support and general-support maintenance units or the appropriate supplies are not available for use in training.

In National Guard and Army Reserve units, geographical separation is often a serious problem. Organic units are frequently training in different armories and have difficulty getting to weekend training sites to train as a unit. Distances often keep units from moving to where training could take place. Insuring that all aspects of the training are arranged—times, areas, instructors, equipment, ammunition, and communication—is made more difficult by this physical separation. The separation complicates effective training management, often depriving Reserve Component units of the supervision needed.

191

Many Reserve Component personnel are not MOS qualified; thus the commanders bear an added training burden. Hard-skill MOSs requiring longer training periods are a particular problem, since many Reserve Component members are unable to take time off from their jobs to attend Army Service Schools.

Complicating the MOS training problem are the unit reorganizations that sometimes occur. When units are converted from one type to another, many personnel need to be retrained in a new MOS. Concentration must then be on MOS proficiency with unit training emphasized later. But the short training time makes attaining MOS qualification most difficult, and the reorganization invariably affects morale adversely.

Often employers do not like their employees to belong to a reserve unit because, in their view, membership conflicts with civilian job performance. Knowing that his employer holds this attitude often dampens the member's willingness to participate. Another distraction is family pressure with respect to absences during what would otherwise be the member's free time. These factors affect the motivation of Reserve Component personnel and have a direct impact on training.

In considering the effectiveness of training, one must be aware of a motivation problem. Many Army Reserve members are highly motivated Army Guard and U.S. Army Reserve members, but also many have joined primarily for the remuneration available. Since Reserve Component personnel are part-time soldiers, it is reasonable to expect that different attitudes toward their assignment will show up. In this respect, guidance from the sociologists who study and write on civilian-military relationships is useful.

This, then, in capsule form, is the training environment with which the Reserve Component commander is confronted. Its very real problems are not easily solved. There are no pat answers. It does appear, however, that Reserve Component training should be geared to the company level with emphasis on individual, section, crew or squad, and platoon in that order. Readiness at company level should be the objective. Whatever goal is set, it must be realistic and reasonably attainable.

It is essential that all involved—DOD, Active Army, Congress, and Reserve Components—determine the purpose of the Reserve Components and the missions they can be realistically expected to fulfill—from the first call to active duty for individuals and small units to the time brigade-size units are engaged in the full range of their missions in a combat environment. A realistic assessment will take into account the time, mission, and training required. For example, support units that will be handling mail, dispensing fuel, and maintaining roads may be ready to deploy much earlier than units expected to fight on arrival in the combat theater. The lives of soldiers will be endangered if Reserve Component units are expected to be fighting even a month from call-up, no matter what the claimed state of readiness is. Some individuals, tank crews, gun sections, and even an occasional platoon might be able to be in combat sooner. But above that level, getting ready will take time. Many legal, personal, medical, and other problems are involved in a call-up and deployment, not to mention the political aspects which cause delay. After all the call-up problems have been accommodated and the unit is assembled in a field environment even company-size units would require at least thirty days of concentrated training to be prepared for combat.

Study any national emergency, any occasion when Reserve Components were called to duty suddenly. All reports indicate that they were not ready, and that it is unrealistic to expect them to be. However, given time, they all went on to make a contribution to national defense. Unfortunately, their lack of instant readiness, occasioned breast-beating and recriminations instead of being recognized honestly as an unavoidable fact of life. Statements that Reserve Component units should be as ready to fight as Active Army units are self-serving and self-defeating. Any unit will fight when it has to; so little is to be gained by proud and optimistic pronouncements.

The recommendation that training be concentrated at the individual and small-unit level might be received with hostility in the Reserve Components. One human problem stands in the way of acceptance, and it needs to be looked at with professional detachment. The Reserve Component structure provides for a number of officers in high rank. It is natural for the senior Reserve Component commanders to feel that if any program succeeded in maintaining individuals and small subordinate elements in a combat-ready condition, these individuals or small units would be called into active service in time of emergency. This would extend the time it would take larger units to be ready. If the theory of a short, violent war is accepted, then the fact that the larger units could seldom be ready for combat in thirty days would keep them out of combat. Reserve Component commanders, eager to show how well their units can do, would be thwarted. Thus, realistic assessments become a victim of policy and ambition rather than need.

Throughout my service I have observed that when the chips are down nothing holds back the best. If a national emergency is of short duration, the individuals or crews who are qualified to do their duty in a combat environment will fare as well as anyone else faced with the same type duty. If the emergency is prolonged and a build-up of forces is required, even if only to impress on an enemy that the U.S. is serious, the calling up of major units of the Reserve Components will achieve that objective. History shows that these larger units need additional time for intensive training. The Army would be remiss to put these units into a combat environment too soon. Certainly, their commanders, recognizing their own lack of military expertise—because they have been doing two jobs, not one—should welcome a period of intensive training. During that time the units would take on a new look, because they would receive personnel from many sources to meet the emergency. In these circumstances, the most competent need not worry about succeeding; the opportunities will be there, and history records the successes of many civilian soldiers. Generals Beightler and McLain of World War II vintage are good examples.

Overoptimistic assessments of readiness capabilities are the root cause of training problems in the Reserve Components. Honest professional appraisals of what is realistic and practical will do much to restore credibility and provide a training environment that will enable the Reserve Components to train for the time when they will be needed. If history is any guide to the future, that time will come.

If the United States is ever defeated in a war, the Congress and the people will not be impressed by the services' educational and social rehabilitation programs.

Quality of Personnel and Personnel Actions

A close relationship exists between the policies and operation of the personnel system and the training conducted at the unit level. Too often when there is reason to find fault with training at the battalion and company levels the blame is not put where it rightfully belongs—at the top policy levels of the Department of Defense and Department of the Army. The quality of the soldier is a major factor in the quality of training, and the Army does not fare as well as the other services in obtaining personnel in the higher mental categories.

There are several reasons for this imbalance. The most obvious is that the Army suffers most of the casualties in time of war. Ground combat missions are prolonged and carried out under the most difficult conditions, and even when combat is not involved the demands are severe. In times past, a civilian who received a note from selective service to report for induction into the Army had only to go to the nearest Air Force or Navy Recruiting Office and apply for enlistment. The enlistment period was longer than the two-year selective service commitment, but the conditions of service and the specialized training that could be used in civilian life made the trade-off a good one. Having a choice, the Navy and the Air Force took the people with the highest educational qualifications. A similar situation exists in the era of an all-volunteer force; the Navy and Air Force now wind up with a much higher percentage of service volunteers in Categories I, II, and III than does the Army. The Army has never achieved comparability with the other services in the higher mental categories. Although leaders have learned that high quality is the key to proficiency, when enlistments lag the speeches about "quality" are forgotten, and the number of soldiers in Category IV starts to climb. Military training pays the bill.

EDUCATIONAL AND SOCIAL REHABILITATION PROGRAMS

Department of Defense Project 100,000 did not make things any better for the Army. This program was designed to absorb into the services a number of men who did not meet the mental criteria or who had minor physical defects that would normally have been a bar to enlistment. It imposed on the services a social rehabilitation program which detracted from their primary missions. Department of Defense quotas resulted in the Army's absorbing a disproportionate share of the disadvantaged: 222,000 compared to the combined total of 132,000 for the Navy, Marines, and Air Force. This situation only added to the imbalance created by those in the higher mental categories who were enlisting in the Air Force and Navy to avoid being drafted into the Army.

One Defense official said, "With the famous 'Project 100,000' we showed, by taking in and training that many Group IV men, many of them not high school graduates, the remarkable extent to which such men could achieve acceptable levels of military job performance. Good training is critically important. A desire to succeed is critically important. The military must not disappoint people who are looking for education and skills."[1] Pronouncements like this are self-serving and deceptive. The question is, "What was the bill?" If "good training is critically important," how much effort was expended on this group of servicemen at the expense of training other servicemen? What percentage achieved "acceptable levels of military job performance?"

The Department of Army staff opposed Project 100,000 and commanders complained about it, but civilian secretaries at defense level were not inclined to listen and implied that those in the field did not know what they were talking about. Or they hinted that the military was not cognizant of its responsibility to make up for the shortcomings of American society with respect to these young soldiers. This was a rather large order in the late 1960s and early 1970s, and I believe that many of the disciplinary and leadership problems in the Army during that period were due to the large number of Project 100,000 people in the Army.

The enthusiasm with which some programs are advocated by proponents

---

[1]Bruce Bliven, Jr., "All Volunteer Armed Forces," *New Yorker* (November 24, 1975), p. 91.

in the civilian secretaries' offices is understandable. Unfortunately, these same civilians, who sometimes find it hard to believe that the military believes in and accepts civilian control, have no idea how effective the military can be, by sheer weight of effort, in making a poor scheme look good once the decision is made. Project 100,000 was one example.

Most on-duty education in units is designed to compensate for the educational deficiencies of soldiers who enlist without a high school diploma or who lack a skill transferable to civilian life. Units of the combat arms and such service units as truck companies absorb the highest number of soldiers without a high school diploma.

The General Educational Development Program outlined in Army Regulation 621-5 states:

> *The minimum Army goal is that every service member during his or her first tour of duty with the first unit of assignment following Advanced Individual Training will be provided an opportunity to participate in on-duty or combined on and off-duty educational programs designed to qualify the individual for a high school diploma. . . .*

This is a demanding minimum goal, but it does not stand alone. At times there are requirements for participation in a predischarge education program and certification or advanced standing in a trade or a skill. All of these programs have merit, but I doubt that many of their advocates ever thought much about their effect on training. If the combat-arms units comply with the regulations, their training effort is seriously impaired and the burden falls on the company-level commanders.

Some senior commanders, reading the regulations from Department of the Army and getting the word on Department of Defense interest, feel constrained to do all that is prescribed and mount education programs second to none. Education is "in," statistics are available, diplomas can be counted. Training that is not being done is not so evident. It is hard to fault an intermediate commander for doing what the regulations prescribe. It is "they" who have taken their eye off the target, not he. Too many senior commanders, including general officers, do not keep the balance in mind. Some develop massive programs that leave little free time for young officers and commanders, who have to spend much of what they have left on these programs, at the expense of unit training.

That is one part of the bill; there is another. The individuals in the lower mental categories include a high percentage of high school dropouts. Statistics and studies indicate that high school dropouts have more adjustment problems, and are more prone to violate the law and use drugs than high school graduates. Non-high school graduates add to the portion of soldiers who get into trouble; carrying their handicapped background into barracks results in a de-

197

terioration of the way of life for all soldiers. An inordinate amount of a company commander's time is devoted to disciplinary matters, and many young commanders have been heard to say, "I spend 90 percent of my time looking after 5 to 10 percent of my troops." The result is that the good soldier is neglected and his training suffers.

No one need tell the military "they must not disappoint people who are looking for education and skills." In the Army, and the other services also, a major effort has been made to raise the educational level of those in the service, but that is not the point. The military must not disappoint the American people and the Congress, who are looking to the military for an effective national defense. If the Untied States is ever defeated in a war, the Congress and the people will not be impressed by the services' educational and social rehabilitation programs.

PERSONNEL SHIFTS AND READINESS

Another facet of the personnel system that adversely affects training is its relationship to the readiness system. Senior military and civilian leaders visiting a command find readiness shortcomings which they want improved without delay. The guidance goes out: "Get the air defense systems in USAREUR operationally ready by —————." "Bring units committed to NATO to ALO 1 by —————." The time allowed is often from two to four weeks. Reassignments are expedited, some retraining is started, and considerable turbulence is created throughout the Army while the emphasis is on those units. These units will retain a high personnel readiness rating for only a few months until some other program is in the spotlight. Unfortunately, in the meantime many soldiers will be moved on extremely short notice and without regard to their family situation. Internal Army pressures are often evident in movement of personnel within units for short periods at about the time a readiness report is due.

These sudden shifts in personnel, which too often are made just so the reports will look better, raise the peaks and lower the valleys in the training status and detract from the stability and coherence of the primary groups, which the sociologists have identified as important in combat situations and therefore important in training. The inconvenience to the soldier as well as the disruption and additional administrative effort is seldom recognized by senior staffs or commanders. Some will assert that they do recognize it, but if so, what is done about it? From experience I would say not much.

An example of self-inflicted wounds within a unit is the assigning of personnel to jobs in an area other than that for which they have received MOS training. However, it is difficult to fault the commanders who are directed to conduct additional programs such as education and equal opportunity, and provide installation support. Much valuable training time will be lost until Army commanders take a stronger stand on this difficult and ever-present problem. Much of the fault lies with the budget and allocation of personnel spaces. Installation support is always one of the "fat" areas that can be cut and still retain the muscle; at least that is what one reads in the paper.

Much of this "fat" consists of individuals who are needed to run education and equal-opportunity programs, and to keep gymnasiums, theaters, and other support activities functioning. Personnel are also used to fill some of the inspection teams created, although this siphoning-off can be stopped by a strong commander. Since people and funds are not provided for these tasks, the only place they can come from is the units—and thus they cannot be available for training. MOS mismatch is the natural result, and once again the young company commanders are held responsible for a situation they can't do much about.

The end result is that soldiers who have received extensive MOS training at considerable expense are put in jobs which do not relate to their primary MOS. Often the position for which a soldier has been given special training is filled by someone with little if any experience for that role. This kind of mis-assignment affects morale adversely, more now than in times past. The soldier who now enlists to be a mechanic does not want to waste his time doing something else. A newly arrived mechanic, who does not find himself repairing the equipment he has been trained to repair is likely to start asking why not.

The effect of personnel actions warrants attention and study throughout the Army school system. First, at the advanced course level commanders should be discouraged from assigning personnel to jobs outside their military occupational specialty. Then, at the Command and General Staff College and Army War College level, commanders and senior staff officers should be taught to recognize the effects of their staff actions down at the unit level. They need to learn that yet another inspection team is not a good solution to all problems.

Also, senior general officers and the Department of Army staff should go to the mat more often with civilian secretaries and Department of Defense policy makers. Somehow the adverse effects of personnel policies pursued for social or cosmetic purposes must be aired and put in the record. Sound personnel policies, properly applied, will solve many training deficiencies.

The quality of personnel is paramount. Those involved in personnel actions contend that if the Army does not enlist up to its authorized strength Congress will cut unfilled spaces from the Army end-strength in the next budget cycle. To avoid the cut they are willing to accept lower quality soldiers. I am not sure that the spaces are certain to be lost, but some very dependable and responsible people believe so.

Another alternative might be for the Army to provide high school level education to trainees at the training centers. Maintaining a centralized civilian-education program at the training centers might be cheaper than supporting civilian educators overseas and on a number of installations. Those soldiers who fail to meet high school requirements after some appropriate period could be separated from the Army at that point. This solution would lift a big burden off unit commanders and provide more men for training in the units. There is no easy solution, but the problem needs attention. The Trainee Discharge Program has been a great help in ridding units of troublesome soldiers. Its effect has borne out my contention that as the quality of soldiers is raised both training and quality of life improve at the unit level.

WOMEN IN THE ARMY

"What are you going to say about the training of women," someone asked me while I was writing this book. I don't have much to say. Women train just as well as men do. The major influence the increase in the number of women in the Army has had on this book is that I used the term "soldier" or "individual" where I might have used "men."

I believe that the increase in the number of women in the Army is a distinct plus. Many jobs that men do women can do too; some they can do better. The biggest advantage that accrues to the Army is that women improve the quality of the Army. So far, all the women who have entered the Army have been high school graduates. As more women are enlisted, fewer men have to be enlisted, which means that the Army can raise its standards for male soldiers. I would like to see the day when the Army enlisted only high school graduates. That alone would improve training in the Army and take a heavy civilian-education load off the company-level commanders.

A question that keeps recurring about women is their role in combat. I do not believe women should be in combat units. It is not that I doubt their courage or tenacity. Women have been effective in guerrilla forces. Some of the toughest members of terrorist groups are women. They will kill and they are ready to die, but I do not think they typify the female of our species.

If our nation is ever in dire straits and national survival is at stake, women will fight for their homes and families alongside the men. Obviously, all Americans hope that the United States will never be in such a position. Until the threat is clear, it would not be prudent to assign women to a combat role.

200

It struck me that the Monday they had been given off was a national holiday. How do you think the troops felt about this compensatory time?

Leadership and Training

Figure 20.1, an extract from an old training note, indicates that leadership is so much a part of the conduct of training that at times it is difficult to tell where one stops and the other starts. Training in leadership never stops, and the execution of a training responsibility provides a good opportunity to teach leadership by example. The examples given on how to develop the chain of command are a part of leadership training as it affects the conduct of training. Perhaps the best way to illuminate the relationship between leadership and training is, again, to give a few examples.

While visiting a unit that had just returned from a major training area, I asked one of the commanders if the men had been given some time off. The unit had been away for seven weeks and had trained all week, including Saturdays and Sundays. The company commander said that they had been given the coming Monday off. He also mentioned that they would possibly get another day off in a week or two. It struck me that the Monday they had been given off was a national holiday. How do you think the troops felt about this compensatory time? Or about the fact that the other day which they might get off was still not confirmed? How can the troops make plans for a free day or weekend if they are not sure when it will be? The question is particularly important to the families of those who are married. When troops return from a long absence at a major training area, two to three days should be spent getting

FIGURE 20.1.
LEADERSHIP

HEADQUARTERS, 4TH INFANTRY DIVISION

Training Note 4-65   29 December 1965

Leadership Training. One of the most important missions of a commander is to train his subordinate leaders in the techniques of leadership. This training is continuous in nature and is best conducted as a part of normal unit training. It is better to allow a junior officer or NCO to learn from his mistakes in training rather than to make these same mistakes in combat when it may be at the expense of men's lives. Some techniques in leadership training are:

On-the-Job Training. Let the junior leader act in a position of higher responsibility. For example, the platoon sergeant may be afforded an opportunity to act as platoon leader for a portion of an exercise. In this way he will gain actual experience in this capacity and will be better prepared to assume this responsibility should he be required to do so in a combat situation. The same principle holds for other positions in the company.

Independent Unit Training. Allow the platoon leader to conduct his own training without constant supervision. Allocate days, on a regular basis, when the leader conducts the training that he feels his unit most needs.

Mission-type Orders. Company commanders should assign missions to their subordinates without elaborating on the details of execution. Let the subordinate use his initiative in working out the details for himself. Never cause the junior leader to feel that he will be condemned for making a mistake; allow him to use his initiative and imagination. After the exercise is over, conduct a critique and offer advice.

Tactical Rides. Commanders will find tactical rides and walks valuable for training subordinate leaders. They can be conducted by battalion commanders for company commanders, company commanders for platoon leaders and platoon leaders for squad leaders. One good technique is to take subordinates over the terrain which they will defend or attack and present various situations which may occur. Junior leaders will be stimulated to think of ways to improve their tactics as well as receiving the benefit of guidance from more experienced commanders. There is no better way for commanders to develop good tactical sense in subordinates than to walk them over the ground and explain strengths and weaknesses of the terrain.

everything back in order and the unit ready to go; but after that there should be time off and the troops should know when it is. There's nothing wrong with providing for time off on the training schedule when the troops have earned it. Surely, after several weeks of hard work and training seven days a week, the troops merit this consideration.

A related matter has to do with promising training holidays for achieving some objective. On several occasions I have been approached by troops who complained that they had not been given the time off they had been promised. Generally these promises had been made at the company/battery/troop level. For one reason or another—an unexpected inspection or a nonconcurrence at a higher level of command—soldiers had been told that they just couldn't have the training holiday which had been promised. Even worse, sometimes the troops had been given no explanation. A training holiday should be planned for and executed with as much resolve as everything else on the training schedule. Subordinate commanders should not make promises about training holidays until they are sure they can deliver. Check with your battalion and brigade commanders if you want to promise something more than the time off normally approved and sanctioned at higher levels of command.

Planning the training schedule, especially for training conducted away from home station, requires considerate leadership. Small groups frequently are overlooked in the effort to follow a program. More often than realized, troops return from three or four weeks of field training only to be sent out a day or two later on some other program that, under the right conditions, could have been both enjoyable and profitable. But when soldiers can't get their laundry done over the weekend, when they don't have dry socks and other clean clothes essential to health and good field service, and when they hardly have a chance to visit with their families before going out again, they are generally unhappy. These matters are fundamental but they are forgotten by some commanders. Poor scheduling leads to negative attitudes and disciplinary problems, and is not in the best interest of the individual or the Army.

These three examples of poor leadership have to do directly with training; they all involve a lack of forethought and consideration. On the other hand, I have seen innumerable instances of good leadership in training. Of the characteristics they had in common these stand out—teaching, patience, and understanding. In these instances the manner of correction, explanation, and teaching conveyed an air of patience, understanding, and concern for the individual, all of which help the learning process.

There was a time when correction was impersonal, frequently loud, often profane, and sometimes demeaning. That type of instruction or leadership has long since ceased to be effective in the United States Army. Each leader develops his own style of leadership, which comes naturally from his personality, education, and training. But the style must be acceptable to soldiers molded by a society which is hostile to authority and highly individualistic. Overcoming this conditioning is an important subject for consideration in noncommissioned officer academies and officer schools.

At times a sharp rebuke, demand for better performance, or reduction in rank is necessary to maintain high standards. Though I often speak of patience in training, there comes a time when patience runs out. When things continue to go wrong or when high standards are not maintained, the troops are the ones who suffer. But there is a balancing point at which personal interest and empathy support discipline and authority rather than undermine them. It has been my experience that most people want to do a good job, and will do a good job if the time is taken to teach them how to do it. That, in essence, is training.

Interchange of ideas within the chain of command is essential to the achievement of training goals. Raising standards at every opportunity and correcting errors in a manner that ensures understanding are all part of the leadership process in training. And since training applies to every aspect of operations —to maintenance and administration as well as to tactics—the synthesis of training and leadership never stops.

With regard to junior officers I suggest that battalion and brigade commanders give guidance somewhat as follows:

> Every commander at company or similar unit level should have a system that enables him to talk to every man or woman in his unit. Set aside one afternoon or evening a week when you can talk to five or six soldiers individually; or set aside a period of one or two weeks during which you can concentrate on talking to every soldier in the company, battery, or troop. It does not have to be for long—ten or fifteen minutes should suffice for each person. Ask them where they are from. How far did they go in school? Are they married? How many children do they have? Where are their families? Is the training interesting? Boring? Demanding enough? How is the chow? Are they getting paid? Make whatever you talk about personal and pleasant and let the soldiers know you are interested in them. Do not challenge them or get on the defensive if they say something is not good—maybe it is not. Ask if they have any suggestions to improve the situation. Once you have talked individually with all members of your unit, it is easy to keep up with the new arrivals—and it will be a natural thing to chat with your troops on the range, in the motor pool, in the chow line, or wherever you meet them as they are about a soldier's business. This is how you keep your fingers on the pulse of your unit. You will learn a lot about your unit and incidentally you will probably cut the time that you are spending on congressional inquiries, IG complaints, and other problems by about 90 percent.

This suggested guidance may not have much to do with the training of units, but it has a great deal to do with training young officers in how to be better leaders. Using it will give them more time to think about training and plans for training.

READING FOR IDEAS

Look back so you can think ahead. Read books such as *The Armed Forces Officer* and S. L. A. Marshall's *Men Against Fire*. Insights of value to trainers and leaders are to be found in works as varied as the superb vignettes of Aubrey S. Newman in *Army* magazine and the scholarly studies of sociologists like Morris Janowitz, Charles Moskos, and Daniel Bell. These readings will stimulate your thinking about human reactions and the attitudes of individuals and groups, which are so important in the military profession. An understanding of the changed attitudes in our society is essential for leaders at every level of the Army.

Browse through some old Operations Research Reports such as "Notes on Infantry Tactics in Korea" and "The Employment of Armor in Korea." There are others on World War II, and some on Vietnam have already appeared. Don't worry about the charge that these are ancient history. If the Operations Research Office material on operations in Korea is studied from the viewpoint of the commander and trainer, a number of small training exercises for keeping weapons systems functioning will come to mind. Most of the weapons these reports mention are no longer used, but similar problems recur with all weapons systems. The studies make you think of the human problems, and the adverse conditions of combat under which soldiers must keep the systems functioning.

Read about the operations and training of foreign armies. Since Rommel said, "The best form of 'welfare' for the troops is first-class training," his *Infantry Attacks* is a good start. The Army has prepared pamphlets on the training of Japanese and German troops in World War II; these along with a recent publication *The Soviet Soldier* will make commanders realize how thorough some foreign forces can be in their training.

The writings referred to are just a few examples of the reading and study necessary to expand your knowledge and understanding of the profession of arms. Expanding your own horizons will enable those who have an interest in minor tactics to generate informal discussions and debate among small groups of officers and noncommissioned officers on the direction Army training should take.

I cannot emphasize too strongly the importance of the basic historical material that recounts combat situations. Often the tide has been turned in a critical battle by an individual or a small group of soldiers who could keep a tank firing after it had been damaged, who could keep a machine gun in a key position operating, or who could keep the guns firing after a battery position had been hit. Often these small actions turned the tide of victory to the side of that Army which had superbly trained individual soldiers and crews. When I read of the critical situations in which a few men prevailed because they were well trained, I am reminded of my earlier comment that too often we neglect training because only a few men are present for duty. Reading historical documents will give you a sense of the importance of each individual soldier and ideas on the many different facets of training that are neglected every day. You have the opportunity and the time to teach the troops now. Take advantage of it. Training time lost can never be regained.

The commander who directs a lot of special effort just because a general is coming had better look to his own standards.

Advice for and about Generals

Frederick the Great said, "A perfect general, like Plato's republic, is a figment. Either would be admirable, but it is not characteristic of human nature to produce beings exempt from human weaknesses and defects." Some stories about generals are true, but most grow in the telling and the extreme becomes the norm. Most of the generals I have known were hard workers and strong characters, and in spite of all the stories they did on occasion take advice. So I don't hesitate to give some.

While discussing with a group of lieutenants and captains some of the problems they encountered in training, one of the lieutenants said, "Sir, when a general visits my unit it creates chaos." I admitted that generals might create a bit of consternation but wondered if calling it chaos wasn't a bit of an overstatement. With this grand opening the other company-grade officers chimed in. They said that whenever the battalion and higher level commanders heard a general was coming, the flurry of activity, sudden changes, and special guidance made things pretty chaotic. Sergeants feel much the same way, and if you want to hear a real tale of woe just listen to the privates.

In many cases this criticism is warranted, and sufficient examples can be cited for those who wear stars to pay heed to their method of operation. As a rule, the generals coming to visit are not the guilty parties. Most often the culprits are ambitious and apprehensive Intermediate commanders—which does include some general officers—who direct all the changes. But to the troops in the units it doesn't make much difference who starts the frantic scurrying. The troops are the victims of the sudden changes and have to do most of the work. To them it can get chaotic, so a little advice is in order. Incidentally, colonels should start acting on this advice now, because those who are fortunate enough to be promoted to general officer will have good habits insofar as the troops are concerned.

Normally, general officers in the chain of command should visit units informally and unannounced, though exceptions to the rule will be cited. As soon as a unit knows a general officer is coming, the problems begin for the soldiers and the company-grade officers. Suddenly there is a surge of activity to put the barracks, dining halls, maintenance shops, and everything else in command inspection order. The troops stay up half the night scrubbing walls and floors and tidying up the barracks. Paint is splattered about, and wasted, on some eye-catching object.

The soldiers who can tell the saddest tale of woe are the electronics repairmen and the mechanics. The former lay out tools and parts in an orderly fashion on the work bench or in the frames provided to repair complex equipment, only to have a sergeant rush in to make sure all the work benches are cleared and cleaned for a visiting dignitary. The mechanics stand about with tools put away as they look at the maintenance shed floor which has been hosed and swept down because "the general is coming by." Clean work benches and wet floors are indicators of poor leadership and hours of lost maintenance time. They are examples of form over substance, external appearance over performance of the job. Form prevails too often over substance in the things we do. It is up to the general officers to recognize the clean benches and wet floors for what they are and expose the stupidity that has led to the practice.

The training schedules get scrubbed just like the barracks. The commander who neglects his day-to-day duties and lacks confidence in his subordinates suddenly starts checking the training schedules for the day of the visit, which is often the next day or the day after. Too often the training doesn't seem promising enough to this concerned commander, especially if it happens to be something like first aid or map reading. He therefore changes the training schedule overnight. New instructors are readied and the training rehearsed, quite often on a crash basis after duty hours, and the chaos the lieutenant was talking about is in the making.

The commander of a unit being visited seldom knows what the general officer is going to look at; the best generals I knew seldom had a preset course, but they certainly knew their business, and mine too. They just sensed where to go next, and their faculty for finding things that needed attention was uncanny. That talent makes the scrambling to get everything in order overnight ridiculous. There is so much to see in any unit that the general officer probably won't get a look at the barracks and dining halls the soldiers worked so hard on in the evening, and the odds are he won't visit the training that has been changed. The soldiers and the junior officers are irritated when he doesn't make an appearance; they know what a great effort has been made to put on a show at their expense. The commander who directs a lot of special effort just because a general is coming had better look to his standards. When you get to be a general and you want to see how good an outfit really is, just drop in unannounced. The soldiers will bless you, and the competent commanders, who have confidence in their men and concern for their well being, will look forward to your occasional visits.

If the visiting general finds things are in horrible shape the chances are he did not need a crystal ball to enable him to pick the one day that everything went wrong. Conditions are no doubt like that every day and the commanders there just don't recognize it. Whenever I made a visit to a unit that showed laxity, I always returned a week or two later to determine what the commander had learned from my previous visit and what he had done about it.

In a good unit, barracks, dining halls and other areas are generally clean and orderly and the training is effective from day to day. A senior officer arriving unannounced should expect to see something occasionally that is marginal or not well done, but he can then take the opportunity to give some help and guidance. Remember that in our business we are always teaching, and a commander's job is to develop his subordinates and teach them all he knows about the subject at hand. Generals can make a major contribution to the development of subordinates. Above all, if you see a unit that has done a good job, compliment it and its commander.

Another advantage to dropping in on a unit is that you don't waste anyone's time. Senior officers often travel by air, and a combination of bad weather and unexpected delays can force a commander to wait for several hours at a helipad or airstrip for a general officer. In such a case, the commander's units would not be getting the attention they needed. When you have three or four stars and visit a unit, you will sometimes find a major general, a brigadier, and one or two colonels standing about awaiting your arrival. What a colossal waste of talent! Their time would be far better used checking on conditions in their units.

I made a standing rule that commanders were not to meet me. It took a while to convince commanders that I meant what I said. If I made my visit during prime training time, I expected commanders to be where some training was going on, and I always hoped I would not find them in their offices. Without fail and at every level of command, whenever I found commanders in their offices during training time, the training and standards in their units were consistently poor. Occasionally, when I wanted to see a commander in person, I notified his headquarters I was coming but suggested that the commander go about his business, designating a sergeant major or staff member to meet me and guide me to the commander.

Arriving unannounced gives you a good opportunity to learn a lot about a unit in a short time. Do the unit's members get the word to the local commander when you first arrive in the unit? How long does it take to dispatch a vehicle? If you have to wait, you have an opportunity to check the facilities and the maintenance at the airstrip. What condition were the fire extinguishers in and could the fire truck move? How about the fuel trucks? Walk through the living quarters with the first sergeant or the charge of quarters. You can learn a great deal about a unit right there.

I often hailed a truck and asked the driver returning to the barracks area to drop me off there. These rides were valuable, and, what is more, I believe the drivers enjoyed having a general officer in the cab with them. Also, by the time I arrived at the barracks area, I had a good idea of how one soldier felt about the food, conditions in the barracks, and pay problems. I would also learn when he had last fired his weapon, and how well he cared for his vehicle. Satisfactory answers in all these areas spoke well for the unit. But if they were on the negative side, a little more digging usually showed whether the problems were pervasive or whether this particular soldier happened to be a Jonah or the type who always complains. In my experience there are not too many of the latter; soldiers are pretty straightforward in telling you how things are. The commanders who have problems are the ones who do not listen to their troops.

I believe the higher ranking you get the more important this guidance becomes. Though I realize that there may be communications or other requirements making it difficult at the Chief of Staff level, still, it would be a great thing if even the Chief could just appear on the scene. As it stands now, the higher the rank, the bigger the entourage; and by the time the unit being visited decides where lunch will be served, who is going to be at the luncheon, and what program is to be set up for all those visiting, a great amount of energy and effort has been expended. The confusion created when the dining hall designated for the lunch has been changed two or three times, as the battalion commanders' choice is changed by the brigade commander and then by the ADC, does not add to the peace and quiet of the installation.

I solved this particular problem in the simplest fashion, although it was not easy on my aides. Most of the time I did not eat any lunch, so I was not committed to arrive at any specific dining hall and eat with any specific group. Simply munching an apple enroute from one unit to another was a great time saver. Also, if I arrived at an installation about lunchtime, it was easy to walk through two or three dining halls for a quick look at the food, the cleanliness, and the attitude of the men. On occasion, there was time to sit down at a table with several soldiers to find out how they felt about any number of things. Such conversations give a commander a good feel for the pulse of a unit.

As a minimum, general officers from one- to three-star rank should circulate freely throughout their commands, trying to see them as they are every day. Privates, NCOs, and young officers like to see the senior commanders on occasion, and it is especially exciting to them when the latter appear without a lot of fanfare. Unfortunately, time and distance being what they are, a general officer will see only a small part of any unit on a visit, particularly if it is doing meaningful training. Nonetheless, if he has a solid background with troops, he can see a lot in a short time. In recent years it has been surprising how seldom intermediate commanders up to battalion level saw their general-officer and brigade-level commanders in the field. They saw them most often at a commander's conference or at some special gathering or training highlight to which several general officers had been invited.

I have given much emphasis to the informal unannounced visit because I believe it will do more than anything to eliminate the false notes and pressures that creep into training, but as in all things there are exceptions. Two that come to mind are the first visit to a unit and command inspections.

In a new command assignment, I always considered a first visit to a unit a protocol visit. I would call the commander and ask him to set up an itinerary without a planned lunch break. My objective was to see as much of the unit and installation as possible and to meet late in the day with representative groups of soldiers, NCOs, and officers. I invariably followed the itinerary and tried to keep to their time schedule, which was always difficult for me since I ask so many questions of the soldiers. Occasionally, as I was being led along a line of barracks or activities, I would ask, "What's in that building over there?" or, "What are those men doing?" and would suggest we take a look. On this type of protocol visit an occasional drift from the predetermined route, to see if conditions on the unexpected detour are comparable to the route on display, is always enlightening. You don't have to make a detour very often, but a good commander should not let himself be led around by the nose.

The other exception pertains to a command inspection. I believe it is a good idea for a division commander to schedule a command inspection for battalion-size units about once a year. That may not sound like much, but such an inspection demands a great deal of a division commander's time; perhaps once every two years might be the best he can manage, if he is lucky enough to have the division that long.

You can be sure the troops work hard with a lot of NCO attention to get everything in first-class shape for the inspection, so on the appointed day the general officer should walk down the line of every unit in the battalion, and look at all the barracks, dining halls, and maintenance shops in the unit area. The division commander will be a lot more exhausted at the end of the day than any of his troops. But the soldiers who have worked so hard to get ready for that inspection will know that the general, about whose wants they have heard so much, has taken the time to see them at their best. His personal attention is good for the soldiers' morale; it is an inspiration for the general officer also.

In recent years general officers have been caught up in community affairs, relations with host nations, luncheons, and a variety of activities that concern the civilian community. With respect to the military, they are swamped by brief- ings, reports, visitors, and enough legal and disciplinary problems to keep them close to the staff and the briefing rooms. A general officer can go to an installation and soon become so wrapped up in these activities that he has little time left for the troops. Usually they get what he can spare, and it is not enough.

Increasingly, more and more officers have come into general officer posi- tions with extremely limited troop duty. They feel more at home in the manage- ment role, where analysis, statistics, and charts are more familiar than guns and stoppages, tracks and maintenance, soldiers, and the ground. They can feel righteous in meeting the demands placed on their time, and they establish relations with the local community that a successor would be hard put to match. I am sure it never occurs to some of these generals that they are neglecting the soldier while they are doing so much for "the Army's image."

I do not want to create the impression that the community should be ignored or that host-country relations are unimportant. That too would be wrong. A commander must show a degree of interest in a local community, but too often this gets all-consuming. Demands on a general officer's time from a community and from his own installation and command will far exceed any time available to him. Attendance at a judicious selection of community activities with staff representation at others, combined with invitations to members of the community to see the soldiers at their training, provides for good balance.

As long as the payroll and budget allocation for an installation keeps flow- ing into a community, that community is going to be happy. A commander should not think that his presence at a large number of functions is what creates good will. The payroll does nine-tenths of that; well-disciplined soldiers with a good attitude do the rest. In foreign nations the discipline and training of our troops stationed there do more for good relations than anything else. Also, there are general officers assigned to these nations whose positions are more political than military; their time is properly devoted to relations between the forces and the nation.

For generals serving with troops, two themes recur throughout this volume: training is all-encompassing; and the atmosphere in which training is conducted is affected by the attention and attitude of senior officers. In pursuing these themes I have asserted that training has been neglected by a large segment of the officer corps, and that the training atmosphere has been corroded by pressure, competition, and lack of knowledge of weapons systems and soldiers. In recent years too many general officers have become involved in too many programs that have little to do with the day-to-day training of troops. And too few have been aware of the total effect of a series of sociological changes on military standards, discipline, and the whole training environment.

It is the responsibility of the top levels in the chain of command—and to me that means the general officers and full colonels—to create an atmosphere in which effective training can be conducted. In brief, what is needed is a relaxation of tensions accompanied by a rise in the standards of performance. That means the senior officers on command assignments must become more familiar with weapons, troops, and the tactical environment. Achieving such familiarity will take a reorientation on the part of senior officers. They must learn to recognize what is merely show and put a stop to it. They must learn to recognize what is form and what is substance. They must learn to create an atmosphere which is tolerant of honest mistakes yet quick to rectify stupidity. They must keep competition in bounds and control overriding ambition while still striving for superior performance. And they must seek to know more about the soldier and what he is called upon to do.

Reorienting in this way also means that general officers who command units must stand up and say that training is the number one business of a peacetime army, and that they believe that *"the commander's* first concern must be to order all the activities of his unit to meet his primary obligation to the Army, his unit, and his soldiers: *produce a unit ready to fight and win now."*[1]

As a general officer you don't have to say much more than that because the commanders will take it from there. But you do have to get out on the ground to see that training is effective and in the process learn what is happening to the troops. If they are carrying any unnecessary burdens, a general can use the stars on his shoulder to lighten their load. The effort won't be wasted, for if a unit ever has to fight, the soldiers will be carrying the general's burdens, and the country's too.

---

[1]FM 100-5 Operations; Headquarters DA, 1 July 1976, pp. 1-5.

22

Could we have defeated our enemies if the force ratios and types of equipment were relatively equal?

Fighting Qualities, National Will, and Training

How well soldiers, airmen, sailors, and marines fight is a delicate nettle. Public figures seldom grasp it firmly; they know the sting can be painful. Political pronouncements imply that Americans will spring to arms when the need arises. The records show, however, that in almost every war large numbers of Americans preferred not to serve and sought ways to have someone else take their places in the ranks.

Defense and congressional officials make statements on the capability of current forces. Most often they overstate the case, whatever they are trying to prove. If it is a matter of shortfalls, these can generally be accommodated by a belief that even if the enemy is stronger, one red-blooded American can beat seven, five, or at least three of any other nationality. How well these claims withstand objective scrutiny is written in the history of United States battle casualties.

Since 1941 there has been more than enough fighting from which comparisons may be drawn. When I reflect on what I have seen, studied, and read on U.S. conflicts in the past thirty years, I cannot claim that American troops were more courageous than those we fought against. In my judgment our forces were not as well trained as those of the enemy, especially in the early stages of the fighting. After the build-up of forces, when we went on the offensive, we did not defeat the enemy tactically. We overpowered and overwhelmed our enemies with equipment and fire power.

Could we have defeated our enemies if the force ratios and types of equipment had been relatively equal? Could we have persevered in the face of the adversity that was the lot of our enemies during the past thirty years? Will we be able to obtain or afford the immense quantities of natural resources that were used for war production in World War II, Korea, or Vietnam? I doubt that many would be able to give positive answers to those questions. I believe that in any future conflict our major potential adversaries will match us in manpower and equipment. Leaders responsible for national security can draw small comfort from a candid evaluation not only of potential enemy military forces, but they must also evaluate the willingness of the American people to make sacrifices in a period which some have described as the end of the American Era.

The American soldier is a product of American society. Wonderful though we like to think we are, and perhaps no group is more patriotic and loyal to the country than the U.S. military, I doubt that anyone in a position of responsibility for national security can feel at ease about the future. What are the underlying trends in our society? The prevailing weight of social theory now emphasizes the individual, and the trend of opinion is against regimentation or controls of any kind. The divisiveness in our society is reinforced by racial animosities and minority movements. A breakdown in law and order has become evident in the inability to control crime or abuse of drugs. Schools—the source of future soldiers—are now confronted with unprecedented vandalism, disregard for authority, and assault on teachers. There are other serious social problems, but those mentioned are enough to suggest the extent of the problems confronting the military leaders who are responsible for defending the nation. An antimilitary bias on the part of the press, liberals, and a large segment of the college faculties makes that responsibility even more onerous.

At the end of World War II, a group of German officers who had fought the Russians on the Eastern Front reported that the Russian soldier "is subject to moods which to a Westerner are incomprehensible; he acts by instinct. As a soldier he is primitive and unassuming—innately brave. . . . These traits make him in many respects an adversary superior to the self-confident and more demanding soldier of other armies." Couple the implications of this comment with the vast improvement in Soviet weapons, the intensive education and physical-fitness programs in Russia, and the devotion to the motherland of the Russian soldier, and you have a partial picture of at least one potential adversary.

How about us? The positive characteristics generally attributed to the American fighting man are initiative, creativity, independence of action, and a high level of technical competence—a combination of mental and manual dexterity—in the maintenance and operation of complex equipment. I believe Americans have these characteristics to a marked degree, and that such attributes are of vital importance to a soldier in land combat. Throughout my service

I have seen superb solutions to difficult problems and situations that derived from these national characteristics. In our army we do not have to do much to develop these capabilities; in fact, sometimes the biggest problem is keeping them under control. Technical competence can be developed in highly regimented societies, but the very nature of a communist society stifles initiative and independence of action. Developing such qualities is most difficult in communist armed forces, but literature and reports on Soviet military training indicates that the Soviet Union is working hard to develop these characteristics through military training.

The positive side of the American fighting man is counterbalanced by characteristics that are detrimental to a military force and earn little respect for the society as a whole. The extremes of these negative characteristics have become more pronounced in the past two decades. Americans are physically soft, undisciplined, and politically immature. They have little respect for authority, are oriented to individual freedom rather than group or collective accomplishments, and are not swayed by appeals to patriotism. And they come to military service from a society with a strong antimilitary bias. By contrast, the Soviet people are in good physical condition, ideologically indoctrinated, thoroughly trained, and highly disciplined. When Soviet soldiers come into the Army they enter with respect for the military service and a high degree of motivation to serve their country.

It is an interesting coincidence that the characteristics Soviet leaders would like to develop in their Army—although they have some reservations about doing so—are just those the American soldier comes by naturally. The characteristics which our forces need to strengthen—physical conditioning, discipline, respect for authority, group as opposed to individual orientation—are ones the Soviet soldier brings to the Army because of his schooling and indoctrination.

For both Russia and the United States—and, on a wider scale, the Communist and Free World—the characteristics to be improved through training are at odds with the general outlook of the respective societies. The Soviets are confronted with a basic problem: To encourage the necessary creativity and independence of actions is to run counter to the fundamental teachings of Communist doctrine. But discipline and respect for authority are not unknown to Americans, and a shift in social attitudes could result in great improvements in the weaknesses in our society that have become so pronounced in the past decade.

I have made a long digression in order to emphasize the importance of training in the Army. Our country is confronted by adversaries who honestly believe their form of government will prevail, and they do not hestitate to say ours will not. They also take actions to confront, confuse, and undermine democratic societies by taking advantage of the freedom of those societies.

216

Our hope for the future is to develop those characteristics that will enable initiative and independence of action to have free rein. Without restraint, however, individual initiative could be a source of great weakness in a combat environment. Those in military organizations must respect authority, be physically tough, recognize the importance of group as opposed to individual action, and maintain a high standard of discipline. All these qualities are needed to accomplish missions under combat conditions.

All can be developed in a realistic and demanding training environment. The Army must improve its training methods and results. The societies of our adversaries lend strength to their armies. Our society forces weaknesses on the Army which must be confronted and corrected. The task can be accomplished if we have the will. That is a commodity that both friends and adversaries of the United States now question.

Demanding training by the Army might spark a regeneration of some of the simple virtues—integrity, physical fitness, discipline, respect for authority, and respect for others—without which no nation can long survive. Putting our training in order is a first step toward creating an Army that is ready to fight tomorrow. It may not win the first battle but it is more important that it not lose the last battle.

The Army must speak plainly on those conditions in our society that are important to our survival as a nation. I believe the Army has a responsibility to insure that civilian leaders know what they are asking and what is reasonably attainable. Developing hard, tough, interesting training is the only way the Army can do its part to insure that our nation might be able to hang on—and survive —in a future conflict. The prospects are not promising unless there is a change in the attitudes of our society. Better training will at least improve the prospects.

INDEX

Lt. Gen. Arthur S. Collins, Jr. (U.S. Army Ret.)

Collins was graduated from West Point in 1938 and received an M.A. in International Affairs from George Washington University in 1964. He served in the U.S. Army for forty years before his retirement in 1974. For twenty years of this service, he closely supervised the training of United States soldiers, as both commander and staff officer. He was a training advisor to the Korean Army. He is a combat veteran of World War II, Korea and Vietnam, having commanded at every level from platoon to field army. The lessons he has learned about training are invaluable to present day leaders in both the military service and civilian life.